ORGANISATIONAL IDENTITY AND SELF-TRANSFORMATION

T0330881

Organisational Identity and Self-Transformation

An Autopoietic Perspective

DAVID SEIDL

Ludwig Maximilians University of Munich, Germany

LONDON AND NEW YORK

First published 2005 by Ashgate Publishing

2 Park Square, Milton Park, Abingdon, Oxfordshire OX14 4RN
711 Third Avenue, New York, NY 10017

Routledge is an imprint of the Taylor & Francis Group, an informa business

First issued in paperback 2018

British Library Cataloguing in Publication Data
Organisational identity and self-tranformation : an
    autopoietic perspective
    1. Group identity 2. Identity (Psychology) 3. Organisational
    sociology 4. Social structure 5. Autopoiesis
    I. Title
    302.4

Library of Congress Control Number: 2005929780

ISBN 978-0-7546-4458-3 (hbk)
ISBN 978-1-138-37893-3 (pbk)

Contents

List of Figures

Acknowledgements

I would like to thank everybody who supported me on my journey through the jungle of distinctions and self-referential loops. I am particularly grateful to Dirk Baecker, Andrew Brown, Geoff Hodgson, André Kieserling and most of all, John Hendry, who did not become tired discussing paradoxes with me. I am also indebted to Suzanne Leão-Grötsinger, Nicola Prinz and Artemis Gause for type-setting and editing the manuscript.

D.S.
Stanford
Spring, 2005

Foreword

Humanity mirrors and reproduces itself through the work of its systems. We may normally think of the systems through which we live and work as providers of structures that direct our thinking and actions or as producers of products that satisfy our needs and cater to our interests, but they perform another, and perhaps more radical, human service: they create and recreate the forms and appearances that constitute the immediate reality of our world. Without the constant work of reproduction and repetition by our systems, the human world would dissolve and disappear and so would its human habitants since we can only know and maintain ourselves as reflections of the objects and structures that serve as props for our daily living. The supermarket has to refill its empty shelves each night in order to ensure its continuation the following day, the newspaper must reassemble the news of the world on a daily basis in order to ensure its repeated publication, and the television station must animate the television screen with the continuous presentation of audio-visual images. The empty supermarket, the newspaper that does not appear, the lifeless television screen simply illustrate the existential shock that would accompany the disappearance of the constitutive forms and meanings of the human world.

The constant work of human systems is thus radically focussed on saving the appearances of the human world. In this interpretation, the objects that support us in the daily work of living are not just instrumental tools to facilitate the tasks of existence or to extend our powers. They are also, and perhaps more significantly, the means for mirroring the human image through projections and extensions of itself into the environment. In this way, the human system talks back to its users to assure them that they are living in a human world. In saving the appearances, the system also saves its human users and reminds them that they are habitants of a human world. A basic strategy in saving human appearances is the fitting together of the human body and its environment so that the human organs and senses, like the pieces of a jigsaw puzzle, can conveniently fit the various spaces into which the body projects itself: the chair is made to accommodate the shape of the body and its tiredness, the book can be held in the hand and within range of the eyes, the telephone connects directly with the ear. Such examples underline the significance of the immediate and continuous presence of the specific contents of the human world as well as their presentability and hence their ready readability. Body and environment are thus organically intertwined. When this organic intertwining breaks down, the meaningful objects and structures of the world dissolve and disappear. Seen from this perspective, human systems are structured connections or organisations of bodily organs and senses with the supportive objects of their environments. Organisations thus can be meaningfully understood as extensions of human organs and senses. This is an old idea which has been lost in the modern stress on organisations as instrumental systems. We see it in the medieval idea of the community as *corporation* which directly reflected the idea of the social body as a *corpus* or an articulated collection of organs and senses. In this radical sense, the human organisation is the work of the body and its organs and senses in constantly creating and recreating connections and correspondences between themselves and the environment. When these connections and correspondences break down, so does the organised world of human appearances.

David Seidl's book can be read as a systematic and meticulous analysis of the work of human systems in the continuous work of saving the structures and appearances of the human world. His focus is on organisations as human systems and more especially on organisations as self-generating systems that maintain a sense of human continuity. The central term in Seidl's analysis for this work of self-generation is *autopoiesis* or self-making. Autopoiesis – a term which originated in theoretical biology – refers to the making of the forms of life in general. Applied to human systems, it means the making of objects and structures that both mirror and reproduce the human world and its occupants. The making of the forms of life is an infinite and never-ending act of creation which exists for itself and not for some external reason. It has no goal or object beyond itself. It is simply the making of making and the forming of forming. All this means that autopoiesis is a fundamental force or power that generates itself. It has to be understood as a generic rather than a specific creative force. As the moving power of human systems and their perpetual regeneration, autopoiesis is less to do with the making of specific objects, of a particular *x* or *y*, and is much more about making as a fundamental life-force whose overall function is to repair, restore and redeem itself and thus save the human world from dissolution and disappearance. Viewed in this way, the work of the supermarket, the newspaper and the television station begins to assume an existential significance rather than a simply practical and instrumental meaning.

The institutions and organisations of the everyday world are now to be re-interpreted as expressions of an ultra-physical life-force rather than the products of rationally focussed human plans and intentions. The factory, the hospital, the school, the university and the department store may present exterior impressions of rational order and directed purpose but this pragmatic interpretation simply conceals their generic origin as human systems that repeatedly create and re-create the forms and meanings of the human world in order to save its existential appearances. This is what David Seidl means when he places autopoiesis in its social context through the work of the sociologist Niklas Luhmann. Luhmann re-interprets the original biological understanding of autopoiesis to reveal its social significance and adds to it insights from a diverse range of intellectual fields such as cybernetics and communication theory. Autopoiesis in its social context is the continuous pursuit of social forms and structures. For Luhmann, autopoiesis in the social context is not about the forms and structures themselves but about the forever unfinished work of reproducing and redeeming them as if the processes of reproduction and redemption were more important than their objectives. The forms and structures of social life are intrinsically unstable; they are momentary events that pass away as soon as they occur. Autopoiesis in the human world is the constant work of preserving some sense of stability and meaningfulness, however fictional, to this arbitrary flow of events. Luhmann's re-working of autopoiesis reminds us at times of Max Weber's view of the world as a *meaningless infinity* on which we impose *convenient fictions*. For Luhmann, the human being is one such fictional product of social autopoiesis; the so-called self-consistency of the human being is a necessary but illusory product of the social system in its continuous attempts to save itself from dehiscence and dissipation.

In Luhmann's interpretation of autopoiesis as the making of cognisable forms and meanings the act of distinction is a primal strategy. All forms and meanings originate in a primal act of *distinction*, an argument which Luhmann borrows from the work of the logician George Spencer Brown. Distinction, for Spencer Brown, is fundamental for the emergence of all forms. In order to indicate a form, we also have to distinguish it from its surrounding context. In this sense, selection is basic to the appearance of forms. Distinction is thus a simultaneous double movement of making something appear *and* making something disappear; it includes and excludes at the same time. The *double stance* of *di*-stinction implies *both* presence *and* absence, the included *and* the excluded. Distinction makes something stand out as a clear and specific form but it requires vagueness and the non-specific out of which it can make things distinct. For Spencer Brown, human knowledge is forever caught in this double movement and can never find a permanent resting place. All distinctions are thus partial and hence suggest that they are simply *tokens* or *expressions* of a more extensive, more tensible space and time which in itself can never be distinguished. Autopoiesis reflects the double movement of distinction in the continuous work of creating its forms out of the immanence and imminence of indistinction. It seems to be actively suspended in a space and time that lacks locatable structures, always deferring and postponing itself as if to ensure its own recurrence. It reveals itself as a permanent process of *becoming* rather than of finished accomplishment; it lives through a sense of anticipation rather than arrival. For such reasons, Spencer Brown conjures up the image of a dog chasing its unreachable tail when summarising his analysis of the relentless project of human knowing.

When we apply autopoiesis to the understanding of human institutions and organisations we begin to see them less as instrumental systems of production and more as expressions of a metaphysical power that both transgresses and redeems itself through the continuous making of making. This is exactly what Luhmann wishes to stress when he reminds us that an organisation is directly dependent for its sense of distinctive and distinguishable unity on what is excluded from its acts of organising. Every decision an organisation makes is a selection from a range of alternatives and thus necessarily relies on the active presence of a wider field of possibilities. This means that the organisation is constantly organised out of a field of uncertainty and tension. In other words, it is the tension of uncertainty that keeps the organisation organising. For Luhmann, the existence of uncertainty is vital for the organisation's autopoiesis. The tension of uncertainty, in whatever degree, is a necessary stimulus for the ongoingness of autopoiesis. The reduction of uncertainty is at best a temporary and transient amelioration of a local problem; uncertainty immediately reasserts its presence as a vital source of autopoiesis in a world that is forever without end. The conventional understanding of organisations and institutions stresses their goals and outcomes. Luhmann's interpretation of autopoiesis in the social context makes us see organisation as the generic production and maintenance of human reality in a context of pervasive uncertainty and even disorganisation. Strangely, autopoiesis even suggests that its self-absorption with the act of making is concerned as much with the creation of uncertainty and dissolution as it is with the making of certainty and organisation. David Seidl's discussion of organisational identity in the context of autopoiesis implies this when it suggests that an organisation creates its identity as a means of finding and re-finding itself or, in other words, of not losing itself in uncertainty and disorganisation. Without uncertainty, there would be no identity. As we have seen, distinction is a way of distinguishing a form from its complementary context of indistinction and is thus basic to any act of indication and identification. Like distinction, identification and identity have to be continually repeated and reasserted in order to save the appearances of reality.

Autopoiesis reminds us that all social systems and structures are temporary and transient and that if we wish to understand them we must think of them as conceptual punctuations momentarily located against a flowing background of disconnected parts and general disunity. Seidl's stressing of self-transformation as being basic to any understanding of organisation as autopoietic process also reminds us that we and our systems are moved by forces we cannot fully grasp. The self-transformation of a system is a creative response to chance-like events and unpredictable possibilities. On this view, organisations and institutions lose their sense of stone-like solidity and rationalised self-belief and appear as systemic reactions to the intrinsic unreadability and ungraspability of the world. Self-transformation redirects our attention from the organisation as a ready-made structure to the compositional acts and gestures that produce it. Autopoiesis displaces our attention from the idea of a finished organisation to its forever unfinished work of composition. At this point everything in the human world has yet to be realised and the conventional distinction between the real and the fictive becomes questionable. When, for example, we strip human being and its settings of their conventional readability and view them as a continuous process of composition, we begin to see the world of human products receding into a horizon of dissipation and disappearance. Autopoiesis dramatically reveals to us this continuous withdrawal of the world as a meaningful reality while at the same time it tells us that it is also saving the world by making and remaking it for the meaningful and readable comprehension of its human habitants. On this basis, Luhmann's comprehensive and probing analysis of the social implications of autopoiesis invites us to re-interpret contemporary views of organisation by opening up radically new vistas for rethinking organisation as a profound human and existential theme.

Robert Cooper
Centre for Culture, Social Theory and Technology
Keele University

Preface

In our 'late modern', 'reflexive modern', 'post-modern', 'post-post-modern' (...) times (the list of terms to refer to one and the same element gets longer by the day), all forms of stability are being dissolved. All areas of knowledge, from philosophy to literary theory to physics, have started to acknowledge instability as the central feature of 'reality'. Against such a backdrop, identity, as a concept for referring to unity, consistency, and sameness over time, becomes particularly problematic. No wonder that now, more than ever before, the concept of identity is being questioned. From the late eighties onwards, concepts of identity have been discussed also in the context of organisation studies. Apart from the general interest in this topic, it was probably also the empirical observation of the dramatic increase in number and frequency of radical organisational changes that stimulated efforts to formulate a concept of organisational identity that would be compatible with the acknowledgement of a fundamental instability.[1] The relevant research has led to several, so far only rudimentary, concepts of organisational identity, which are still being tested for their viability.

The purpose of this work is twofold: first, it aims to contribute to the study of organisation a new concept and, ultimately, a new understanding of organisational identity. Second, it aims to put forward a theory of self-transformation – in other words, of change of identity – that is based on a radically new understanding of 'reality' and of the researcher's role in observing and describing it. The theoretical framework on which this study is based is that of New Systems Theory. According to this view, the objects of our observation are understood as systems that determine themselves and their relation to their environment in a *self-referential* way. This implies a renunciation of the traditional distinction between input and output, or cause and effect: outputs serve as their own inputs, effects as their own causes. Thus, such an approach implies an active engagement with paradoxicality.

For the purpose of our study we will focus on two theoretical works in particular. These are Niklas Luhmann's theory of social systems and George Spencer Brown's *Laws of Form*. Drawing on Luhmann, we will conceptualise social systems as communicative systems that reproduce themselves through their own communications. Accordingly, organisations will be understood as systems that reproduce themselves on the basis of *particular* communications; that is to say, decision communications. Spencer Brown's work will serve as a theoretical tool for analysing those self-referential systems. In contrast to traditional logic, the *Laws of Form* constitutes a three-valued logic, which is able to deal with paradoxical forms associated with self-referential systems.

---

[1] On reasons for the current interest in organisational identity see also Albert (1998); Albert et al. (2000); Brown (2001).

This approach to analysing organisational identity has been chosen not only because New Systems Theory generally provides genuinely new insights,[2] but also because it seems particularly suitable for our specific purpose. New Systems Theory is one of the very few theories that are able to combine the opposing ideas of stability and instability. According to this theory, stability, as associated with identity, can be conceptualised as the product of principally unstable processes.

In the first chapter we shall give an introduction to recent developments in systems-theoretical thinking: we shall explain Maturana's and Varela's theory of autopoiesis, as well as Luhmann's theory of social systems, and Spencer Brown's *Laws of Form*, and relate them to each other. In the second chapter we shall outline a general theory of organisations as autopoietic systems. To a large extent we shall draw on Luhmann's own writings on this topic. At several points, however, we will develop the theory further – particularly with regard to the concepts of organisational interaction and organisational culture. In the third chapter we shall explore the concept of organisational identity. We will take Luhmann's own theoretical work on this issue as a starting point for developing the concept and the theory further. We shall present a concept of organisational identity as a self-description by which the organisation refers to its own unity. In the fourth chapter, we shall analyse the logic of self-transformation, that is to say, the change of identity. We will identify the 'paradox of self-transformation' and explore organisational mechanisms for dealing with it. In the last chapter we shall develop an evolutionary model of self-transformation.

Due to the novelty of the issues and concepts presented, the following work can only be an exploratory study that opens up possibilities for further research. It does not presume to present a detailed and elaborately worked-out theory. Furthermore, due to the great extent to which *theoretical* issues have to be tackled, empirical investigations have to be dispensed with. For empirical substantiation of the theory we have to rely on further research.

---

[2]   According to Weick (1987) theories should be chosen on the basis of their capacity to stimulate new observation, rather than confirm what we have already seen.

Light | *Darkness*

Chapter 1

Autopoiesis, Luhmann, Spencer Brown

If there is anything like a central intellectual fascination in this century it is probably the discovery of the observer.[1]

Introduction

Under the title of 'new systems theory' the last decades have seen the development of a host of promising concepts, which propagate a radical departure from our current understanding of the world.[2] These ideas were developed in the spirit of the General Systems Theory, an explicit aim of which was to develop abstract, general concepts that were applicable to many different disciplines. Nevertheless, the concepts of new systems theory have found hardly any recognition in the wider research community. Possible reasons for this apparent negligence might be found, on the one hand, in the complexity of the ideas and thus the effort that is necessary to become acquainted with them, and on the other hand – and probably more importantly – in the 'revolutionary' novelty of the ideas, which made them (almost) impossible to grasp within the conventional frame of mind.[3]

In the social sciences, in particular, there were initially some half-hearted attempts at applying the new concepts, but when the first results proved inconsistent the efforts were soon dropped. In this respect, Luhmann's theory of social systems constitutes an important exception. It can be understood as a rigorous and consistent application of the new concepts to the social domain.

We begin the chapter with an account of new developments in systems theory, in particular Maturana's and Varela's biological theory of autopoiesis. In Section 2 we will present and explain Luhmann's theory of social systems, which can be understood as an application of the principles of autopoiesis to the social domain. In the Section 3 we will present and explain Spencer Brown's *Laws of Form*, which can serve as an analytical tool for exploring the self-referential loops of autopoietic systems.

---

[1]   Baecker (1996), p. 17 (my translation).
[2]   On the topics discussed in this chapter see also Seidl (forthcoming a) and Seidl and Becker (2006).
[3]   Luhmann speaks of 'paradigm change'. See Luhmann (1995a), pp. 1ff.

1.   New Systems Theory: The Concept of Self-Referential Autopoietic Systems

a.   Systems Theory as Transdisciplinary Paradigm

'General Systems Theory' as an area of academic research was founded by the biologist Ludwig von Bertalanffy and others in the early fifties. The aim was to create a genuinely transdisciplinary field of research.[4] On the grounds that different academic disciplines often dealt with very similar theoretical problems, it was believed that there was scope for synergies to be exploited. The idea was to abstract the solutions found within a specific field of research to a general level in order for other disciplines to be able to re-specify and apply them to their respective fields.[5]

The common ground on which those synergies were to rest was a specific approach to the objects of research: the systems approach. It was argued that the conventional approach of explaining characteristics of an object of observation solely on the basis of an analysis of its parts lead to 'analytical reductionism': many objects of observation possessed properties that could not be explained on the basis of the properties of their parts. An understanding of these so-called 'emergent' properties required a view of the object as a whole: as a system.

In contrast to an earlier phase of systems theory, which was based on a notion of *closed* systems and only analysed the internal relations between parts and whole, the General Systems tradition, as formulated by Von Bertalanffy, assumed an *open* systems model. It replaced the conceptualisation of systems according to the difference between *whole and parts* with that between *system and environment.*[6] This was often explained in terms of the findings in thermodynamics. According to the second law of thermodynamics the entropy of a closed system always increases. Thus, any closed system sooner or later dissolves. At the centre of the open systems model was the idea of systems transforming inputs from the environment into outputs into the environment. The system could be described as a particular input-output relation.[7]

A 'surpassingly radical further step'[8] within the systems tradition was taken in the seventies with the development of the concept of *self-referential systems*. In contrast to the open systems model, the concept of self-referential systems was not so much concerned with input-output relations as with the self-determination of the system through its own operations. The theory of self-referential systems

> maintains that systems can differentiate only by self-reference, which is to say, only insofar as systems refer to themselves [...] in constituting their elements and their elemental operations.[9]

---

[4]   See Von Bertalanffy (1973). For short summaries see Luhmann (1995a), pp. 1-11, or Skyttner (1996).

[5]   A particularly important aim was the development of a transdisciplinary terminology.

[6]   Luhmann (1995a), p. 6.

[7]   The black box model was developed in connection with the idea of open systems.

[8]   Luhmann (1995a), p. 8.

[9]   Luhmann (1995a), p. 9.

One of the most important contributions to this new phase of systems theory was the theory of autopoiesis, developed by the two biologists Humberto Maturana and Francisco Varela, which will be explained in the next section.[10]

b.   *Maturana's and Varela's Theory of Autopoiesis*

The theory of autopoiesis was developed by the two Chilean cognitive biologists Humberto Maturana and Francisco Varela in the sixties and early seventies. They were trying to answer the question: what is life? Or: what distinguishes the living from the non-living? Their answer was: a living system reproduces itself. This self-reproduction they referred to as *autopoiesis* (< Greek: αυτός = 'self' and ποείν = 'to make', 'to produce'). An autopoietic system is a system that recursively reproduces its elements through its own elements. Varela explains:

> An autopoietic system is organised (defined as a unity) as a network of processes of production (transformation and destruction) of components that produces the components that:
>
> 1.   through their interactions and transformations continuously regenerate and realize the network of processes (relations) that produces them; and
> 2.   constitute it (the machine) as a concrete unity in the space in which they exist by specifying the topological domain of its realization as such a network.[11]

Central to the concept of autopoiesis is the idea that the different components of the system interact in such a way as to produce and reproduce the components of the system. That is to say through its components the system reproduces itself. A living cell, for example, reproduces its own elements: proteins, lipids, etc. are not just imported from outside.

> [O]ne, perhaps the, major function of the living cell [is] the constant re-creation of itself from within.[12]

In contrast to *allopoietic* systems (< Greek: άλλος = 'other' and ποείν = 'to make', 'to produce'), the elements of autopoietic systems are not produced by something outside the system. All processes of autopoietic systems are produced by the system itself and all processes of autopoietic systems are processes of self-production. In this sense, one can say that autopoietic systems are *operatively closed*. There are neither elements entering the system from outside nor vice versa.

---

[10]   A second pillar of new systems theory is second-order cybernetics developed by Heinz von Foerster, see particularly Von Foerster (1981). The general ideas of second-order cybernetics are very similar to those of autopoiesis. However, due to their different background – second-order cybernetics is rooted in physics and engineering, and autopoiesis is rooted in biology – they present two distinct areas of research which have not yet completely merged.

[11]   Varela (1979), p. 13.

[12]   Rose (1970), p. 78.

A system's operative closure, however, does not imply a closed system model. It only implies a closure on the level of the *operations* in that no operations can enter or leave the system. Nevertheless, autopoietic systems are, also open systems. All autopoietic systems have contact with their environment. Living cells, for example, depend on an exchange of energy and matter without which they could not exist. The contact with the environment, however, is regulated by the autopoietic system; the system determines, when, what and through what channels energy or matter is exchanged with the environment.

This simultaneous openness and closure of the autopoietic system becomes particularly important when considering cognitive processes. For Maturana and Varela the concept of living is directly linked to the concept of cognition.

> Living systems are cognitive systems, and living as a process is a process of cognition.[13]

In this sense, the operations of an autopoietic system are defined as its cognitions; life and cognition are one and the same. Hence, everything that has been said about life applies to cognition: cognition is a self-referential, autopoietic process.

In light of this, we might take a further look at the relation between system and environment. The operative closure of the cognitive system means that the environment cannot produce operations in the system. Cognitions are only produced by other cognitions of the same system. The operative closure does not, however, imply a solipsistic existence of the system; on the contrary. As Maturana and Varela argue: operative closure is a precondition for interactional openness. On the level of its operations, the autopoietic system does not receive any inputs from the environment but only *perturbations* (or irritations), which might *trigger* internal operations in the system. The particular processing of the perturbations from outside is entirely determined by the system itself.[14]

Maturana and Varela generally distinguish between a system's *organisation*[15] and *structure*. 'Organisation' refers to the interrelations between the components of the system, which – independently of the components themselves – define the system as a distinct system in a given space-time continuum. In this sense, the organisation of the living system is autopoiesis. In order to speak of the same system the organisation of the system has to remain the same.

> The relations between components that define a composite unity (system) as a composite unity of a particular kind, constitute its organization. In this definition of organization the components are viewed only in relation to their participation in the constitution of the unity (whole) that they integrate.[16]

---

[13]   Maturana and Varela (1980), p. 13 (original emphasis).

[14]   One can speak of a replacement of the conventional input/output-modus through the perturbation/compensation-modus. See Mingers (1995a), pp. 33f.

[15]   Note that Luhmann does not share this terminology. See Luhmann (1992b), p. 184 fn. 15.

[16]   Maturana (1980b), p. xix.

'Structure' refers to the actual components and the actual relations between them:

> The actual components (all their properties included) and the actual relations holding between them that concretely realize a system as a particular member of the class (kind) of composite unities to which it belongs by its organization, constitute its structure.[17]

In contrast to the organisation, the structure is not constitutive of the system. Structures can change, and yet one can still speak of the same system. A caterpillar, for example, changes its structure radically during its transformation into a butterfly but is still the same animal. Hence, the theory of autopoietic systems distinguishes strictly between the continuation of autopoiesis and the stabilisation of particular structures.[18]

Closely connected to the distinction between organisation and structure is the shift from thinking in terms of structures to thinking in terms of processes. While conventional, stucturalist theories take their point of departure from the identification of structures and conceptualise processes as some sort of outcome of the structures,[19] the theory of autopoiesis[20] starts off with processes and describes structures as their product. Although themselves dependent on structures, processes can be seen to be primary as they can produce new structures.[21]

A central element of the theory of autopoiesis is the concept of *structural coupling*, with which Maturana and Varela refer to the relation between systems and their environments.[22] As explained above environmental events can trigger internal processes in an autopoietic system but the concrete processes triggered (and whether any processes are triggered at all) are determined by the structures of the system. For example, some animals have certain neuronal structures that allow certain electromagnetic waves in their environment to trigger internally the sensation of different colours; other animals possessing different neuronal structures might not be stimulated by such waves, or might be stimulated by them in other ways. A system is said to be structurally coupled to its environment (or other systems in its environment) if its structures are in some way or other 'adjusted' to the structures of the environment (or systems in the environment), i.e. if the structures of the system allow for reactions to 'important' environmental events.[23] Animals living above ground, for example, are structurally adapted to a different environment from those living underground. The former possess

---

[17] Maturana (1980b), p. xx.

[18] Luhmann (2000), p. 54. This is a major difference between the theory of autopoietic systems and structuralist theories, where the system is defined by its structure.

[19] Although so far they have not been able to explain how structures produce processes.

[20] Similar to that of Giddens (1984). For a comparison between autopoiesis and Giddens's theory of structuration see Mingers (1995b; 2004).

[21] Later on, Luhmann will speak of the primacy of operations over both structures and processes. Structure and process mutually presuppose each other and, ultimately, have to be explained on the basis of operations. Cf. Luhmann (2000), pp. 45-46.; Luhmann (1995a), p. 44.

[22] Maturana (1978), p. 35; Maturana (1980a), p. 70.

[23] It is important to note that every autopoietic system that exists is already adapted to its environment (and vice versa). Otherwise it would not exist. Cf. Luhmann (1992a), p. 563.

structures that can be stimulated by electromagnetic waves which produce differentiated impressions of colour, while the latter are more likely to possess structures that can be stimulated more easily by vibrations which produce equally differentiated impressions.

The structures of the autopoietic system are not given but are themselves the result of the autopoietic reproduction of the system in its environment. Varela writes about structural coupling that

> the continued interactions of a structurally plastic system in an environment with recurrent perturbations will produce a continual selection of the system's structure. This structure will determine, on the one hand, the state of the system and its domain of allowable perturbations, and on the other hand, will allow the system to operate in an environment without disintegration.[24]

It is important to note that in the concept of structural coupling adaptation is mutual. Not only is the system structurally adapted to its environment but also the other way around.[25]

c.   Summary: Input-Type Description vs. Closure-Type Description

New systems theory can be understood as a suggestion for a new way of approaching one's objects of observation.[26] In this sense it is one among several possible approaches, and as such it might be more or less suitable depending on the purposes of observation.

The traditional approach to observing a system focusses the attention on the interaction between system and environment. Input and output of the system are the most important dimensions. The internal processes and their relations are comparatively less important. That approach leads to an *input-type description* of the system:

> By an *input-type description* I mean that the definition of the system's organization is given by the *specific* ways in which it interacts with its environment, through a well-defined set of inputs followed by a transfer function. This [...] has been the standard mode of description in system's theory and cybernetics.[27]

New systems theory reverses the focus of attention. Instead of the interactions between system and environment, a system's internal interconnections become relatively more important. External influences – which are at the centre of the

---

[24]   Varela (1979), p. 33.
[25]   Maturana and Varela (1992), p. 102. This is particularly important if one considers the relation between two autopoietic systems, which constitute environment for each other. Cf. Varela (1979), pp. 48-49.
[26]   One can, of course, also conceive of autopoiesis as descriptions of the objects of observation. Hence the question is whether we conceive of something as a description or as a concept, which can be used for a description. In this respect, see also Luhmann (2000), p. 55.
[27]   Varela (1984), p. 25 (original emphasis).

input-type description – are marginalised and merely treated as perturbations for the internal processes. While the traditional approach views the interaction between system and environment as constitutive for the system, new systems theory puts more emphasis on the *self*-determination or *self*-assertion of the system. It therefore leads to a *closure-type description* of the system.

> The main consequence of changing from an input- to a closure-type stance for defining the organization of a system is that we concentrate on the inner coherences, and thus what used to be specific to the environmental inputs is bracketed as unspecific perturbations or simply noise. An input becomes a perturbation when it is no longer necessary to specify the system's organization, i.e. it has become noise.[28]

While both approaches acknowledge the importance of *both* external and internal influences, there is a major difference in the emphasis each puts on them: while the traditional approach treats the external influence as crucial and the internal influence merely as noise, new systems theory treats the internal influence as crucial and the external influence as noise.

2. Luhmann's Theory of Autopoietic Social Systems

a.   Luhmann's Transdisciplinary Concept of Autopoiesis

With his theory of social systems the sociologist Niklas Luhmann tries to make use of the concept of autopoiesis for the description of social phenomena.[29] In contrast to the attempts of other social scientists, who applied Maturana's and Varela's concept of autopoiesis directly to the social domain,[30] Luhmann abstracted the concept of autopoiesis from its physical-biological roots. In line with other concepts on the level of the transdisciplinary systems theory, he derives from this process a *general* concept of autopoiesis that leaves open the basis on which it is realised.[31] Luhmann explains his procedure:

---

[28]   Varela (1984), pp. 25-26 (original emphasis).
[29]   Maturana and Varela themselves were generally sceptical about the fruitfulness of such attempts. Explicitly: Varela (1981), p. 38. Varela (1979) suggests instead a modified version of autopoiesis, which he calls 'operational closure'. Maturana (1980c; 1988), in contrast, suggests treating the social merely as a medium in which the autopoiesis of living systems is realised. For social theories based on Maturana's view see e.g. Von Krogh and Roos (1995). For a general introduction to different applications of autopoiesis to the social sciences see Mingers (1995a).
[30]   E.g. Beer (1980); Zeleny and Hufford (1992); Robb (1989); Robb (1991). For criticisms see e.g. Mingers (1992); Mingers (1995a), pp. 123-128, Geyer (1992). Other researchers have suggested a metaphorical use of the concept of autopoiesis in the social sciences, most notably Morgan (1997). For criticisms on such a use see Mingers (1995a), pp. 151-152; Luhmann (2000), p. 49, fn. 31.
[31]   Luhmann (2000), p. 48. Luhmann complains that the close adherence of the concept of autopoiesis to biochemical processes has often led the discussion in the wrong direction.

[I]f we abstract from life and define autopoiesis as a general form of system-building using self-referential closure, we would have to admit that there are non-living autopoietic systems, different modes of autopoietic reproduction, and general principles of autopoietic organization which materialize as life, but also in other modes of circularity and self-reproduction. In other words, if we find non-living autopoietic systems in our world, then and only then will we need a truly general theory of autopoiesis which carefully avoids references which hold true only for living systems.[32]

Luhmann suggests that we speak of autopoiesis whenever the elements of a system are reproduced by the elements of the system.[33] This criterion, as he points out, is also met by non-biological systems. Apart from living systems, Luhmann identifies two additional types of autopoietic systems: social systems and psychic systems. While living systems reproduce themselves on the basis of life, social systems reproduce themselves on the basis of communication and psychic systems on the basis of consciousness. Furthermore, living systems can be differentiated into three subtypes: cells, brains and organisms. Equally, social systems can be divided into the three subtypes: society, interaction and organisation (Figure 1.1).

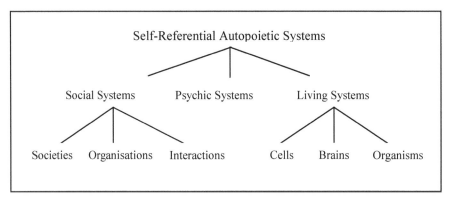

Figure 1.1 Types of autopoietic systems[34]

On the basis of this typology of systems one can derive a hierarchy of three levels of analysis.[35] On a first level we find statements that concern autopoietic systems in general without reference to any particular mode of reproduction. On this level we can find the general concept of autopoiesis. Statements on this level are equally valid for living as for social and psychological systems (and their respective subtypes). On a second level we find different applications of the general theory of autopoiesis. There are three such areas: research concerned with the particular

---

[32] Luhmann (1986), p. 172. See also Luhmann (1992a), pp. 131-132.
[33] Luhmann (1992a), p. 128.
[34] Luhmann (1986), p. 173.
[35] Luhmann (1986); Luhmann (1997), pp. 79-80.

characteristics of social systems, psychic systems, and living systems. Most of Maturana's and Varela's research can be placed on this level (in the area of living systems). It produces general statements concerning all types of living systems (cells, brains, organisms), but is not applicable to social or psychic systems. Psychological research is concerned with the particularities of systems that are reproduced on the basis of consciousness. Sociological research on this level is concerned with the particularities of systems reproducing themselves on the basis of communication. Statements produced in this area concern all three types of social systems. On a third level, in the biological field one can distinguish research concerning the particular mode of reproduction of cells, brains and organisms, while in the social field one can distinguish research concerning the particularities of societies, interactions and organisations. That is to say, for each type of system the particular mode of reproduction has to be defined and the consequences of the particular mode of reproduction analysed.[36] Thus, in social research in particular, one can identify four different areas: research on the general level of social systems[37] and research on the particular types of social systems – on the societal system,[38] on the organisation,[39] and on the interactional system.[40]

Against the backdrop of categorisation of analytical levels, the transformation of the original autopoiesis concept into the concept of autopoiesis of particular types of social systems becomes clear. Instead of just transferring the concept from the field of biology to the field of sociology, it is first *abstracted to a general concept on a transdisciplinary level*, before being re-specified into social autopoiesis and the autopoiesis of particular types of social systems.[41] Here, we cannot examine the abstraction of the concept of autopoiesis in detail, but merely want to highlight two important modifications: the *temporalisation* and *deontologisation* of the concept of element.

Luhmann's general concept of autopoiesis *radicalises the temporal aspect* of autopoiesis.[42] While Maturana and Varela conceptualise the elements of biological

---

[36] The particular modes of reproduction for the three types of social systems are: decision in the case of organisations, communication amongst people present in the case of interactions, and communications in the case of society (Luhmann (1995a). Society in this conceptualisation has an exceptional position, as it is both one type among others, and the one system that encompasses all other social systems. See Luhmann (1997), p. 80.

[37] E.g. Luhmann (1995a).

[38] E.g. Luhmann (1997).

[39] E.g. Luhmann (2000).

[40] E.g. Luhmann (1993a), pp. 81-100; Kieserling (1999).

[41] In a strict sense, Luhmann's theory of social systems is not an application of Maturana's and Varela's *biological* concept of autopoiesis. Consequently, it cannot be criticised against the backdrop of this *biological* concept as, for example, in Mingers (1995a), pp. 148-150 and Mingers (2002; 2003). Criticism, instead, either has to focus on its abstraction to the general level or its re-specification in the social domain.

[42] Of course, Maturana and Varela also refer to the temporal aspect of autopoiesis, i.e. when they speak of operations (operations are elements seen from the temporal perspective. See Luhmann [1997], p. 65). But while Maturana and Varela start off from the fact 'dimension' and integrate the temporal dimension into it, Luhmann intends to do the

systems as relatively stable chemical molecules, which have to be replaced from time to time, Luhmann conceptualises those elements as momentary *events* without duration[43] that vanish as soon as they come into being; they 'are momentary and immediately pass away'.[44]

> Events are elements fixed as points in time. [...] They occur only once and only in the briefest period necessary for their appearance (the 'specious present').[45]

Through this shift from a reproduction of relatively stable elements to a reproduction of momentary events, Luhmann radicalises the concept of autopoiesis. Because the elements of the system have no duration, the system is urged to constant production of new elements. If the autopoiesis stops, the system disappears.[46]

In addition to temporalisation, Luhmann *deontologises* the concept of element. Elements are defined as such merely through their integration into the system. Outside or independently of the system they have no status as elements; that is to say, they are 'not ontically pre-given'.[47] Elements can, of course, be composed of different components, which can be analysed independently of the system, but as elementary units they are only defined through the functions they serve for the system as a whole.[48] Luhmann writes:

> [W]e have deontologized the concept of element. Events [...] are not elements without substrate. But their unity corresponds to no unity in the substrate; it is created in the system through their connectivity. Elements are constituted by the systems that are composed of them [...][49]

As a consequence of deontologising the concept of element, the concept of 'production' (as in 'self-re-*production*') gets a functional meaning. Production refers to the *use* of an element in the network of elements. The important point in this conceptualisation is that the element and the use of the element are not two different issues, but two sides of the same coin. It is not that we first have the element and then the system makes use of it: only by being used (i.e. by becoming

---

reverse: start off from the temporal dimension and integrate the fact 'dimension' into it (see our explanations of the three dimensions of meaning below in Section d).

[43] This shift to the general level of autopoiesis is not always explicit. It can, however, be clearly inferred from his analysis on the lower level of social systems. For an explicit statement see Luhmann (2000), pp. 45f. Luhmann's conceptualisation of the basic elements as events shows many similarities with Whitehead's cosmology (1979).

[44] Luhmann (1995a), p. 287.

[45] Luhmann (1995a), p. 67.

[46] If one accepted Luhmann's suggestion for a development of the concept of autopoiesis on the level of the general theory, the theory of living systems would have to be adjusted accordingly. Ironically it is Luhmann who now questions Maturana's and Varela's original concept of autopoiesis in living systems. See Luhmann (2000), p. 53.

[47] Luhmann (1995a), p. 22.

[48] Luhmann (1997), p. 66.

[49] Luhmann (1995a), p. 215 (endnotes omitted); see also pp. 21-22.

integrated in the network of other elements) does an element become an element. Thus, one can say: the element is *produced* as a result of being used.[50] One can, of course, analyse the substratum on which an element rests, and find a whole range of *causal* factors which are involved in bringing it about, but the particular unity, as which the element functions in the system, can only be *produced* by the system.

b. Communicative Events as Elements of Social Systems

After our introduction to autopoiesis as a general concept on the transdisciplinary level, we now want to take a closer look at the realisation of autopoiesis in the social domain. In this and the following sections we are not concerned with the general principles of autopoiesis, but with the particularities of *social* autopoietic systems. The statements on this level of analysis, however, are still unspecific with regard to the particular realisation of autopoiesis in the three types of social systems (society, interaction, organisation).

The first decision Luhmann as a theoretician has to make for constructing his general sociological theory is, what to treat as the basic element of the social system. The sociological tradition suggests two alternatives: either persons or actions. Luhmann rejects both as incompatible with the concept of autopoietic social systems. Instead, he chooses a completely different element: communication; that is to say, the promotion of a 'conceptual revolution'.[51] He writes:

> Social systems use communications as their particular mode of autopoietic reproduction. Their elements are communications which are recursively produced and reproduced by a network of communications and which cannot exist outside of such a network.[52]

In order to understand this conception of social systems, we have to clarify Luhmann's *concept of communication*, which differs considerably from the conventional notion of communication as an asymmetrical process of transferring meaning or information from a sender to a receiver.[53] Building on the speech theories of Karl Bühler,[54] Luhmann conceives of communication as a combination of three components: information, utterance and understanding,[55] each of which is regarded as a selection.

In accordance with Shannon and Weaver,[56] *information* is defined as a selection from a repertoire of possibilities.[57] Every communication selects *what* is

---

[50] Luhmann (1997), pp. 65-66.
[51] Luhmann (1986), p. 178.
[52] Luhmann (1986), p. 174.
[53] Cf. Shannon and Weaver (1949).
[54] Bühler (1934).
[55] However, in contrast to Bühler – and later Austin and Searle – Luhmann does not conceive of these components as 'acts' or 'functions', but as selections. See Luhmann (1986), p. 188, fn. 2; Luhmann (1995b), pp. 117-118.
[56] Shannon and Weaver (1949).

being communicated from everything that could have been communicated.[58] Luhmann uses the term *utterance* to refer to the form of and reason for a communication: *how* and *why* something has been said. One can say that the utterance selects a particular form and reason from all possible forms and reasons. *Understanding* is conceptualised as the distinction between information and utterance. For a communication to be understood the information has to be distinguished from the utterance: what is being communicated must be distinguished from how and why it is communicated. For example, if alter says to ego[59]: 'I am tired', ego has to distinguish the information from the utterance (the words alter is using and the reason why alter is saying it). Understanding, here, includes *mis*understanding.[60] Ego might misunderstand the information: he or she might later realise that alter had said, 'I am tired of what I am doing'. It is also possible that ego might misunderstand the utterance: alter had actually wanted some advice on what to do about his tiredness. Thus, understanding can be understood as a selection of one particular distinction between information and understanding from all possible ones.

While most communication theories refer only to the first two elements (information and utterance), for Luhmann the third element, understanding, plays a central role. Instead of approaching a communication from an 'intended meaning' of the communication, Luhmann reverses the perspective: communications are conceptualised as determined through understanding. Von Foerster calls this the 'principle of hermeneutics'.[61]

> [This principle states] that not the speaker but the listener decides on the meaning of a message, since it is the latter whose understanding of the set of possibilities constrains the possible meaning of the message, no matter what the speaker may have had in mind.[62]

A central point in this concept of communication is that the three selections form an insoluble unit. The unit can be divided analytically into the three components, but only as a unit does it constitute a communication. As a consequence, a communication as this particular *unit* cannot be attributed to any one human being (psychic system). Instead, it constitutes an *emergent* property of the interacting psychic systems. In this sense Luhmann writes:

---

[57] Luhmann (1995a), p. 140. Similarly, Bateson (1972), p. 315: 'a difference which makes a difference'.

[58] The possibilities are defined by the system in which the communication takes place. Cf. Baecker (1999a; 2001).

[59] Luhmann reverses the usual perspective: the situation is not looked at from the perspective of the speaker but from that of the listener. See below.

[60] Conceptually there is no difference between understanding and misunderstanding.

[61] Von Foerster and Pörksen (1998), p. 100.

[62] Baecker (2001), p. 66. Similarly, Luhmann writes: 'Communication is made possible, so to speak, from behind, contrary to the temporal course of the process' Luhmann (1995a), p. 143.

[Communication] is a genuinely social (and the only genuinely social) operation. It is genuinely social in so far as it presupposes the involvement of a multitude of psychic systems but (precisely because of that) it cannot be attributed as a unit to a single psychic system.[63]

Thus, although human beings are necessarily involved in bringing about communication, the communication (as a unit) cannot be understood as the product of any one of them.

In order to render more precisely Luhmann's concept of communication, we have to take another, closer look at his concept of understanding. Understanding, as we said above, is the distinction between utterance and information; but whose understanding is of relevance here? Again, for Luhmann it is not the psychic system that is of interest, but the understanding implied by the ensuing communications – in the same way that the concrete meaning of a word in a text is only defined through the words following it in the text. Thus, the meaning of a communication – that is to say, what difference a communication makes for later communications – is only retrospectively defined through the later communications. For example, whether a 'yes' is understood as an approval or as a question or as a neutral acknowledgement of the given information is only determined through the reaction of the connecting communications. For instance, 'I'm happy you agree', 'you don't believe me?', or 'what is your own opinion?' (again, the meaning of these communications as such is only defined through the communications that are linked to them). In other words, Luhmann does not refer to any form of psychic understanding, but to an understanding on the level of the communications. What the 'involved' psychic systems think during the communication processes, that is to say, how the psychic systems understand the communication, is (at first) completely irrelevant to the communication. For example, the psychic systems might understand the 'yes' as a question, while the ensuing communications treat it as an approval. Of course, what the psychic systems think about the communications might ultimately influence the communications because of the structural coupling between the two systems: different thoughts about the communications might lead to the psychic systems causing different perturbations in the social system and thus might ultimately lead to different communications coming about. But it has to be stressed again that the psychic systems cannot determine what communications come about.

This retrospective determination of the communication through ensuing communications is connected with a fourth type of selection. With understanding, a communicative event as the synthesis of the three selections (utterance, information and understanding) is complete.[64] However, if the social system is not discontinued a fourth type of selection will take place: acceptance or rejection of the meaning of the communication.[65] This fourth selection is already part of the

---

[63] Luhmann (1997), p. 81 (my translation). Cf. also Luhmann (1992a), pp. 23ff.
[64] Understanding marks the temporal point at which the event takes place. A written communication, for example, is realised at the moment it is read. See Luhmann (1997), p. 72.
[65] Luhmann (1995a), pp. 147ff.

next communicative event. It is important not to confuse the third and fourth selections: understanding does not imply acceptance! For example, a pupil understands when the teacher says: 'do your homework' but he or she might still reject the communication, answering: 'No, I won't'. There might be communicative structures that make acceptance more likely than rejection, but the *concept* of communication is not focussed on acceptance – in contrast, for example, to Habermas's concept of communication.[66] On the contrary, every communicative event provokes the selection between acceptance and rejection. This distinction between understanding (as part of the first communication) and the selection acceptance/rejection (as part of the ensuing communication) adds a dynamic element, which bridges the gap from one communicative event to the next.

This leads to a very important point: the (re-)production of communications. In accordance with the general concept of autopoiesis, communications only 'exist' as communications through their relation to other communications. As explained above, a communication is only defined through the ensuing communications – in the same way that the meaning of a word in a text is only defined through the context of other words. This does not mean that without the relation there is nothing at all (there are, for example, words and sounds), but they have no status as communication. In this sense, one can say that it is the network of communications that 'produces' the communications. In other words, it is the context of other communications that makes it count as a communication at all. Luhmann thus famously said: 'Only communications can communicate.'[67]

While, as an operation, the three components of communication form an undecomposable unity, *further* communications (themselves being undecomposable for the moment) distinguish between information and utterance. They refer *either* to the information, i.e. the 'what' of the previous communication, *or* to the utterance, i.e. the 'how' and 'why' of the communication.[68] Focussing on either of these does not make the other irrelevant; on the contrary, it is a necessary background for the other. The relation is one of figure and ground.

c.   Self-Reference and Other-Reference

According to the distinction between information and utterance, communications distinguish between other-referentiality[69] (reference to something else) and self-referentiality (reference to itself). While information *refers* to something beyond the communication,[70] the utterance refers to the communication itself. For example, if alter says: 'My dog has died', the information (the dog is dead, it is not alive) refers to something beyond the communication system. The utterance, in contrast, refers to the communicative situation (alter said it, because he or she was

---

[66] Habermas (1987).
[67] e.g. Luhmann (2002), p. 169; Luhmann (1992a), p. 31.
[68] Luhmann (1986), p. 175; Luhmann (1995b), p. 118.
[69] The German term for this is *Fremdreferenz*, which in some texts is also translated as 'hetero-reference' or 'allo-reference'.
[70] Unless the communication becomes reflexive.

asked and he or she used particular words because the communication system provided a particular language). Thus, by distinguishing between utterance and information, communications distinguish between the communication system and its environment.

While the system itself distinguishes between self-reference and other-reference the entire process is essentially self-referential. Even other-reference is self-reference. Information cannot be imported from the environment. As Foerster famously said: 'the environment contains no information; the environment is as it is.'[71]

Information can only be created by the system itself. This is particularly evident in the definition of information as a 'change in system states',[72] that is to say, as 'a difference that makes a difference' for the system. It is the system itself that determines what can effect a change in its states. Luhmann writes:

> Information appears as a selection from a domain of potentialities that the system itself devises and holds to be relevant; but it appears as a selection that not the system but the environment carries out.[73]

Thus, it is not that the environment has no effect on the information, but it is the system that defines in what way it is to be affected by the environment. With regard to self-reference of the social system we have to distinguish two levels.[74] First, we can speak of a general self-reference on which the reproduction of the social system rests: communications only connect to communications; they cannot connect to anything outside the communication network. Second, communications distinguish between self-reference and other-reference as different aspects of communications. Other-reference and self-reference in this second case, however, are only attributions which the communication process itself makes. The communication process itself treats certain aspects of the communication as determined by the system and others as determined by the environment, although *both* are ultimately determined by the system.[75]

The distinction between the two levels of self-reference corresponds with two different kinds of boundaries between system and environment. First, the communication system is clearly distinguished from the environment through its elements: everything that is (a particular type of) communication is part of the system, while everything else is environment. Thus, with every communication the communication system redraws the distinction between system and environment as that between communication and everything else.[76] *Inside* the system the

---

[71] Von Foerster (1981), p. 263.

[72] Luhmann (1995a), p. 67.

[73] Luhmann (1995a), p. 68.

[74] To speak of 'levels' here, is just a way of dealing with the paradox that self-reference is both self-reference and other-reference.

[75] Cf. Luhmann (1997), p. 87.

[76] In the case of society the distinction is drawn as communication/non-communication (there is no communication outside the society). In the case of organisation the distinction is drawn as decision-communication/everything else, and in the case of interaction systems it is drawn as communication-among-people-present/everything else. See sections below.

distinction between communication system and environment is observed or represented as the distinction between self-reference and other-reference – a case of distinguishing between utterance and understanding. One could say that the distinction between system and environment is copied into the system.[77] In comparison with Maturana's and Varela's concept of boundary, here we can draw two conceptual differences: first, while for Maturana and Varela particular components of the system serve a boundary spanning function (e.g. membranes in the case of the cell),[78] for Luhmann there are no specific boundary elements: *every single operation redraws the boundary* just by virtue of being a (particular) communication (thus belonging to the system) and not something else (and thus belonging to the communication).[79] Second, while for Maturana and Varela the boundary can only be observed by an external observer (the system's operations simply take place inside the system 'unaware' of any boundary), for Luhmann the observation of the boundary according to the distinction self-reference/other-reference is an integral part of the autopoiesis of the social system.

d. Meaning

Meaning is 'the basic concept'[80] in Luhmann's social theory. It applies both to psychic and social systems and distinguishes them from the third type of autopoietic systems, i.e. living systems. Just as the autopoiesis of living systems is based on life, the autopoiesis of psychic and social systems is based on meaning. They can thus be called *meaning-constituted systems*.

As originally developed by Husserl,[81] the concept of meaning denotes the *surplus of references* to *other possibilities* of an experience or action. The meaning of 'knife', for example, is its reference to actions and experiences like cutting, stabbing, eating, operating, cooking etc. Thus, the knife is not only 'knife' as such but 'knife' with regard to something beyond the knife. In this context, Luhmann writes:

> The phenomenon of meaning appears as a surplus of references to other possibilities of experience and action. Something stands in the focal point, at the center of intention, and all else is indicated marginally as the horizon of an 'and so forth' of experience and action.[82]

Formally, meaning is defined as the difference between the real and the possible, or between actuality and potentiality. A momentarily actual experience or action refers to other momentarily not actual but possible experiences. The significance of this distinction becomes clear, if one looks at it from a dynamic perspective. While the one side of the distinction indicates what is momentarily

---

[77] Cf. Luhmann (2000), pp. 42f.
[78] Varela et al. (1974), pp. 192-193.
[79] It is, however, not a physical but a meaning boundary. See explanations below.
[80] Luhmann (1990b).
[81] Cf. Husserl (1948), pp. 23ff.; Husserl (1950), pp. 57ff., 100ff.
[82] Luhmann (1995a), p. 60.

actual, the other side indicates what could become actual next.[83] The (not actualised) possibilities are thus not unreal but not real *yet*. In this context, Luhmann speaks of the *virtualization of possibilities*:[84] the non-actual possibilities are virtually real and hint at their realisation at a later point in time.

Meaning is an event that disappears as soon as it appears. It marks a merely temporal point after which something else has to follow. The combination of this instability with the co-presentation of possible ensuing events results in the particular dynamic of meaning. Every meaning event disappears as soon as it takes place, but it *produces* further meaning events to succeed it. For Luhmann this 'auto-agility' of meaning events is 'autopoiesis par excellence'.[85]

Meaning processes can be described as the processing of the distinction between actuality and potentiality. A meaning event actualises one particular possibility, which it distinguishes from those possibilities that it leaves unactualised. After the event has taken place a new meaning event will have to select and actualise *one* of the presented possibilities. In this way, it will create a new distinction, and a new possibility will be actualised while everything else will be presented as possibility.

Meaning events not only distinguish between the actualised and the unactualised possibilities, but also differentiate between the unactualised possibilities; that is to say, they make 'suggestions' which of the given possibilities are to be actualised next. Luhmann writes:

> [E]very specific meaning qualifies itself by suggesting specific possibilities of connection and making others improbable, difficult, remote, or (temporarily) excluded.[86]

A particular meaning event suggests a multitude of possibilities for ensuing events, but is not the ensuing event in itself. In this sense, the suggestion of possibilities is not in the selection yet. Only the ensuing event can make the selection. As Luhmann writes:

> [T]he form of meaning, through its referential structure, *forces* the next step to *selection*.[87]

Luhmann distinguishes between three dimensions of meaning. In other words, the differences between the *possibilities* are 'redifferentiated'[88] according to three dimensions: fact dimension, temporal dimension and social dimension. The *fact dimension* distinguishes the surplus of reference into 'this' and 'something else'.[89] Something is 'this' and not something else. A knife is a knife and not a spoon, or

---

[83] Luhmann (1995a), p. 74.
[84] Luhmann (1995a), p. 65. On the concept of virtuality, see also Baecker (1999b), pp. 132-136; Esposito (1995).
[85] Luhmann (1995a), p. 66.
[86] Luhmann (1995a), p. 61 (endnote omitted). See also Luhmann (1990b), p. 48.
[87] Luhmann (1995a), p. 60 (original emphasis).
[88] Luhmann (1995a), p. 75.
[89] Luhmann (1995a), p. 76.

fork. The *temporal dimension* divides the reference structure into 'before' and 'after', as well as into the two horizons of past and future.[90] The *social dimension* refers to the differentiation of references according to the distinction of 'ego' and 'alter'. It is a distinction between different social perspectives.[91] In every meaningful event the three dimensions can only take place in combination.

e.   Structure

The concept of structures in Luhmann's theory of social systems is an important, but, notably, not its basic element. Structures are important in the sense that no social system can reproduce itself without structures, but they are not 'basic', as structures are conceptualised and explained as the *product* of the autopoiesis of the system.[92] Thus, with regard to autopoietic systems, one distinguishes between the *autopoiesis* of the system as the reproduction of operations through operations, and *self-organisation* as the production of particular structures as a *result* of the autopoiesis of the system.[93]

In contrast to most theories, structure is not defined as the relation between elements, as this would mean that the structures disappeared from moment to moment together with the elements that they related. This would contradict the central notion that structure endures beyond temporal points.[94] Instead, Luhmann suggests conceptualising structure as the *selection* of relations between elements. Luhmann writes:

> [R]elations acquire structural value only because the relations realised at any given time present a *selection from a plurality of combinatory possibilities* [...] And only *this* *selection* can be held *constant* across change in elements, that is, can be reproduced with new elements.[95]

The concept of structure does not therefore refer to the concrete relation between elements but to a *selection* of the concrete relation as one among several possible relations. While the concrete relation is bound to the concrete elements, the *selection* of a concrete relation is abstracted from the concrete elements.

In the form of structures autopoietic systems make (pre-)selections with regard to permissible relations for later situations and thus relieve those situations of some of the burden of selecting. In later situations there are still selections to be made (otherwise the autopoiesis would end), but the set of permissible relations is constrained. The effort of every event having to select between *all* possible

---

[90]   Luhmann (1995a), pp. 77-78.
[91]   Luhmann (1995a), pp. 80-81.
[92]   Luhmann (1995a), pp. 281-282.
[93]   Luhmann (2000), p. 47. See also Cooper (2006).
[94]   Luhmann (1995a), p. 283.
[95]   Luhmann (1995a), p. 283 (original emphasis).

relations would be too big for the reproduction of the system to be possible.[96] In connection to this, Luhmann writes:

> [O]nly by structuring that constrains can a system acquire enough 'internal guidance' to make self-reproduction possible.[97]

Structures of social and psychic systems are conceptualised as *meaning structures*. Every meaning event presents, as explained above, all possible connections. Structures now lead to a differentiation between these possibilities: some connections are 'more' probable than others.

The structures of *social* systems materialise as *expectations*. In social systems it is expectations that select possibilities for different communicative events to connect to each other.[98] For example, if alter asks ego for the time, ego is expected to tell him the time (or to tell him that he or she does not know the time), but he or she is not expected to tell him about the weather (although ego *could* tell him about the weather). Structures *suggest* certain connections between elements but they do not make the selection. If an expectation is disappointed, there will be other expectations, dealing with the resulting situation; for example, expectations about punishment.[99]

Luhmann conceives of a recursive relationship between structure and operation that is analogous to that of Giddens:[100] on the one hand, structures (pre-)select possibilities for operations and in this way both enable and restrict operations. On the other hand, operations reproduce or change structures. In the case of social systems, expectations 'guide' the emergent communications: to the extent that the realised communications meet those expectations, the expectations are confirmed and thus reproduced; to the extent that they do not meet those expectations, the expectations are changed.[101] For Luhmann, as for Giddens, structures have no independent existence apart from their realisation in the concrete operations; they only exist in the 'surplus of references' of the realised operations.

f. Interpenetration: The Relation between Social and Psychic Systems

The relation between social system and 'human being' is a very controversial aspect of Luhmann's theory. It is also the most misunderstood aspect. For an

---

[96] If all possible connections were equally probable, the system would be in an entropic state. See Luhmann (1995a), p. 285.

[97] Luhmann (1995a), p. 283.

[98] Apart from behavioural expectations there are also other expectations, which refer to non-social phenomena; social systems, for example, expect the functioning of clocks, cars, technology. See Luhmann (1995a), pp. 96-97; pp. 293ff.

[99] Luhmann (1992a), pp. 136ff.

[100] Giddens (1984). In contrast to Giddens, however, Luhmann does not assume any kind of human agency (see Section b above).

[101] Luhmann distinguishes between 'cognitive' and 'normative' expectations, which differ in their stability in the face of deviant operations. On this point see Chapter 5, Section 4.

adequate appreciation of Luhmann's theory it is thus necessary to outline carefully this relation.

First, we have to take a closer look at the concept of the 'human being'. In Luhmann's theory 'human beings' are not conceptualised as systemic unities, although they may appear so to themselves or other observers.[102] Instead, they have to be understood as conglomerates of different systems: psychic systems and organic systems,[103] which are operatively closed with regard to each other.

However, although the 'human being' does not constitute a systemic unity, the social system treats it as such: it constructs it as a *person*. In other words, persons do not exist as such – they are not systems. Persons are merely a construct of the social system that it uses to refer to the conglomerate of organic and psychic systems. A social system might for example construct the person 'John Smith'. Whenever the 'corresponding' conglomerate of organic and psychic systems causes perturbations in the social system, the social system will refer to it as caused by 'John Smith'. In the course of time, a social system will develop certain expectations about when and how this conglomerate might cause perturbations. These expectations become part of the construct 'John Smith'. Ultimately, we could say that a person is nothing other than a complex of expectations that a system has vis-à-vis a specific conglomerate of organic and psychic systems. Luhmann defines 'person' in this sense as the 'social identification of a complex of expectations directed toward an individual human being'.[104]

Particularly important for the social system is the psychic system. Like social systems, psychic systems are meaning-constituted systems. However, in contrast to social systems, the meaning events do not materialise as communications but as thoughts. In other words, psychic systems are closed on the basis of consciousness: only thoughts can produce thoughts.[105] However, systems are not only closed with regard to other kinds of systems – for example social systems – but also with regard to each other. No psychic system has direct access to another psychic system.[106]

The connection of one thought to another can be conceptualised in a similar way as in social systems. While a thought is an undecomposable unit in its capacity as an operation, *other* thoughts can decompose it and distinguish with regard to it between self-reference and other-reference:[107] they distinguish the thought itself (self-reference) from the content of the thought (other-reference).[108] As an operation, for example, a thought about justice is a unit, but other thoughts distinguish between the thought as such and justice as the content of the thought. Consequently, ensuing thoughts have two points to connect to: the thought as such

---

[102] Luhmann (1995a), p. 40.

[103] Luhmann (1995a), p. 210.

[104] Luhmann 1995a, p. 210.

[105] Not even events in the brain can take part in the autopoiesis of psychic systems: a nerve impulse is not a thought.

[106] Luhmann (1995b), p. 58.

[107] The distinction between self-reference and other-reference is, of course, itself self-referentially constituted. See above, Section c.

[108] Luhmann (1995b), pp. 62, 64.

– for example, they might think about reasons for thinking about justice – or the content – for example, they might think about ways of achieving justice.[109]

As operatively closed systems, psychic and social systems constitute 'environment' for each other: thoughts cannot become communications and communications cannot become thoughts. Mutual influences are restricted to the structural level. There merely exists a relation of structural coupling: both types of systems are *structurally* adapted to each other in a way which allows for mutual perturbation. In the case of psychic and social systems these perturbations are constitutive of each other. Luhmann calls it *interpenetration*.[110] He writes:

> By 'interpenetration' we mean that an autopoietic system presupposes the complex achievements of the autopoiesis of another system and can treat them as if part of its own system.[111]

The simultaneous (but separate) autopoiesis of psychic systems is constitutive for the autopoiesis of the social system. Without psychic systems social systems are impossible.[112] Every communicative event presupposes 'parallel' events in the psychic systems. For the perception of utterances, the social system already depends on the psychic system: the social system cannot hear spoken words, nor read letters. Furthermore, psychic systems serve as a memory as they can remember communicative events beyond their momentary point of existence. Because of their 'structural complementarity',[113] social systems can expect their communications to cause perturbations in the psychic systems and to receive perturbations from the psychic systems when necessary. They can, for example, count on psychic systems to trigger new communications after every communication. Although psychic systems trigger communication processes and vice versa – we repeat this point, since it is very important – the processes of the psychic system and the social system *do not overlap in any way*.

The most important evolutionary achievement for the coupling of social and psychic systems is language.[114] Language ensures that psychic systems are perturbed by the communication processes. Articulated speech, for example, normally disturbs people even if it is not actively involved in the communication more than mere noise is.[115] In this sense, Luhmann writes:

---

[109] Cf. Luhmann (1995b), p. 63.

[110] Luhmann's concept of interpenetration is not identical to that of Parsons. See Luhmann (1995a), pp. 546-547, endnote 5.

[111] Luhmann (1995b), p. 153 (my translation). On the relation between consciousness and communication, see also Baecker (1992).

[112] Consciousness is to some extent possible also without the social system, but probably only for some time and not in general. Cf. Luhmann (1995b), p. 39.

[113] Luhmann (1995b), p. 45.

[114] Luhmann (1995a), p. 272. This, however, does not mean that communication is only possible with language. One can also communicate, e.g. through laughing, through questioning looks, through dress etc. See Luhmann (1995a), p. 151.

[115] Luhmann (1995a), pp. 142-143.

Crucial [for the coupling between social and psychic systems] is [...] the differentiation of specific objects of perception which stand out and fascinate as they have no resemblance at all with anything else perceptible [...]. Language and writing fascinate and preoccupy consciousness and in this way ensure that it comes along, although consciousness's own dynamic does not necessitate this and always provides distractions.[116]

Although language is a purely social phenomenon (psychic systems do not think in language[117]) thought processes are mostly structured in a complementary way to language. Particularly during communication processes, thought processes are structured similarly to language: thoughts are broken down to sentences and words. To put it differently, psychic processes are synchronised with communication processes and, in this way, they 'know' when to contribute perturbations to the communication process in order to make the reproduction of the social system possible.[118]

Although Luhmann's strict distinction between social and psychic systems runs counter to our everyday beliefs and almost all social and psychological theories, it has an important theoretical advantage. It allows for a concept of the social which is clearly distinguished from that of the psychological. Consequently, social and psychic phenomena can be analysed in their own right. This does not lead to a marginalisation of the psychic with regard to the social system. On the contrary, through the differentiation it can be clearly shown that, and in what way, both systems depend on each other. The treatment of human beings as 'environment' of the social system (and not as part of it), as Luhmann writes,

does not mean that the human being is estimated as less important than traditionally. Anyone who thinks so (and such an understanding underlies either explicitly or implicitly all polemics against this proposal) has not understood the paradigm change in systems theory.

Systems theory begins with the unity of the difference between system and environment. The environment is a constitutive feature of this difference, thus it is no less important for the system than the system itself.[119]

g.   Communication and Action

While Luhmann suggests treating communications – and not actions – as the elements of social systems, the concept of action does not become completely irrelevant. On the contrary, Luhmann assigns it an important role in the reproduction of the system. The fact that not only sociologists but the social systems themselves use the concept of 'action', means that it cannot be ignored.

---

[116] Luhmann (1995b), p. 41 (my translation).

[117] Luhmann (1995a), p. 272.

[118] The adjustment of psychic structures according to social structures and particularly to language is captured in the concept of socialisation. See Luhmann (1995a), pp. 240ff.; Luhmann (1995b), p. 51.

[119] Luhmann (1995a), p. 212.

Many social theorists treat communication as some kind of action; in this sense Habermas, for example, speaks of 'communicative action'.[120] But, communication – and this is very important – is not a kind of action. As explained above, communication is constituted as a synthesis of a threefold selection of utterance, information and understanding. The concept of action cannot account for all three selections. It might capture the first two selections but certainly not understanding.

[T]he perfection of communication implies understanding and understanding is not part of the activity of the communicator and cannot be attributed to him.[121]

Thus, a central element of communication would be missing if communication were interpreted as action. Apart from that, according to Luhmann the original intention of an action is not important for the communication. For example, looking at one's watch might be understood as communicating one's boredom, although one only wanted to know what time it was.

Luhmann suggests treating action as a concept of social systems for *observing* their communications; that is to say, social systems observe their communications not as communications but as actions. They (falsely) *attribute* the selectivity of the communication to an 'actor' (to a person) and in this way shift the responsibility for the selection onto him/her.

In this way, the social system creates a second version (or description) of itself as a nexus of actions.[122] This second version constitutes a simplification of the system and this is also where its function lies. The simplified version of itself serves as orientation for its (re-)production: first, actions are easier to recognise and deal with than communications. While an orientation according to communications presupposes a clear distinction between utterance, information and understanding, an orientation according to action only has to deal with the specific rules of attribution.

The simplification lies in the fact that only actions and not fully communicative events serve as connective points, in that an abstraction suffices to communicate action or simply connective behaviour, and in that one can to a great extent omit the complexities of the complete communicative occurrence. The fact that one need not examine (or need examine only under very specific conditions) which information an utterance referred to and who understood it takes some of the load off.[123]

Second, the description of communicative processes as connections of actions leads to clear-cut temporal relations between different elements. Communications are completed only once understanding has taken place; that is, the communicative

---

[120] Habermas (1987).

[121] Luhmann (1986), p. 178.

[122] Luhmann (1986), p. 178; Luhmann (1995a), p. 165.

[123] Luhmann (1995a), p. 168.

occurrence is 'held in suspense'[124] between utterance and understanding, whereas actions mark one point in time (determined by the utterance). As a consequence, the different events are also much more clearly differentiated from each other:[125] while communications are heavily entangled with each other – with later communications retrospectively defining earlier ones – actions appear to be self-defined and do not presuppose other actions.

3. A Theory of Observation: Spencer Brown's *Laws of Form*

Having presented and explained the essential features of recent developments in systems thinking, we will now turn to Spencer Brown's mathematics of distinctions, which can serve as a tool for analysing the complex operations of self-referential systems. From the classical perspective of two-valued logic, self-referential operations are incomprehensible: they constitute a paradox, which requires a third value. Even from the perspective of Hegelian dialectics, which in principle is capable of dealing with such forms, one would quickly lose orientation in the web of self-referential loops. The *Laws of Form*, in contrast, are complex enough to deal with self-reference, but at the same time of such simplicity that, if one makes the effort of acquainting oneself with them, they can elucidate even the deepest jungle of self-referential connections.[126] This analytical rigour can only be won at the cost of an extremely dry and abstract format. However, in view of its advantages we consider a presentation and explanation of the *Laws of Form* at this point indispensable.[127]

a. The Observer

Spencer Brown suggests treating *observation* as the most basic concept for any analysis. As a concept it is supposed to be even more basic than, for example, that of thing, event, thought, action or communication.[128] This means, of course, that the term 'observation' is not used in its usual sense as referring merely to optical perception. Instead, 'observation' is used as an abstract concept referring to any operation from communication to thought and even to the operation of a machine;[129] even the observer is treated as an observation.[130]

Spencer Brown's concept of observation does not focus on the object of observation but on the observation itself as a *selection* of what to observe. In this

---

[124] Luhmann (1995a), p. 169. This is particularly extreme in the case of written communication, where the understanding often takes place considerably later than the utterance: e.g. the writing of the letter. See Luhmann (1997), p. 72.

[125] Luhmann (1986), p. 178.

[126] Cf. Baecker (1993a), p. 20; Luhmann (2000), p. 8.

[127] Luhmann himself and Baecker, in particular, make use of the *Laws of Form* for the analysis of self-referential systems.

[128] Luhmann (2000), p. 126.

[129] Even the concept of observation itself is an observation. See Luhmann (2000), p. 126.

[130] Spencer Brown (1979), p. 76.

sense, the underlying question is not: *what* does an observer observe, but *how* does an observer observe; *how* is it that an observer is observing what he or she is observing, and not observing something else.[131]

Every observation is constructed from two components: a distinction and an indication. An observer chooses a *distinction* with which he or she demarcates a space into two spaces (states or contents). Of these two states he or she has to choose one which he or she *indicates*. That is to say, the observer has to focus on one state, while neglecting the other. It is not possible to focus on both simultaneously. In this sense, the relation between the two states is asymmetrical. We have a *marked* state and an *unmarked* state.[132]

Spencer Brown illustrates this rather abstract idea with an example. Let us imagine a uniform white piece of paper. On this paper we draw a circle. In other words, we draw (!) a distinction which creates an inside of the circle and an outside of the circle. It is important to note that it is the act of drawing the circle that establishes the two different states: without us drawing the distinction, the *two* states as such do not exist.[133] We can now indicate one of the two states: either the inside or the outside. Let us choose the inside. The inside becomes the marked state and the outside the unmarked state. While we can see the marked state, the unmarked state remains unseen. With the metaphor of figure and ground we can say: the inside becomes figure and the outside ground.

Spencer Brown calls the distinction with *both* sides the *form* of the distinction.

> Call the space cloven by any distinction, together with the entire content of the space, the form of the distinction.[134]

Thus, in contrast to the common use of the term, form does not refer merely to the marked state. The form of something is not sufficiently described by the de-fined – the marked state – but the unmarked state is a constitutive part of it.[135] In our example, the form of the circle is the inside together with the outside of the circle. In this sense Spencer Brown declares:

> *Distinction is perfect continence.*[136]

A distinction has thus a double function: like any boundary it both distinguishes and unites its two sides.[137]

---

[131] The switch from 'what'-questions to 'how'-questions is also characteristic of Luhmann's work. See Luhmann (1993b), pp. 14-30.

[132] Distinction and indication have to be conceptualised as taking place simultaneously. For reasons of clarity, however, we have presented them in a temporal sequence.

[133] On this point, see also Cooper (1986); Chia (1994).

[134] Spencer Brown (1979), p. 4.

[135] Cf. Simon (1993b), p. 46; Luhmann (1993b), pp. 17ff.

[136] Spencer Brown (1979), p. 1 (original emphasis).

[137] On the theoretical implications of understanding boundaries as both separating and joining, see also Cooper (1986).

Another important element of the *Laws of Form* is the unwritten distinction (*unwritten cross*), which defines the space within which the distinction is drawn.[138] In the above example it is the distinction between the piece of paper and the rest of the world. As the border of the unmarked state it remains equally unobserved as the unmarked space. Now we have a complete unit of observation: a space defined by an unwritten cross is divided by a distinction into two states; the relation between the two states becomes asymmetrical by indicating one state as the marked state in contrast to the other, which becomes the unmarked state.

The central point in this concept is that once you have drawn a distinction you cannot see the distinction that constitutes the observation – you can only see *one* side of it. With Heinz von Foerster this can be referred to as the 'blind spot'[139] of observation. The complete distinction with *both* its sides (the inside *and* the outside), can only be seen from *outside*; if you are inside the distinction you cannot see the distinction.

Two orders of observation can be distinguished: first-order and second-order observation.[140] So far we have been explaining the operation of first-order observers, who cannot observe the distinction they use in order to observe. Second-order observers are observers who observe other observers. They use different distinctions from the first-order observers: in order to observe the other observers, they have to draw distinctions that contain the distinctions (the marked and the unmarked state) of the first-order observers in *their* marked state. Second-order observers can see the blind spot, the distinction, of the first-order observers. They can see *what* the first-order observers cannot see and they can see *that* they cannot see.[141] Particularly, they can see that the particular vision and blindness of the first-order observers is due to their using particular distinctions and not other ones. They see that they could also have used other distinctions and, thus, that their observation is *contingent*.[142] In this sense, a second-order observation is more than a first-order observation, because it does not only see its object (first-order observation), but it also sees, what this object sees, and how it sees; and it even sees, what it does not see, and sees, that it does not see, that it does not see, what it does not see.[143]

Since second-order observers need distinctions to observe the distinctions of the first-order observers, they themselves are first-order observers, who could be observed by other second-order observers. In this sense, second-order observation is only possible as first-order observation.[144]

---

[138] Spencer Brown (1979), p. 7.
[139] Von Foerster (1981), pp. 288-309.
[140] Von Foerster (1981). Spencer Brown himself does not explicitly speak of first-order and second-order observers, but this is implied.
[141] Luhmann (1991c), p. 75.
[142] 'Contingent', here, in the sense of 'also possible differently'.
[143] Luhmann (1993b), p. 16.
[144] Luhmann (1993b), p. 15.

b. *The Calculus*

In his *Laws of Form* Spencer Brown does not only offer a concept of observation, but, most importantly, he also describes how observations are connected to each other. He presents different 'laws' for relating observations to each other. In other words, the *Laws of Form* constitutes a mathematics for 'calculating' observations.

In order to formalise this concept, Spencer Brown introduces a specific notation to refer to the distinction, 'the mark of distinction' or the 'cross': ¬.[145] Spencer Brown writes:

Let a state distinguished by the distinction be marked with a mark ¬ of distinction.[146]

This sign symbolises a boundary that distinguishes two sides. Connected with this sign is the instruction to cross the boundary from the right (convex) to the left (concave) side, by which the left side becomes the marked and the right side the unmarked side.

It is important to understand that the 'cross' has *two* meanings here: an operative and a descriptive meaning.[147] Firstly, the cross stands for an *instruction* to cross (!) the distinction from unmarked to marked state. Secondly, the cross stands as a *sign for* the marked state. In this sense Spencer Brown writes:

In the command
let the crossing be to the
state indicated by the token
we at once make the token doubly meaningful, first as an instruction to cross, secondly as an indicator (and thus a name) of where the crossing has taken us.[148]

In terms of the calculus the cross is used both as operator and operand: on the one hand, it gives instructions to calculate and, on the other hand, it is the element that is calculated.[149] This double meaning might be confusing but as Spencer Brown writes:

It is the condensation [of the two meanings into one symbol] which gives the symbol its *power*.[150]

After the first distinction has been drawn, all following observations (distinctions) have to start off from this first marked state. There are only two operations that can follow: the same distinction can be repeated, or the distinction

---

[145] Spencer Brown also uses the terms 'mark', 'sign' and 'token' to refer to the cross.

[146] Spencer Brown (1979), p. 4.

[147] Cf. Kibéd and Matzke (1993), pp. 59f.

[148] Spencer Brown (1979), p. 81.

[149] Because of this double meaning of the cross Spencer Brown is able to develop his mathematics with just one single symbol.

[150] Spencer Brown (1979), p. 81.

can be cancelled. Spencer Brown's two (only) axioms deal with these two alternatives.[151]

The first axiom is the *law of calling*

Axiom 1. The law of calling
The value of a call made again is the value of the call
That is to say, if a name is called and then called again, the value indicated by the two calls taken together is the value indicated by one of them. That is to say, for any name, to recall is to call.[152]

Formally: ¬¬ → ¬.

If we draw a distinction with a marked and an unmarked state and then we indicate the same distinction again, there is no change in the distinction. Thus, it is as if the distinction had been drawn only once. Observing the same thing twice is the same as observing it once. Axiom 1 corresponds with the *descriptive* aspect of the cross: once we have drawn a distinction we can *indicate* or *name* it many times without changing the distinction.[153] With regard to our example from above, the law of calling states that we can name the circle several times ('circle', 'circle') without changing anything about the circle.

The second axiom is the *law of crossing*:

Axiom 2. The law of crossing
The value of a crossing made again is not the value of the crossing
That is to say, if it is intended to cross a boundary then it is intended to cross again, the value indicated by the two intentions taken together is the value indicated by none of them. That is to say, for any boundary to recross is not to cross.[154]

Formally: ⫟ →   .

In contrast to the first axiom, the *law of crossing* corresponds with the *operative* aspect of the cross. Having crossed to the marked state, the only possible second crossing is from the marked state back to the unmarked state. Thus, the first distinction is dissolved.[155] With regard to our example from above, the law of crossing states that while a first instruction 'cross the boundary!' leads us into the circle, a second instruction 'cross the boundary!' can only lead us out again. Thus, the meaning of the two instructions taken together is the same as no instruction at all.

---

[151] Spencer Brown's entire calculus rests on these two axioms.

[152] Spencer Brown (1979), p. 1 (original emphasis).

[153] It is important to understand that the cross is not meant as instruction here. As instruction it would not make sense: having crossed to the inside, one can only cross to the outside (see axiom 2).

[154] Spencer Brown (1979), p. 2 (original emphasis).

[155] Kibéd and Matzke (1993), pp. 67f., emphasise that the double crossing does not mean an indication of the unmarked state.

Based on the two axioms, observations can be presented as combinations of distinctions. An observation can either be presented simply with one cross or as an 'arrangement'[156] of several crosses. That is to say, arrangements of crosses can be transformed into other arrangements without changing their meaning. In this sense, the *Laws of Form* can be understood as a *calculus*, which allows the 'calculation' of observations. Spencer Brown writes:

> Call calculation a procedure by which, as a consequence of steps, a form is changed for another, and call a system of constructions which allows calculation a calculus.[157]

Spencer Brown distinguishes two basic transformations: Through an *expansion of reference*[158] an arrangement of distinction is transformed into a longer arrangement, and through a *contraction of reference*[159] it is transformed into a shorter one. Both axioms can be used both for an expansion and a contraction of reference.

According to the law of calling we get an expansion of reference through the repetition of the same distinction ($\neg \rightarrow \neg\neg$). This operation is called *confirmation*. A contraction of reference according to the law of calling is achieved through the elimination of one distinction ($\neg\neg \rightarrow \neg$). This operation is called *condensation*. According to the law of crossing we get an expansion of reference through the introduction of double crossings ($\rightarrow \neg$). This operation is called *compensation*. A contraction of reference according to the law of crossing is achieved through the cancellation of a double cross ($\neg \rightarrow$). This operation is called *cancellation*.

This means that if we want to indicate a certain state we can do so in a simple way by just using *one* sign. We can, however, indicate the same state through an expansion of reference by repetition of the same sign or the introduction of double crosses. Neither form of expansions of reference changes the value of the state indicated. In the other direction all arrangements of distinction can be simplified to one single state – either marked state or unmarked state.

c. The Re-entry

The most interesting idea in the *Laws of Form* – at least in our context – is the concept of *re-entry*, which deals with self-observation, that is to say, the concept of a distinction being used for observing the distinction used.

The concept of re-entry offers a new solution for dealing with paradoxes.[160] Let us consider Epimenides's paradox: 'this statement is false.' If the statement is false it is true, and if it is true it is false. For the conventional, two-valued logic such

---

[156] Spencer Brown (1979), p. 4.
[157] Spencer Brown (1979), p. 11.
[158] Spencer Brown (1979), p. 10.
[159] Ibid.
[160] Cf. Spencer Brown (1979), pp. xiii ff.

paradoxes are an impossibility: a (meaningful)[161] statement is *either* true *or* false, but it cannot be *both* true *and* false – *tertia non datur*. The solution offered to this problem by Whitehead and Russell was the 'Theory of Types',[162] which simply 'disallowed' paradoxes in logic. In our example one can, according to the Theory of Types, distinguish a statement (the statement stating something) and a meta-statement (the statement *about* the statement), which have collapsed into one statement. The Theory of Types states that both types of statements belong to different levels and must be *strictly* distinguished from each other.

Spencer Brown's 'solution' to the problem of paradox, however, does not need such an (arbitrary) 'rule':[163] instead, a paradox is conceptualised as a distinction that re-enters itself. We can analyse the above statement accordingly. The statement constitutes an observation in Spencer Brown's terms: it observes by drawing a distinction between true and false indicating false. With this distinction (true/false) the observation observes its own observation, i.e. on the inside of the distinction, the distinction includes the distinction true/false, indicating true. Thus, the statement distinguishes not only false from true but also true from true (Figure 1.2).[164]

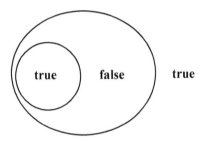

Figure 1.2 The logical structure of the statement 'This statement is false'

The problem, now, is that an observation cannot indicate both sides of the distinction at the same time. As we have seen in the last sections, an observer first has to cross to the other side (and thus dissolve the original distinction), before he or she can observe the unmarked state. In other words, the observer is either on the inside or the outside but not on both sides at the same time.

---

[161] The classical logic has an implicit third value: a sentence is either true or false or meaningless. See Spencer Brown (1979), pp. xiv-xv.

[162] Whitehead and Russell (1913).

[163] Russell saw the Theory of Types as refuted by the *Laws of Form*. See Spencer Brown (1979), pp. xiii-xiv.

[164] The analysis of the structure of the sentence could also have started differently: the statement itself is the first distinction between true and false indicating true (it is presented as a true sentence). On the inside of the distinction (true) the sentence contains the distinction true/false indicating false. Thus, taken together the sentence distinguishes false from both true and false. For our argument it does not make a difference from where we start.

Spencer Brown's solution to the problem of the observation of the outside from within is the introduction of a *tunnel* connecting both sides of the distinction. This enables the observer to get to the other side without having to cross the boundary and hence without dissolving the distinction (Figure 1.3).

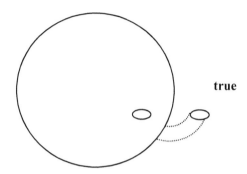

Figure 1.3 The tunnel connecting marked and unmarked state

With the tunnel metaphor two important points are expressed: first, one can get to the other side without having to cross the boundary, i.e. without creating a double crossing. Second, as the tunnel runs underneath the boundary, there is no point on the way through the tunnel from which both sides of the distinction can be observed simultaneously. When *entering* into the tunnel one observes the one side and when *leaving* the tunnel one observes the other. In other words, the two sides of the distinction can only be observed at different *times*. This is a crucial point: with the concept of re-entry time is introduced into the calculus. Getting from one side of the distinction to the other takes time – Spencer Brown also says: it 'constitutes' time.[165] In this sense, the paradox is dissolved into an oscillation in time.

The observation of our above example can thus be described as an oscillation between true and false: when it is true it becomes false, which makes it true and as a consequence false. The two-valued logic (true/false, inside/outside, marked/unmarked) is thus expanded by an additional value: the *imaginary value*.[166] If a statement is neither true nor false (neither inside nor outside, neither marked nor unmarked), it has an imaginary value, which describes an oscillation between the two sides of the distinction.[167]

In Von Foerster's terms the concept of re-entry deals with an observation serving both as first-order and second-order observation for itself. Every observation, as we have said above, uses a distinction for observing, which it

---

[165] Spencer Brown (1979), pp. 58ff.

[166] Spencer Brown (1979), p. 61. Varela (1975) introduces a new sign for the imaginary value: ⌐, which was probably derived from Spencer Brown's own sign. See Spencer Brown (1979), p. 65.

[167] Cf. Baecker (1993b), p. 28.

cannot see (its blind spot). The distinction used for observing can only be seen from outside. Hence, in order to observe its distinction the observation has to get onto the outside of the distinction. In this sense, self-observation can be conceptualised as re-entry, as the outside re-enters the inside. The observer has to oscillate between both sides of the distinction that he or she uses for his or her observation. Hence, he or she oscillates between a first-order and second-order observation. As a consequence of this process taking time, the observer can only see him/herself with a time lag: the observer whom he or she observes is the observer from a little time ago. Thus, the distinction he or she observes is not identical with the distinction he or she uses in order to observe. In this respect, Spencer Brown, distinguishes between 'cross' and 'mark':[168] the mark stands for the cross but it is not the cross.[169]

4.   The *Laws of Form* and the Theory of Social Systems

On the basis of the calculus of forms, Luhmann described autopoietic systems as distinction-processing systems. Every operation of an autopoietic system constitutes an observation, i.e. a distinction and indication. Take, for example, communication: every communication communicates something (marked state) while at the same time having to leave everything else unsaid; in particular all other possible communications (unmarked state). These other possibilities of communication, however, are not just other communicative options which just happen not to have been realised, but are constitutive for the realised communication: the meaning of the communication depends to a large extent on what has not been communicated. In other words, one needs to know what could have been communicated (i.e. the context of the communication) in order to establish the meaning of the communication. These other possibilities are on the unmarked side of the communication – as they have not been communicated. Other communications (second order observation), however, can communicate about the communication (first order observation) and its unmarked state, but only at the cost of producing yet another unmarked state. Thus, the communication can never fully communicate about its own conditions of communication.

Not only the operations but also the system itself can be conceptualised as observation, i.e. distinction and indication. A system is constituted as a distinction between system and environment, of which the system is the marked state and the environment the unmarked state. In accordance with Spencer Brown's concept of observation, system and environment are the two sides of the same distinction and as such are constitutive for each other.

While an observer can draw his distinctions where he or she likes and thus define what to treat as a system and what as environment, the concept of

---

[168] Spencer Brown (1979), pp. 64-65. Cf. Baecker (1993a), pp. 23, 25.
[169] The re-entered distinction is the same and not the same. See Luhmann (1992a), pp. 379-380.

autopoiesis assumes that the system/environment distinction is not drawn by an external observer but by the system itself. Luhmann in this sense writes:

> If we describe [something] as an autopoietic system, we are dealing with the production and reproduction of a distinction (in systems-theoretical terms: the distinction of system and environment), and the concept of autopoiesis says that an observer using it assumes that the difference is produced and reproduced by the operations of the system itself.[170]

How are we to understand this reproduction of the system/environment distinction? Every operation of an autopoietic system constitutes a distinction between that which it is, i.e. an operation of the system, and that which it is not, i.e. an operation of the environment. The operations of the social system are communications. Every communication constitutes a distinction between that which it is (marked state), i.e. a communication and thus an element of the social system, and that which it is not (unmarked state), e.g. a thought. In this sense, every single communication (re-)draws the distinction between communication system and environment. Thus, in actual fact, the reproduction of communications is the reproduction of the distinction communication/non-communication, i.e. of the distinction between communication system and environment. According to this conceptualisation every single operation of a system reproduces the 'boundary' of the system.

This conceptualisation of the system's boundary as reproduced by every single operation implies an operative closure of the system: every operation constitutes a distinction between the operation and everything else (i.e. between system and environment). It can only be this operation that constitutes the one side (marked state) of the distinction and not the other (unmarked state). For example, a communication is only a communication (marked state) to the extent that it is not something else (unmarked state). In this sense, operative closure of a system means that the system (i.e. system/environment distinction) is only reproduced by operations that are themselves constituted as a system/environment distinction. The 'communication system/environment' distinction, for instance, can only be reproduced by operations constituted as communication/non-communication distinctions. Other distinctions, for example, thought/non-thought (communication is here included in the unmarked space), cannot be reproduced in this manner. The integration of other distinctions, in which communication is included in the unmarked space, would dissolve the 'communication system/environment' distinction and thus dissolve the system. In other words, the system cannot enter its environment, nor could the environment enter the system; otherwise the distinction between system and environment would disappear.

We can also describe the autopoietic reproduction of elements through their own elements with Spencer Brown's two laws: drawing on the 'law of calling' we can say that every communication (being constituted as a system/environment distinction) confirms the system/environment distinction. Or, the other way around,

---

[170] Luhmann (2000), p. 55; my translation.

we can say that all communications taken together condense into the system/environment distinction.

The 'law of crossing' offers the basis for an argument – in terms of a rigorous logic – for conceptualising social systems as operatively closed. As explained, a system is created by communications drawing a distinction between system and environment, indicating the system. If any other type of operation (a different distinction indicating something else) connected to the communications, it would constitute (together with the communication) a double distinction leading out of the system, and the system/environment distinction would be dissolved.

Finally, we can apply the concept of re-entry. Although autopoietic systems can only operate on their inside (marked state) and have no contact to their outside (unmarked state), the system/environment distinction can re-enter the system: every single operation distinguishes between other operations of the same system and other events outside the system. In other words, every operation has a self-referential aspect and an other-referential aspect. Take, for example, the communication as an element of a social system. Every communication can be divided on the one hand into the utterance, i.e. how and why something is expressed, which is (treated as) determined by the communication system (self-reference), and on the other hand into the information, i.e. what is expressed, which is (treated as) referring to events in the environment (other-reference). For example, A says to B: 'my dog is dead'. Here we can distinguish between the utterance (i.e. the words A uses, what other communications this communication refers to, etc.) as the self-referential aspect, and the information about a dog being dead as referring to something outside the communication network (other-reference). The important point here is that the re-entered distinction is not identical with the distinction itself: first, the utterance/information distinction is not the system/environment distinction – a communication is not a system – and second, the information about the dog being dead is not the dead dog.

Chapter 2

Organisation as Autopoietic System

Introduction

For our present purpose of studying organisational identity and self-transformation it seems necessary that we first clarify the concept of organisation on which the study is to be based.[1] If we do not have a clear concept of organisation in the first place, we cannot expect to develop a meaningful concept of either *organisational* identity or *organisational* self-transformation. Yet, given the ubiquity of organisations, both as a 'reality' in social life and as a topic of research, one will be surprised to find hardly any (explicit) definition of organisation in the relevant literature. Take for example, the opening of the classic book on 'organisation' by March and Simon:

> This book is about the theory of formal organizations. It is easier and probably more useful, to give examples of formal organizations than to define the term. [...] [F]or present purposes we need not trouble ourselves about the precise boundaries to be drawn around an organization or the exact distinction between an 'organization' and a 'nonorganization'.[2]

In a similar way most studies presuppose the concept of organisation as commonsensical and start directly with the analysis of specific phenomena *in* organisations. While for some purposes such a procedure might indeed be fruitful, we cannot rest content with this position.

On the basis of his theory of social systems, Luhmann develops a concept of organisation that allows us to conceive of it as a unified system and to distinguish it clearly from other social systems. The important point in Luhmann's approach is, not to infer a classifying distinction from outside but to look at the way the organisation distinguishes *itself* from its environment.[3]

In the following sections we will first elaborate on the concept of organisation as an autopoietic system that operates on the basis of decisions (or to be precise:

---

[1] On the topics of this chapter see also Seidl and Becker (2006) and Seidl (forthcoming a; forthcoming b).

[2] March and Simon (1958), p. 1. Later in the text, however, March and Simon come close to defining organisations, when they contend that the influence that organisations impinge on the individual is '*specific*' in contrast to the '*diffuseness*' of many other influence processes in society (pp. 2-3).

[3] Luhmann (2000), p. 45. For a general review of the potential contributions of Luhmann's autopoiesis theory to organisation theory see Hernes and Bakken (2003).

decision communications). In the second section we will relate the concept of organisation to society as the all-embracing system of communication. In the third section we will analyse the relation between organisation and interaction. In the last section we will suggest a new conceptualisation of organisational culture.

1. Organisation and Decision

In this section we will outline Luhmann's concept of organisation. We will first explain its central building blocks: the concept of decision, which constitutes the elements of the organisation (Section a), the concept of uncertainty absorption, which describes the processes within an organisation (Section b) and the concept of decision premise, which describes the structures of an organisation (Section c). Bringing these three elements together we will describe in the last part (Section d) Luhmann's concept of organisation as an autopoietic system of decisions.

a. The Elements of Organisations: The Concept of Decision

Luhmann argues that the central element around which any viable concept of organisation has to be built is *decision*.[4] Yet, the concept of decision generally seems even less clear than that of organisation.[5] Mostly decision is defined as 'choice'. This, however, means decision is defined through a synonym that is equally unclear. Sometimes the definition is specified somewhat more describing it as a choice among *alternatives*. The concept of alternative, however, is itself only defined in relation to choice: Alternatives are those possibilities among which one can *choose* – the choice defines the alternatives.[6] Thus, we have a tautological definition, which in this form does not really help very much. In order to arrive at a more fruitful concept, Luhmann argues that one has to unfold the tautology and analyse its particular form.[7] As he demonstrates, this analysis can be done both from a factual and from a temporal perspective.[8]

In the fact dimension, the chosen alternative and excluded alternatives can be conceptualised as the two sides of a distinction – with the former constituting the marked side and the latter the unmarked side. However, in contrast to a normal distinction both sides of the distinction – both the chosen and the excluded alternatives, that is – are observed. This can be expressed by drawing an additional

---

[4] The importance of the concept of decision for organisation is, of course, not new and has been widely acknowledged; explicitly so, for example, in the title *Decision and Organisation* by March (1989). In Germany the importance of decision for organisation is particularly prominent in the decision theories of organisation as developed especially by Edmund Heinen and his disciples: see for example Kirsch (1970-1971). Yet, the radicality with which Luhmann bases his concept of organisation on decision has no parallel.

[5] Cf. e.g. Mintzberg and Waters (1990).

[6] Luhmann (2000), p. 125.

[7] For another analysis of the concept of decision based on the *Laws of Form* see Chia (1994).

[8] See Chapter 1, Section 2.d on dimensions of meaning.

distinction, which includes the original distinction (with both its sides) on its marked side. In Spencer Brown's terms we get an 'arrangement' of two distinctions. A primary distinction distinguishes between the alternatives and the rest of the world. A secondary distinction located within this primary distinction distinguishes chosen and excluded alternatives (Figure 2.1).[9]

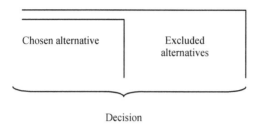

Decision

Figure 2.1 The form of decision in the fact dimension

The important point here is that the decision cannot be located on either side of the (secondary) distinction – it is not the selected alternative – but in the entire distinction with *both* its sides. To make the paradox more explicit we can say: a decision is the unity of the difference between chosen and excluded alternatives.[10]

   In the time dimension the form of decision looks quite different. Here it is not about the relation between chosen and excluded alternatives but between two different time horizons: before and after the decision. After a decision has been made the situation is different from before. Before the decision we have a situation in which any one of the alternatives can be chosen. After the decision we have a situation in which *one* alternative *has been chosen* and all other alternatives have been excluded. These 'excluded' alternatives do not disappear, but continue to exist as excluded *possibilities*. Thus, both before and after the decision we have situations of contingency (in the sense of 'also possible otherwise'), but they are different kinds of contingency: before the decision we have 'open contingency' and after the decision 'fixed contingency'.[11] In this sense, decision is conceptualised as the distinction between open and fixed contingency (Figure 2.2).

---

[9]   Cf. Luhmann (2000), pp. 133f. See also Meyer (1990) and Baecker (1992), p. 224.
[10] Luhmann (1993e), p. 289; Luhmann (2000), pp. 135f.
[11] Luhmann (1984), pp. 593f.; Luhmann (1992b), p. 170; Luhmann (2000), p. 170.

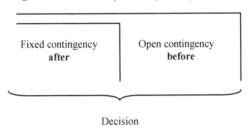

Decision

Figure 2.2 The form of decision in the time dimension

The important point, again, is that the decision is neither an open nor a fixed contingency, but the unity of the distinction between the two. Thus we can summarise: both in the fact dimension and in the time dimension decisions are paradoxically constituted.

Since decisions, for Luhmann, are social phenomena, they have to be conceptualised as a particular type of communication. It is not that decisions are first made and then communicated, but *decisions are communications*. What has been said about communications in general, also applies to decision communications: they are not produced by 'human beings' but by a social system; in this case, the organisation.

What is particular about decisions is that they are 'compact communications'[12] which communicate their own contingency ('contingency' here in the sense of 'also possible otherwise'). In contrast to an ordinary communication, which only communicates a specific content that has been selected (e.g. 'I love you'), a decision communication communicates also – explicitly or implicitly – that there are further alternatives that could have been selected instead (e.g. 'I am going to employ candidate A and not candidate B'). As such, decision communications are always paradoxical: the more they communicate that there are real alternatives to the one that has been selected, the less the selected alternative will appear as justified, and thus the less the decision will be accepted as 'decided'. Equally, the more the selected alternative is justified as the right selection, the less the other options will appear as alternatives, and thus the less the decision will appear as a 'decision'. To put it in linguistic terms, every decision communication contains a performative self-contradiction: the 'report' aspect and the 'command' aspect[13] of the decision communication contradict each other. The more clearly the decision is communicated as a selection among possible alternatives (report aspect), the less the decision will be accepted by later communications as a decision (command aspect).

Because of their paradoxical nature, decision communications are very delicate, calling for their own deconstruction by ensuing communications. Without any other communicative provisions, decision communications would have a very high 'failure rate'. So, why does the organisational communication not break down all

---

[12]   Luhmann (2000), p. 185.
[13]   Ruesch and Bateson (1951).

the time? Luhmann gives two answers to this question. First, organisations totalise decision as the organisational form of communication – organisations are operatively closed on the basis of decisions. Thus, even the deconstruction of a decision in an organisation has to be communicated as a decision. In other words, the rejection of a decision can itself only be communicated as yet another decision – otherwise it would not be part of the organisational autopoiesis.[14] Second, decision communications in organisations usually can refer to other (successfully completed) decisions – 'decision premises' (see below) – to stabilise the decision; that is to say, decisions prohibiting the rejection of certain other decisions.[15] We will get back to this point in Chapter 4.

b. *Organisational Processes: The Concept of Uncertainty Absorption*

Within organisations, decision communications are always integrated into a process of connecting decisions – the actual autopoiesis of the organisation. Every decision is the product of earlier decisions and gives rise to ensuing decisions. Luhmann describes this process of decisions connecting to each other with the concept of *uncertainty absorption*,[16] the idea of which he takes from March and Simon who describe it in the following way:

> Uncertainty absorption takes place when inferences are drawn from a body of evidence and the inferences, instead of the evidence itself, are then communicated.[17]

For a decision to be made information is needed on the basis of which one alternative can be chosen over the others. An investment decision, for example, is based on information on the availability of financial resources, on current interest rates, current market demand etc. We can also say that a decision is 'inferred' from the given information. Yet, the important point is that no decision can rely on complete information; some uncertainty inevitably remains. In our example, there is uncertainty concerning future market demand, investment projects of competing firms, future inflation figures, and so on. All this uncertainty, however, is absorbed by the decision: all given information and all remaining uncertainty is transformed into the selection of one alternative over the others. In other words, once a decision has been made the uncertainty involved in making the decision becomes irrelevant; what counts is merely which alternative has been chosen. Thus, uncertainty absorption takes place in the *connection* between decisions.[18] Decisions do not impart any information about the uncertainties involved in making the decision but merely about selected and excluded alternatives, so ensuing decisions that connect

---

[14] Luhmann (2000), p. 145.

[15] Luhmann (2000), p. 142.

[16] Cf. Luhmann (1993e), pp. 299-303; Luhmann (2000), pp. 183ff.

[17] March and Simon (1958), p. 165. They present it, however, as a relatively insignificant concept. Weick (1979) was the first to recognise its theoretical potential and developed his concept of reduction of equivocality from it. On the development of the concept of uncertainty absorption, see Luhmann (2000), p. 184.

[18] Luhmann (1993e).

to them cannot 'see' the uncertainties. That is to say, from the perspective of further decisions orienting themselves toward the first decision, the uncertainty of the first decision is absorbed.[19]

On the basis of such a processual understanding of decision, we can distinguish between two 'states' of a decision: before and after subsequent decisions have connected to it. As Baecker argues, a decision is only completed, when subsequent decisions connect to it. Before that, the decision is merely *virtual*,[20] because the realisation of the decision in subsequent decisions is expected, but not yet realised. Let us illustrate this with an example: a manager makes the decision to manufacture a particular new product – in contrast to producing another new product or not producing anything new at all. This decision is only virtual until subsequent decisions have completed it as a decision by orienting themselves according to it. The marketing manager, for example, might decide on the advertisement of the new product.[21] In other words, a decision is completed when it has absorbed the uncertainty that concerns subsequent decisions.

c.   *Organisational Structures: The Concept of Decision Premise*

A concept closely related to uncertainty absorption is that of decision premise – originally introduced by Herbert Simon.[22] The concept of decision premise refers to the *structural* preconditions that define – or create – a decision situation. For example: the alternatives given, the objectives of the decision and so on. While one could include in the term everything that influences the decision situation, Luhmann argues that such a concept would not be very fruitful.[23] Instead, he restricts the term to those structural preconditions that themselves 'result' from decisions, which means that a decision takes previous decisions as decision premises. In other words, every decision serves as a decision premise for later decisions. With regard to the previous section, here we have reversed our perspective: we are not looking at the transformation as it progresses from the initial decision situation towards the connection of subsequent decisions. Instead, we are looking 'back' from the point of a given decision towards the decisions that had preceded it. When we examine their relevance to that decision, we can see that preceding decisions serve as decision premises. To bring the concepts of uncertainty absorption and decision premise together we can say: uncertainty absorption takes place, when a decision is used by subsequent decisions as a decision premise.[24]

---

[19] Luhmann (2000), pp. 184f.; see also Baecker (1994), pp. 148ff.

[20] Baecker (1999b), p. 138.

[21] Connection does not imply acceptance: a connecting decision could also decide to reject the decision. Cf. Baecker (1999b), p. 140; Luhmann (1992b), pp. 172f.

[22] Originally Simon called them 'behavioral premises'. See Simon (1957), p. 201, and Simon et al. (1950), pp. 57ff.

[23] Cf. Luhmann (2000), p. 223.

[24] Uncertainty absorption and decision premise are two sides of the same phenomenon. See Luhmann (2000), p. 172; Luhmann (1993e).

An important aspect of the concept of decision premise is its double function as both creating and restricting the decision situation. Decision premises create the decision situation in the first place: they define the decision situation as such. Without decision premises there is no occasion for decision making. At the same time, decision premises restrict the decision situation by creating a particular decision situation and not a different one. If decision premises define a decision situation as a choice between alternative A and alternative B, one cannot decide between X and Y. In terms of our analysis, as presented in the last section, we can say that decision premises draw the primary distinction between alternatives and the rest of the world.

By applying the concepts of decision and decision premise recursively to each other Luhmann creates, in a second step, a concept of *decision premises in the narrower sense*: apart from the factuality of every decision becoming a decision premise for subsequent decisions, *decisions can decide on decision premises* for other decisions, i.e. decisions on decision premises. In this case, we have to distinguish between, and relate to each other, two different components of such a decision: on the one hand there is the decision on the decision premise and on the other hand there are the decision premises on which the decision is being made (these decision premises, again, have to be distinguished from the decision's own decision premises). The crucial point of this constellation is that a decision can decide on decision premises which are not only binding for immediately succeeding decision situations, but for a multitude of later decisions. They serve 'some sort of anticipated, generalised uncertainty absorption.'[25] In this way, decisions on decision premises can influence other decisions that take place much later in the decision process. These decision premises in the narrower sense are the organisation's *structures*.[26]

Luhmann identifies three types of such decision premises in the narrower sense:[27] programmes, communication channels, and personnel. *Programmes* are decision premises that define conditions for correct decision making; they are often also called 'plans'. There are two different kinds of programmes: conditional programmes and goal programmes. Conditional programmes[28] define correct decision making for the case that some specified conditions are met. They have the general form of 'if-then' – '*if* this is the case, *then* do that.'[29] Goal programmes, in contrast, define correct decision making by identifying specific goals that are to be achieved – for instance, 'increasing the market share'. Neither type of programme, however, removes the uncertainty from the decisions it engenders: programmes do

---

[25] Luhmann (2000), p. 261.

[26] See note on structures in general Chapter 1, Section 2.e.

[27] Luhmann later suggests that we speak of decision premises only when they are explicitly decided upon, i.e. the mere factuality of every decision serving as a decision premise for subsequent decisions is not enough because it is too similar to the concept of uncertainty absorption. See Luhmann (2000), p. 223.

[28] March and Simon (1958), pp. 141-150 describe something similar with their concept of 'performance programs'. This is probably where Luhmann took the idea from.

[29] Luhmann (2000), p. 263.

not 'decide' those decisions (otherwise they would not be decisions).[30] In the case of conditional programming there is uncertainty about whether the conditions are actually met by the decision situation – there usually is considerable scope for interpretation. In the case of goal programming the main uncertainty concerns the causal link between alternatives and goal.[31] Apart from that, in both cases there is uncertainty on whether the programmes should actually be applied to the decision situation, as it is always possible to find reasons for making an exception.[32]

The decision premise of *personnel* concerns the recruitment and allocation of personnel. In this respect, organisations decide on the commencement and termination of membership, as well as on the transfer of members to different positions within the organisation – both with and without promotion.[33] 'Personnel' is a decision premise in that the question of who is in charge of a decision is of significance. An experienced manager is likely to influence decision making differently from a newcomer.[34] In this sense, organisations have expectations concerning the behaviour of different persons, which serve as a basis for selecting their personnel.

The decision premise of *communication channels* concerns what can be called the *organisation* of the organisation.[35] Not everybody can communicate with everybody at all times (all-channel net). Instead, the communication is restricted to certain channels.[36] The hierarchical structure, in which the communication channels only run vertically, is a classic example of this. Decisions on one level inform decisions only on the next lower or next higher[37] level, but not decisions on the same level. That is to say, decisions can use as decision premises other decisions only on the vertical axis but not on the horizontal axis. There are several other forms of communication channels besides hierarchies;[38] for example the matrix-organisation.[39]

---

[30] In any case one can always decide not to comply with the programme. See Luhmann (1984).

[31] Luhmann (2000), pp. 266ff.

[32] Luhmann (2000), p. 261.

[33] Luhmann (1993a), p. 366; Luhmann (2000), Chapter 9.

[34] This recognition of different individuals making a difference for the organisation does not contradict the concept of autopoiesis. Different individuals are only considered for the difference in irritations that they cause.

[35] Luhmann (2000), p. 302. Kirsch and Meffert (1970) write: the organisation *is* an organisation and it *has* an organisation.

[36] Luhmann (1975), p. 42.

[37] One often reads that decisions travel from the top to the bottom of the hierarchy, while information travels in the opposite direction. Luhmann (2000), p. 325, in contrast, argues that both communications – top-down and bottom-up – have the form of decisions.

[38] Some hierarchical elements can, however, almost always be found. See Baecker (1999b), pp. 198ff.

[39] Galbraith (1971), Davis and Lawrence (1977). On alternatives to hierarchies see also Herbst (1976).

The three decision premises – programme, personnel and communication channel – are coordinated through *positions*.[40] Positions are nodes at which the three decision premises meet and are specified with regard to each other. Every position executes a particular programme, is filled by a particular person, and is located somewhere in the communication network.[41] Positions coordinate decision premises in two respects. On the one hand, they coordinate them with regard to concrete decisions. On the other hand, they serve as an orientation for decisions based on new decision premises: only the new decision premises that fit into the existing structures of positions, or for which new positions can be created, can be integrated.[42]

d. The Organisation as an Operatively Closed System

With the concepts of decision, uncertainty absorption and decision premise we have the necessary building blocks for understanding Luhmann's theory of organisation as a particular type of autopoietic system. For Luhmann, the organisation is a social system that reproduces itself on the basis of *decisions* (or to be exact: decision communications). In this sense he defines organisations as

> systems that consist of decisions and that themselves produce the decisions of which they consist through decisions of which they consist.[43]

The concept of uncertainty absorption describes the self-reproduction (i.e. autopoiesis) of the organisation. It describes how decisions produce other decisions, which in turn produce further decisions. Every decision produces new decisions; on the one hand, by reducing uncertainty, and on the other hand, by producing new uncertainty, which brings forth the need for a further reduction of uncertainty in the form of a further decision. In this sense, the organisation can be seen as pulsating between reduction and production of uncertainty.[44] Let us illustrate this with an example: a decision to produce a new product reduces the uncertainty concerning different possible new products, but at the same time produces new uncertainty – concerning the marketing of the product, for instance. A new decision is therefore necessary, in order to decide between alternative ways of marketing it. The decision on marketing reduces in its turn the uncertainty involved in this step but produces new uncertainty – concerning the different ways of financing the marketing campaign, for instance; and so on.

While this example might give the impression that uncertainty is reduced with every decision until only certainty remains, this is not the case for organisations. If all uncertainty were removed, the organisation would cease to exist and no further decisions would be produced. The organisation *needs* uncertainty for its

---

[40] Luhmann (2000), p. 232.
[41] Luhmann (1992b), p. 178; Luhmann (1975), pp. 41-42; Luhmann (2000), pp. 231ff.
[42] See also Chapter 5, Section 3.
[43] Luhmann (1992b), p. 166 (italics in the original; my translation).
[44] Luhmann (1992b), p. 172.

autopoiesis. The reduction of uncertainty is not a process that leads to a final 'solution'. Although one might sometimes find decision hierarchies or goal-oriented decision processes that lead to a final decision,[45] these decision processes have to be seen as part of a greater decision network which is not organised in such a teleological way.[46] There are always new uncertainties that have to be absorbed by new decisions.[47]

What we have described here is a *primary closure* on the level of decisions. The organisation is operatively closed in that only decisions can reproduce the system. The environment cannot contribute any decisions to the organisation. A thought in the mind of an individual cannot serve as an organisational decision – it might influence the organisational decision making, but just as a perturbation. Neither can a decision in one organisation serve as a decision in another.[48]

In addition to this primary closure on the level of operations, organisations – like all cognitive systems[49] – possess also a *secondary closure* on the level of structures: not only their decisions but also their decision premises (i.e. their structures) can only be produced through their own decisions. That is to say, the decision premises do not come from outside the organisation but are the organisation's own product – decision premises are explicitly defined as a result of decisions (see above).

We can analyse this double closure with the help of the *Laws of Form*. The primary closure concerns the primary distinction between organisation and environment. Every decision reproduces the distinction between organisation and environment, as it reproduces the distinction between decision and everything else. As the environment is located on the unmarked side of the distinction, the organisation cannot observe it. Decisions can observe other decisions, but they cannot observe anything beyond decisions. That is to say, on the level of its decisions the organisation is 'blind'. On this level, the organisation is only 'concerned' with the continuation of the reproduction of decisions;[50] on this level it does not make a difference whether it is a decision on a new product or on the colour of the toilet doors. As long as any decision – irrespective of its content – is produced, the organisation is reproduced.

The 'blindness' of decisions is, however, compensated through the decision premises; that is to say, the structures of the organisation on the structural level. These decision premises influence which decisions are produced. For example, a business programme will lead to particular business decisions being made and not to decisions on the colour of toilet doors. In other words, decision premises

---

[45] Such processes sometimes are called *projects*: see Luhmann (1993e), p. 298.
[46] Luhmann (1992b), p. 172.
[47] The most important source of uncertainty is the environment.
[48] This has important implications for the conceptualisation of organisational networks. Organisations in a network do not overlap with regard to their operations; they are merely very sensitive with regard to each other's operations. See also Luhmann (2000), Chapter 13 Section 7; Baecker (1998), p. 42; Wimmer (1995).
[49] See Von Foerster (1981), pp. 304-305; Von Foerster (1993); Baecker (1999b), pp. 147ff.
[50] Baecker (1999b), p. 153.

channel the reproduction of decisions. With relation to individual decisions, the important point about decision premises is that they serve as a substitute for orientation according to the environment as such. That is to say, instead of observing their environment (which they cannot do) and observing what decisions would make sense in view of that, they observe the organisation's premises. The decision premises in this sense *represent the organisation/environment distinction within the organisation.*

In terms of the *Laws of Form* the organisation/environment distinction re-enters into the organisation. Let us, for example, take the goal programme 'increasing the market share'. This decision premise refers to the distinction between organisation and environment: the 'market share' distinguishes the organisation from the environment, and at the same time relates them to each other. Thus, by observing this decision premise, the organisation observes the organisation/environment distinction. On the basis of this decision premise, the organisation can observe its decisions with regard to their effect on the relation to their environment. Every decision can be evaluated on the basis of its particular contribution to an increase in the market share. However, the re-entered distinction is not the original distinction: the 'market share' is not the distinction between decision and non-decision, but merely an internal construct that represents it. The decision premise, in this sense, is a marker but not a cross.[51]

The implications of the organisation's double closure are twofold: on the one hand, double closure implies autonomy. It is the organisation itself that determines its structures. Without the ability to decide on its own structures the organisation would be the continuation of the environment.[52] On the other hand, double closure implies unavailability. As the organisation can only operate on the inside of the organisation/environment distinction (that is to say, it possesses no mode of operation other than decisions), the distinction itself ultimately remains unavailable. All internal representations of the distinction are ultimately merely internal constructs.[53]

2. Organisation and Society

In this and the next sections we will look at the relation between organisation and the other two types of social systems – society and interaction. In Luhmann's work this part remained underdeveloped and partly inconsistent. We believe that Fritz Heider's concept of medium and form offers a fruitful way to capture these relations. Luhmann himself suggested such an approach at one point but did not develop it significantly any further.[54]

---

[51] Baecker (1999b), pp. 156f.
[52] Luhmann (2000), p. 229.
[53] Cf. Baecker (1999b), p. 126.
[54] See particularly Luhmann (1994), Chapter 9.

a.   Medium and Form

The distinction between medium and form goes back to Fritz Heider's theory of human perception (there, however, as a distinction between medium and thing).[55] Heider asks why it is that we attribute the cause of our acoustic and visual perceptions directly to the perceived object, and not to any of the many other factors which are causally involved in our perception, such as light waves or air waves. He writes:

> Our perception points to one particular link of the [causal] chain. With regard to causality, all links of the chain are equal; with regard to perception they are not: there is, rather, one highlighted link, namely our object of perception.[56]

Heider explains this with the difference in constitution between the object of perception – the *thing* – and the other causal factors – the *medium*. The difference between thing and medium is conceptualised as the difference between the loose and tight coupling of elements. Due to the loose coupling of its elements (that is to say, its openness to a multitude of possible connections), the medium can be conditioned through the thing. In other words, certain couplings between elements in the medium can be understood as enforced through the thing and hence be interpreted as 'signs' for the thing.[57]

In his writings, Luhmann[58] takes up Heider's idea but gives it a much more general meaning. Most importantly, he separates the concept from its reference to the physical world and, instead, relates it strictly to an observer. The difference between medium and form becomes a schema of observation according to which something is *seen* as either an open (loose coupling) or a determined multitude of possible connections between elements (strict coupling).[59] 'Form' refers to the selection of *particular* connections that we observe, among a multitude of *possible* connections, which constitute the medium. It is important to understand medium and form as relational concepts: a medium is only a medium with regard to form, so it is not a pure scattering of elements. Equally, a form is a form in a medium, it is not a selection that is apparent in itself.[60] This distinction, however, contains an asymmetry: the medium can only be observed from the perspective of possibilities for producing a form, not the other way around. In other words, it can only be observed as the contingency of the form and cannot be observed directly.[61]

With regard to the observation according to the schema of medium/form, Baecker speaks of an epistemological paradox: on the one hand, the medium itself is excluded from the causal explanation of the form; that is to say, the selection of

---

[55] Heider (1926). An abridged version has been published in English translation: Heider (1959).
[56] Heider (1926), p. 113 (my translation).
[57] Heider (1926), p. 120.
[58] See especially Luhmann (1998a), Chapter 3.
[59] Luhmann (1998a), p. 168.
[60] Luhmann (1994), p. 303.
[61] Luhmann (1998a), p. 168.

a particular form is not considered as motivated by the medium. On the other hand, however, it is ultimately included in the causal explanation as a restriction of possible forms.[62]

When analysed according to the *Laws of Form*, the difference between medium and form is itself a form.[63] It is a distinction with two sides.[64] Medium/form is a form that also contains form on one of its sides – which makes it a re-entry. In other words, the form/medium distinction is repeated on both sides of the distinction. The elements of the medium are themselves forms in another medium, and the forms in a medium can themselves be a medium for further forms.[65] We can thus speak of a hierarchy of medium/form relations.[66] However, it is only levels in direct succession within the hierarchy that can serve respectively as medium and form for each other.[67]

b. Society as Form in the Medium Meaning

If we apply the distinction form/medium to the analysis of systems, we can distinguish two different levels. Firstly, the system itself constitutes a form which is realised in a particular medium. Secondly, the operations constitute forms in the medium of the system. With regard to the societal system this means, we have to distinguish between the society as a particular form in a (yet to be determined) medium, and a communication as a particular form within the medium of society.

Let us start with the first level. What is the medium of society? Drawing on Luhmann we can answer the question with the concept of meaning.[68] Meaning[69] is the medium in which actuality and potentiality can be distinguished; it is medium in the sense that it restricts the production of forms to the distinction actuality/potentiality, but leaves open the question of *which specific* actuality/potentiality distinctions are realised. The concept of meaning is paradoxical as the specific actuality/potentiality-distinctions (that is to say, the forms in the medium of meaning), are themselves also instances of meaning. Furthermore, the distinction actuality/potentiality is itself an actual distinction that is distinguished from other potential ones. In this sense, meaning is not only medium but also form in itself.[70] Because of this cyclical closure, meaning has to be conceptualised as the lowest level of the medium/form-hierarchy (at least for meaning-constituted systems, such as human beings) that cannot be further

---

[62]   Baecker (1999a), pp. 174f.

[63]   Luhmann (1995b), p. 146; Luhmann (1999), p. 59; Baecker (1999a).

[64]   It is, however, not a simple but a double distinction. The distinction between medium and form is itself distinguished from the 'rest of the world'.

[65]   This is exactly the point where the distinction between form and medium differs from the old-European, metaphysical distinction between form and matter, where matter is conceptualised as completely undetermined in itself. See Luhmann (1992a), p. 53.

[66]   Luhmann (1998a), p. 172.

[67]   Luhmann (1992a), p. 399.

[68]   Luhmann (1997), p. 51.

[69]   See Chapter 1, Section 3.d.

[70]   Luhmann (1997), p. 50. Cf. Ort (1998).

deconstructed: meaning is realised in the medium of meaning and this medium is itself form in the medium of meaning.

Although we, as meaning-constituted systems, cannot descend further the hierarchy of medium/form relations, we can nonetheless ascend it and identify different forms in it. On the next higher level we can distinguish the societal system and psychic systems as two forms. In the following pages we will restrict ourselves to the analysis of the societal system.

Society is a form as it realises a particular system/environment distinction in the medium of meaning. This, however, does not suffice to describe it as a form: society is that form of system/environment, which distinguishes all communications[71] from everything else. Society is a meaning form that imprints itself into the medium of meaning as it actualises *one particular* (system/environment) distinction among all potential distinctions (including distinctions other than system/environment distinctions). Meaning provides the *possibilities* for the creation of form, but it also restricts the creation of forms to 'meaningful forms'.[72] However, as is characteristic of a medium, the particular form that society realises is not determined by the medium of meaning.[73]

We can now examine the particular 'strict coupling', i.e. the forms, in the societal system.[74] First, we have the communication. A communication unit is a combination of three elements of meaning: utterance, information and understanding. Only in this coupling do these elements constitute the form 'communication'. This is the first coupling of elements of meaning. From this follows a second coupling: any communication is coupled to other communications (meaning forms) in such a way that a further synthesis of utterance, information and understanding has to connect to either the utterance or the meaning of the previous communication, and thus either accept or reject it.[75]

We can now look at the next higher level of medium/form relations: the relation between society and *particular* communications. Society can be understood as a medium which provides the possibilities for forming communications. To put it differently, society restricts all forms to communications – for example, no thoughts can be formed in society. As with any medium, society makes communications possible but does not determine them. However, in society not all communications are possible. In our modern society, for example, other communications are possible than in the society of two thousand years ago. In this sense, different structures of society imply a different medium; that is to say, different possibilities for communication. We can thus say that a particular

---

[71] More precisely: all communications that relate to each other.

[72] Cf. Luhmann (1984), p. 96ff.; Luhmann (1997), pp. 51ff.; Hahn (1987).

[73] But only by itself. In this sense society already has to exist in order to produce itself. See Luhmann (1997), p. 440.

[74] The arguments below are based on the explanations in Chapter 1, Section 2.

[75] The coupling of the three meaning elements – utterance, information and understanding – and the coupling of different communications to each other can be separated analytically. Both types of coupling, however, constitute a circularly connected phenomenon. Communication only exists within a connection of communications (Luhmann 1986, p. 174).

historical society not only restricts all possible forms to communication, but also restricts *the scope of possible* communications (Figure 2.3 summarises our explanations so far).

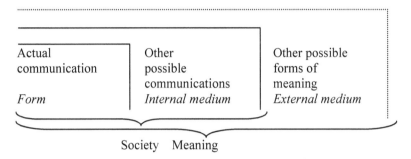

Actual communication	Other possible communications	Other possible forms of meaning
Form	*Internal medium*	*External medium*

Society   Meaning

Figure 2.3 The relation of meaning, society and communication[76]

c.   Organisation as Form in the Medium Communication

In Luhmann's theory, society is conceptualised as the system that encompasses all other social systems. That is to say, all other social systems take place *within* the social system and besides reproducing themselves also reproduce society.[77] This constellation can be understood as a medium/form relation: with its possibilities of communication, society provides a medium in which the organisation constitutes a particular form.

We can understand the relation between society and organisation analogously to the relation between meaning and society. Society constitutes a medium as it provides possibilities for the coupling of communications. Organisations can be understood as forms in this medium as they strictly couple these communications into networks of decisions. Two types of coupling can be distinguished and related to each other. First, the coupling of communications to the form 'decision': every decision is a coupling of several different communications – the communication of the set of alternatives, of the chosen alternative, and of the instruction to consider the selection as a precondition for further decisions.[78] In this sense, decisions constitute 'compact communications'.[79] Second, there is the coupling of decisions into the form of a decision network (i.e. an organisation): every decision is coupled to other decisions in the sense that it serves as a decision premise for ensuing decisions and uses previous decisions as its own decision premises – and it is only through this coupling that these decisions become decisions.[80]

---

[76] Cf. Baecker (1999a).
[77] Luhmann (1997), pp. 78ff.
[78] See Section 1.a.
[79] Luhmann (2000), p. 185.
[80] See Section 1.d.

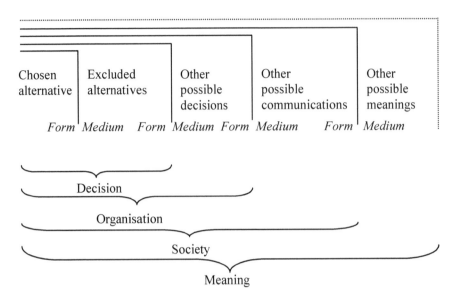

Figure 2.4 The relation of meaning, society, organisation and concrete decision

If we move to a higher level of medium/form relations, the organisation itself can be understood as a medium in which forms can be created: this is the form of a concrete decision. The relation between concrete decision and organisation is analogous to that between concrete communication and society. The organisation provides a set of possibilities, in which the form of concrete decisions can be created. However, we must be careful not to confuse the set of possible decisions with the set of alternatives that is defined through the decision.[81] The set of possible decisions defined through the organisation refers to the possibilities of defining different sets of alternatives between which to decide. While the set of alternatives is included in the decision, the decision possibilities are not. We are not talking about the alternatives A and B of a decision, but about the possibility to decide between A and B *or* between D and E (Figure 2.4 summarises the different medium/form levels as an arrangement of distinctions).

d. Decisions and 'Other' Communications in the Organisation

In the theory presented above, organisations are conceptualised as systems of decisions which reproduce themselves through their own decisions; the organisation is closed on the basis of decisions. Empirically, however, one can observe that many important communications 'in' organisations are not really decisions. One finds, for example, 'ordinary' communications preparing decision

---

[81] See Section 1.a.

makers for a decision or communications explaining the meaning or consequences of a decision. Apart from communications that are directly related to decisions, we also find communicational forms such as gossip within organisations.[82] All these communications are important for the organisation, but are not themselves decisions.

How can one account for such non-decision communications in a concept of organisation that is purely based on decisions? On the one hand, Luhmann himself writes

that organisations *do not 'consist' of anything but* the communication of decisions.[83]

Hence, the concept of decision is totalised in the concept of organisation. On the other hand, the idea of totalisation *seems* to be negated, when he acknowledges:

In organisations [...] *also other* behaviours [than decision] can take place, for example gossip.[84]

Apparently organisations also consist of 'other' communications, apart from decisions. Luhmann, however, makes clear that, although these communications take place 'in' the organisation, they do not take part in the *autopoiesis* of the organisation. Luhmann illustrates this idea with an example from biology:

[I]n living cells [there are] also some minerals [...] which do not take part in the autopoiesis of the system but which nevertheless serve important functions.[85]

The example is, however, problematic, since it seems to imply a substantialistic notion of organisation, which contradicts the concept of organisation as the reproduction of decision events. How can one speak of 'something else' *taking place inside* the organisation, when the organisation is just the reproduction of decisions through decisions? The concept of medium and form seems to offer a solution to this problem.

Analysed according to the schema medium/form, these communications that have no reference to decisions are not forms on the level of the organisation. They are merely the loosely coupled elements of its medium. They are not strictly coupled with other decisions into a network of decisions. Organisations can, however, create a strict coupling. In other words, they can create forms out of them, by *interpreting them retrospectively* as decisions. That is to say, later decisions may interpret those 'normal' communications retrospectively as decisions by using them as their decision premises. If we look at this phenomenon in its temporal succession we first have a 'normal' communication, which is not understood as decision form. If a decision follows, which interprets the non-

---

[82] Cf. March and Sevón (1989), Drew and Heritage (1992), Boden (1994), Fuchs (1995), and Kurland and Pelled (2000).
[83] Luhmann (1997), p. 833 (my emphasis, my translation).
[84] Luhmann (2000), p. 68 (my emphasis, my translation).
[85] Luhmann (2000), p. 68 (my translation).

decision communication as a decision by using it as a decision premise, the communication is transformed into a decision. In this sense, Luhmann writes:

> In the first place, the reality of these 'other' decisions is only guaranteed through the reality of the reference to them. Hence, the process of constitution does not result in *all* decisions being *decided upon*, but in *every* decision being able to *assume* that all decisions are decided upon.[86]

Assuming that decisions are produced through decisions the question arises where non-decision communications originate. In order to answer this question, we have to examine a lower level of medium/form relations and look into the regeneration of the medium of the organisation. These communications are not produced by the organisation, but by the societal system. They are forms on the level of the societal system. As with any communication, decision communications give rise to further communications. In this way, every decision communication also leads to the communication of acceptance or rejection of the communication, or to communications that ensure understanding – without the communication necessarily taking the form of a decision. Not the decisions, but the communications that are coupled in the decisions produce these non-decision communications.

These communications sometimes develop a certain dynamic that goes beyond the basal conditions of communicative reproduction – for example, as in the form of gossip. In this case, the communications that are bound in the decisions lead to further communications, which in their turn produce further communications without direct focus on the production of further decisions.[87] These communications are 'influenced' by the organisation, as they originate in communications bound in decisions, but they are not produced by the organisation – they are produced by the societal system. In principle, these communications can be integrated into the decision network. However, the further these communications are removed from the original communications that are bound in decisions, the more difficult and the more unlikely their integration becomes.

For those reasons, we have to differentiate between the reproduction of elements on the level of the medium and the reproduction on the level of the organisation. That is to say, two different system references have to be distinguished: organisation and society. The society ensures that communications are produced in such a way that further communications can be connected to them. It guarantees the reproduction and consequently the availability of the medium. The organisation itself would not be able to serve this function. The reproduction of the medium on the basis of the reproduction of decisions is not enough in itself. In this sense, society produces some communications in between decisions, which are necessary but 'invisible' to the organisation.

---

[86] Luhmann (1993a), p. 353 (my translation, original emphasis).
[87] In a similar context, Heider (1926), p. 133, speaks of the medium's inherent oscillations [*Eigenschwingungen*].

The organisation has to take the operations of the society for granted, as it specialises in the production of forms *within* the network of communications. The organisation ensures that after every decision a further decision follows; this, however, does not have to follow immediately. In between decisions a multitude of other communications take place, which are normally invisible to the organisation. In order to be recognised by the organisation they have to be interpreted as decisions; that is to say, they have to be coupled into forms of decision. Since these communications originate in communications that are bound in decisions, they can often be integrated relatively easily into the decision process if later decisions use them as decision premises. In this sense one might speak of 'latent decisions'.

3. Organisation and Interaction

On the basis of our foregoing analysis of the relation between medium and form, in this section we will suggest a new way of conceptualising *organisational interactions*. In terms of Luhmann's theory, no convincing conceptualisation has emerged so far.[88]

a. Interaction as an Autopoietic System

Like all social systems, interactions are systems that reproduce themselves on the basis of communications. In contrast to society, however, these are communications of a particular kind, which are based on the perception of the physical presence of their participants.

There is no doubt that perception as such is clearly a psychic phenomenon – communications cannot perceive. However, reflexive perception gives rise to communication.

> If alter perceives that alter is perceived and that this perception of being perceived is perceived, alter must assume that alter's behavior is interpreted as communication whether this suits alter or not, and this forces alter to control the behavior as communication.[89]

Thus, every communication refers to the fact that all participants perceive each other as present – a face-to-face contact is a precondition.[90] However, not everyone who is physically present will also be treated as present by the communication. Although physically present, people at other tables in a restaurant, for example, might not be considered present by the interactional communication. Similarly, not all perceptible behaviour will necessarily be treated as perceptible – or present – by

---

[88] See however Kieserling (1994a; 1999); Seidl (forthcoming b).

[89] Luhmann (1995a), p. 413.

[90] Cf. Luhmann (1993a), p. 81. This necessity of a 'face-to-face' contact can, however, with the help of new information technology be relaxed; in this way the telephone, for example, can make even physically absent people perceptibly present for the interaction.

the interaction; blowing one's nose, for example. In other words, every interactional communication distinguishes between what to consider as present and what to consider as absent. Making this distinction qualifies the communication as interactional. One could also say that the interactional communication carries the code presence/absence.

The interaction can be conceptualised as an autopoietic system in the sense that only interactional communications reproduce interactional communications. Every interactional communication draws the distinction between interaction and environment, as well as that between communications based on the difference between present/absent and 'everything else'. This distinction between interaction and 'rest of the world' is observed internally as the distinction present/absent. In other words, according to the distinction present/absent the interaction distinguishes between self-reference and other-reference.[91]

b. Organisational Interaction

After these general remarks on Luhmann's theory of interaction systems, we can now analyse *organisational* interactions on the basis of the concept of medium and form. In a first attempt, we could try to conceptualise organisational interactions as interactions that use the organisation as a medium for coupling their specific forms, analogously to the relation between organisation and society. Such a concept implies that the interaction creates a strict coupling between the open possibilities of coupling decisions to each other. Empirically, however, we can observe that it is often non-decision communications in particular that are characteristic of organisational interactions.[92] Often no decisions at all are made in such interactions. Furthermore, it may be the case that part of an interaction is organisation-related while other parts have nothing to do with the organisation: a business meeting may end in bed; colleagues may discuss their evening at the pub during work; after their shared coffee break, colleagues make their way back to a meeting.[93] In all these cases it is not that one interaction is terminated and a new interaction is started: it is all part of the same interaction. For that reason, it is not possible to conceptualise organisational interactions as a specific *type* of system.

It is clear that we have to choose a different approach. As the direct medium of the interaction, one probably has to take society. The interaction is not a form in the medium of the organisation, but rather a form in the medium of society. The possible communications, rather than the possible decisions, are the medium in which the interaction creates a strict coupling. The interaction couples possible communications among people present. From this perspective, organisations and (organisational) interactions take place on the same medium/form level.

The theoretical problem one faces with such an approach is that interaction and organisation partly 'use' the same elements of the medium, the same communications. That is to say, interaction and organisation do not exist side by

---

[91] Luhmann (1997), pp. 815-816.
[92] Cf. Kieserling (1999), p. 355 ff; Kieserling (1994a).
[93] See e.g. Atkinson et al. (1978).

side but are entangled with each other. In interactions, decisions are made, which are forms for the organisation, as they refer to earlier decisions and prepare for further decisions. At the same time they are also forms for the interaction, as they are communications among people present.

We are thus dealing with two different kinds of forms, which partly 'use' – or create – strict coupling between, the same components. The relation between the forms can be explained with a metaphor of sand-cakes and sandcastles: the sand is the medium, the grains are the elements of the medium and the cake and the castle are forms that are created within the medium. If we make sand-cakes we create strict couplings between the otherwise loosely coupled sand grains. If we now want to build a sandcastle at the same place, with the same sand grains that we used for the sand-cakes, we have to either dissolve the strict coupling of the cakes or integrate the couplings of the cakes into the coupling of the castle, by using the cakes as towers of the castle, for instance. It is important that the couplings in the form of the cakes are preserved, although in the context of the castle they would no longer be recognised as such. The metaphor becomes more dynamic if one imagines that the sand-cakes and sandcastles are built simultaneously. Both forms present each other with strict couplings that have to be integrated into each other's couplings respectively.

Analogously to the sand in the metaphor, the communication possibilities of the society are the medium in which interaction and organisation create strict couplings. The organisation is presented by the interaction with strict couplings, which it can integrate into its own form. This happens when the organisation interprets communications produced in interactions as organisational decisions.

So far we have analysed the relation between organisation and interaction in general. We can now try to conceptualise organisational interactions in particular. Organisational interactions are interactions which reproduce themselves in an organisational 'context'. We could also say that the communicative medium through which they reproduce themselves is 'de-fined' (in the original sense of the word) through the organisation: in the social dimension, potential participants of the interaction are confined to members of the organisation:[94] in this sense, the interaction among visitors to an organisation would not be considered 'organisational'. In the fact dimension the communications are confined to 'organisational' topics, that is to say, the topics have to be in some way related to the organisation. In this sense, if members met and communicated about their private lives this would not be considered an *organisational* interaction. In the time dimension communications have to have some sort of temporal relation to the organisational processes. Such communications would normally take place during 'office hours'; or, in exceptional cases also outside of these hours, but, in such cases, with a clear reference to those hours. An example of this would be members discussing an important issue after work because they have to reach an agreement before 'office hours' commence next day.

---

[94] In exceptional cases they might include *in addition* to members also some non-members, e.g. consultants.

The important point is that the interaction is 'aware' of the organisational 'context'. That is to say, the interactional communications observe both the interaction and its organisational context. As Kieserling writes, such interactions take place on the level of second-order observation, in which interactional behaviour and decision process are both distinguished from and related to each other.[95] In the case of organisational interactions we have a re-entry of the interaction/organisation distinction into the interaction. The participants of the interaction are addressed as members of the organisation, the topics are understood as being of some relevance to the organisation, and the communications are 'aware' that they might contribute to the organisational decision processes: and it is this reference to the organisation that provides the interactional communications with their specific meaning.

We generally can distinguish between 'formal' and 'informal' organisational interactions. Informal organisational interactions are interactions that take place in the organisational context and observe the organisation, but are themselves not observed by the organisation. That is to say, the organisation takes no notice of them and, most importantly, their interactional communications are not reinterpreted by the organisation as decisions. Often such informal interactions try actively to evade being observed by the organisation, as in the case of interactional communications in the form of gossip. In terms of the medium/form distinction, we could say that the interaction observes the forms that the organisation creates from the societal medium, and locates itself *in between* the organisational forms, where the societal medium is still loosely coupled.

In the case of formal organisational interactions, the interactional communications are also observed by the organisation.[96] Furthermore, the organisation uses the interactional communications to derive its decisions from them. That is to say, the interactional communications are re-interpreted as decisions and as such reproduce the organisation. The important point is that both organisation and interaction are aware of their mutual use of the same communicative components: the organisation is aware of the interactional basis of its decisions, and the interaction is aware of the organisation's reinterpretation of its communications as decisions. We can say that organisation and interaction both reintroduce the distinction between organisation and interaction into their respective systems and use this distinction as a structure for producing their operations.

In terms of the medium/form distinction, this means that the interaction observes the forms which the organisation creates from the communicative medium (i.e. organisational decisions) and locates itself in the still loosely coupled medium in between. In contrast to informal interactions, however, this is done in such a way that the organisation takes notice of them and creates forms out of their interactional communications; that is to say, couples them to decisions. The

---

[95] Kieserling (1999), p. 362.
[96] On formal interactions, or 'deciding' interactions as he calls them, see also Kieserling (1999), pp. 371ff. Kieserling, however, is not explicit on the relation between organisation and interaction.

interaction may even highlight certain 'culmination points'[97] in its communications in order to signal to the organisation possible points for the creation of decisions – for instance, the formal opening of a meeting or the announcement of a ballot.[98] Yet, as organisation and interaction are two different types of systems, there can never be a 'one-to-one relation' between interactional and organisational operations, in the sense that every interactional communication is coupled into a decision. Instead, even during formal interactions many interactional communications will remain unobserved by the organisation – the encouraging nods of listeners, for example.

Let us summarise: in the case of formal interactions the autopoieses of three types of systems are interlinked without, however, intersecting each other. We might refer to this conglomerate of different systems as a *meeting*[99] – in contrast to 'organisational interaction' as merely *one* of the linked systems. In the 'meeting' the society produces a communication process. From these communications the interaction forms interactional communications creating an interactional communication process. In this interactionally pre-formed communication process (not in the interactional communication process!), the organisation creates an 'interactionally framed decision process'.[100]

c. *Conditioning of Organisational Interactions*

For the organisation, the possibility of using interactional communications for creating its decisions has important advantages: it means that the interactional complexity can be instrumentalised for the organisational reproduction.[101] Certain decision processes are only possible because of the complexity of the interaction.[102] In order to be able to 'use' interactions in this way, however, the organisation needs to *condition* them first.[103] There are several ways in which an organisation can condition interactions with relation to the three dimensions of meaning: time dimension, social dimension and fact dimension.[104]

Conditioning in the *time dimension* is particularly focussed on the beginning and end of an interaction. The organisation can decide to start an interaction and it can also decide on a certain time limit, after which the interaction is to come to an end. For example, a meeting can be scheduled for a certain time – from three to four o'clock. The organisation could also decide on a sequence of interactions – every Monday from three to four o'clock.[105] However, as the organisation has no

---

[97] Luhmann (1993a), p. 339.

[98] Cf. Kieserling (1999), pp. 358f.

[99] Analogously to the 'human being' as a conglomerate of organic and psychic systems (however, the relation between the systems is not identical).

[100] On interactionally framed decision processes see Chapter 4, Section 4.c.

[101] In this respect, we might speak of 'interpenetration' between organisation and interaction analogously to the relation between social and psychic systems (cf. Seidl, forthcoming).

[102] See Chapter 4, Section 4.c

[103] Cf. Kirsch (1992), p. 271; Zu Knyphausen (1991).

[104] On dimensions of meaning see Chapter 1, Section 2.d.

[105] Cf. Luhmann (1997), p. 818.

direct access to the interactional operations, it cannot start or terminate them directly;[106] only the interaction itself can produce its own beginning and its own end. Yet, organisations can condition participation, and thus indirectly 'stimulate' interactions to produce a beginning and an end. That is to say, the organisation can decide on a certain time span for which members are to come together. The beginning of the interaction can be conditioned in so far as the organisation can arrange for members to come in face-to-face contact, on the basis of which an interaction is likely to form.[107] The end can be conditioned through the decision to withdraw the participants after the time has run out. The interaction can observe this prospect of their participants being withdrawn after a certain time, and in expectation of that produce its own end. When the specified time has run out, the participants of the interaction say 'good bye' to each other.

In the *social dimension*, the organisation can condition the interaction by deciding on participation. That is to say, the organisation can influence interactional communications by deciding who is to participate, and, consequently, what social perspectives become available in the interaction.[108] In this respect, the perspectives that open up through the participants' different organisational roles are of particular importance: an interaction between senior managers, for example, is likely to be different from one between shop-floor workers.

By deciding on participants, the organisation can condition the interaction but does not have control over it. Only the interaction itself can determine who is considered present and who is considered absent. In this sense, even people physically present might be considered absent by the interaction. Similarly, the interactional communications might not acknowledge the formal organisational roles of the participants.

Conditioning in the *fact dimension* concerns the organisation's influence on the selection of topics. An example of explicit conditioning in this dimension would be a decision about the agenda of a forthcoming interaction. The selection of topics can also be indirectly influenced through decisions on the participants. If many marketing managers were involved in the interaction, for example, the communication would be likely to focus on marketing issues.[109] Another way of conditioning the selection of topics is to set in advance certain output categories for the interaction, by specifying that certain decision have to be made. An important form of conditioning concerns *constraining* the range of possible topics. Instead of influencing the interaction in a way that makes the selection of a specific topic

---

[106] Unless the organisation, for example, decided to blow up the interaction with a bomb, in which case the interaction would not be terminated by the interaction itself, but by the elimination of its (necessary) environment of psychic systems.

[107] Kirsch (1992), pp. 271ff. In this context, Kirsch speaks of the 'creation of necessary and sufficient initial and contextual conditions' for the emergence of interactions.

[108] Cf. Kieserling (1999), p. 378.

[109] One has to be careful not to confuse the social and fact dimensions. Here we discuss specific topics of communication – the sales figures. When we speak about the social dimension, we are looking at the particular ways in which a specific topic is exchanged.

more likely, the organisation can also make the selection of certain topics more unlikely; for example, by withholding information.

Although here we have treated the different dimensions of conditioning separately, they are to a large extent interdependent. By starting an interaction for discussing recent sales figures, for instance, the organisation might condition the interaction in all three dimensions. In the object dimension, the organisation might pre-select a particular topic of communication: sales figures. In the social dimension it might pre-select the participants: the marketing managers. In the time dimension it might schedule the meeting for a particular time.

4. Organisational Culture

a. *Organisational Culture as Medium*

For the last thirty years a host of different phenomena have been discussed and analysed under the label of organisational or corporate culture.[110] Even so, the concept of organisational or corporate culture remains rather vague.[111] Apart from that, the concepts that have been developed cannot be directly integrated into Luhmann's theoretical design. In the following section, we shall re-describe the existing approaches from a Luhmannian perspective, and attempt to arrive at a more precise definition, at least within regard to our context.[112]

In Luhmann's theory of organisation, the concept of organisational culture is almost completely absent. Only in his last writings does he introduce the concept briefly.[113] Luhmann follows the suggestion of Darío Rodríguez[114] that we conceptualise organisational culture as 'undecidable' decision premises, in contrast to the 'decidable' decision premises explained above. Luhmann writes

> [Undecidable decision premises] are not attributed to particular decisions, nor are they aimed at preparing or carrying out particular decisions. One cannot, therefore, point out how they came into being.[115]

---

[110] The literature on organisational culture is vast. For some good reviews of the field, see Smircich (1983), Schulz (1994), Linstead and Grafton-Small (1992), Alvesson and Berg (1992), and Martin and Frost (1996).

[111] Organisational culture is often defined with reference to the concept of 'symbol'; see e.g. Pettigrew (1979), pp. 574-575. The concept of 'symbol' itself, however, remains vague. Thus, one vague concept is replaced by another. On this criticism, see Luhmann (2000), p. 242. Czarniawska-Joerges (1992), pp. 159ff., speaks with regard to organisational culture of an 'umbrella concept', under which very diverse phenomena are subsumed.

[112] Cf. Luhmann (2000), p. 242.

[113] Luhmann (2000), pp. 239ff.

[114] Rodríguez (1991), pp. 140f. Rodríguez himself refers to the definition of culture as 'basic assumptions' by Schein (1984; 1985).

[115] Luhmann (2000), p. 242 (my translation).

This suggests that we are faced with decision premises which come into being in connection with decision processes, but are themselves not interpreted as decided upon.

Luhmann's remarks concerning organisational culture are in many respects reminiscent of our explanation of the concept of medium. Undecidable decision premises influence the decision network without themselves being decisions, or rather, forms. Here we are dealing with restrictions on the creation of forms, but not with the production of forms. As is characteristic of a medium, the undecidable decision premises usually remain invisible. Only by observing the decision processes with regard to their contingency do they become visible.

The observation of contingency depends on comparison. One can observe the restrictions at work in one situation, by comparing the situation to another situation where these restrictions do not apply. That is to say, for the observation of the restriction on possibilities one needs other spaces of possibility as contrast. The concept of culture becomes therefore a concept for comparison. Similarly, Luhmann writes that the concept of culture has the primary function of making comparison possible.[116] The decision possibilities in an organisation can be compared with those in other organisations, or with those in the same organisation but at different points in time or in different 'areas'. For that reason, the concept of culture is somewhat complicated: it indicates the medium but it does so from a comparative perspective.[117]

b.   Different Organisational Cultures in Different Parts of Society

In the literature on organisational culture one often finds comparisons of organisational cultures in geographically different parts of society, for example in different countries. In this context, culture is treated as an independent variable with respect to the organisation, which stems from outside but is imported in the organisation.[118] The cultures of organisations in Japan are often compared with those in the USA, for example.[119]

All these comparisons ultimately focus on what organisational decision processes are *possible* in different parts of society.[120] In this sense, they can be understood as studies of the organisational *medium*, in that they compare in what way the communication structures in different countries restrict (or make possible) organisational decision processes; in other words, they compare the available possibilities for coupling.

---

[116] Luhmann (2000), pp. 246f. On the concept of culture in general, see Luhmann (1995), pp. 31-54.

[117] For Luhmann (1995), p. 38 culture in general is conceptualised as a comparison consisting of three elements: the 'own culture', the 'other culture' and the points of reference according to which they are compared.

[118] Smircich (1983), p. 343.

[119] E.g. Ouchi (1981).

[120] Cf. Smircich (1983), p. 343.

Similar comparisons can be made between organisations in different *functional systems of society*. Organisations in the economic system (e.g. firms), have very different possibilities of reproducing their decisions from organisations in the legal system (e.g. courts).[121] In firms, decisions can be coupled to a great extent on the basis of the code income/expenditure, which is not possible in courts. Courts, in contrast, can create decision processes with regard to the code justice/injustice, which is not possible in firms. Hence, functional systems provide certain structures that influence decision processes without being perceived as being based on decisions. In this sense, basing decisions on the distinction between income and expenditure is not considered a decision in a firm. Similarly, basing decisions on the distinction between justice and injustice is not considered a decision in a court.[122]

Although most organisations are located within one particular functional system this is not a precondition.[123] Organisations can also be placed in two or more functional systems at the same time, or they can be located entirely outside any functional systems. Universities, for example, are often located in the educational system, in the system of science, and in the economic system at the same time. For that reason, different social structures from different functional systems exert their influence on decision processes. The way in which organisations are affected by these societal structures varies from organisation to organisation. Organisations, in this case, might be differentiated into different parts, each of which is placed in one particular functional system – resulting in different organisational subcultures.[124] Alternatively, all parts might be placed in all the functional systems simultaneously.[125] In our schema of medium and form the placing of an organisation in several functional systems simultaneously can be conceptualised as a form in an inhomogeneous medium.

On the basis of our form/medium distinction we can also analyse the effect of changes in societal structures on the organisation. For the organisation a change in societal structures means a change of its medium and therefore a change of the possibilities of coupling, through which the decision processes can be formed. The effect of societal change on the organisation is only of an indirect nature: the

---

[121] Cf. Luhmann (1994), Chapter 9, where Luhmann analyses the relation between economy and organisation according to the distinction between medium and form.

[122] In the reverse case, if a firm started to base its decisions on the distinction of justice and injustice, or a court started to base its decisions on the distinction of income and expenditure, it would most likely be considered a decision.

[123] Luhmann (1997), pp. 828f. See also Tacke (1999), p. 64 fn. 18; see Drepper (forthcoming) on the problem of the 'container metaphor' of organisations existing 'within' the function system.

[124] Gregory (1983), for example, analysed how different functional groups in an organisation reflected different occupational cultures.

[125] In a manner similar to our conceptualisation of organisations being placed in several societal subsystems at the same time, Martin and Frost (1996), p. 604, describe the organisational culture as 'a *nexus* where environmental influences intersect, creating a nested, overlapping set of subcultures within a permeable organizational boundary'. See also Martin (1992), pp. 111-114.

possibilities for creating forms are changed, but no specific form is determined by the change. The organisation might not change at all, because the forms it actualises are not affected by the change in societal structure. Changes in the decision processes that result from such societal changes normally take place without being recognised, as they cannot be attributed to any particular decisions.

c. *Organisation-Specific Culture*

So far we have been concerned with the restrictions that societal structures pose to organisations, without distinguishing between different organisations. We have so far posited that two different organisations in the same part of society face identical restrictions. The possibilities for coupling have so far been considered external, a priori restrictions. The organisational decision processes, however, also affect their medium. Through the particular reproduction of decisions, organisations generate changes in their medium. Consequently, every organisation creates its individual medium. In the course of the organisation's history certain couplings are recreated so many times that they become routine. They can no longer be dissolved, so the original number of possibilities of coupling in the medium is reduced. If the same decision is repeated over and over again, for example, the organisation might start to conceive of it as a necessity and no longer treat it as a decision. This might explain why organisations tend to become inflexible with age.[126] It may also be the case that the possibilities of the medium are enlarged through the decision processes. The organisation might become aware of its routines and break them.

In order to indicate the organisational culture in our arrangement of distinctions we have to draw an additional distinction. The direct medium of the organisation includes only a selection of the communication possibilities available in society (Figure 2.5).

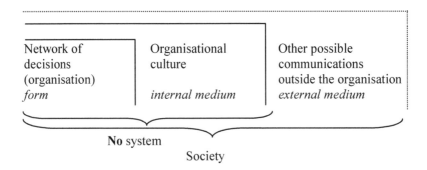

Figure 2.5 Organisational culture as part of the societal communication possibilities

---

[126] Cf. e.g. Abernathy (1978); Hannan and Freeman (1984).

It is important to note that organisational culture, or rather, the communication possibilities among which the organisation can create its forms, is not a system in its own right. That is to say, the distinction between organisational culture and other possible communications outside the organisation is not reproduced as a systemic boundary.[127]

d. 'Culture Management'

The initial euphoria with which the concept of organisational culture – and corporate culture in particular – was met in the eighties can probably be explained by the paradox it entailed: it allowed the indication of that which in itself evades indication. Following the concept of medium in general, the concept of organisational culture allows us to include the excluded as excluded into the explanation of the form. The concept of organisational culture provided a means for indicating culture as something that influenced the decision processes without being itself part of the decision processes. All of a sudden it became possible to explain why in different organisations different decision processes were possible. Decisions no longer had to be attributed solely to other decisions. Not only did the students of organisation acquire a new concept with which to refer to the medium, but organisations themselves also acquired a concept to refer to their own preconditions.

Given the possibility of indicating the excluded influence factor, the temptation was very strong to try to include the excluded as included. Organisations started to take care of their medium – their culture; they started to 'manage' it.[128] Many books were written in the eighties to promote the management of organisational culture, many of which have become bestsellers.[129] Communication structures, which both enabled and restricted decision processes, were analysed, evaluated and contrasted with ideal structures. This led to the belief that it was possible to create a 'successful' organisational culture through carefully composed measures, often with the help of consultants.[130] In other words, there was an effort to include organisational culture in the decision process.

Naturally, this attempt could not but fail, as the explanations of form and medium above make clear:[131] the medium cannot be made into a form, since for the form the medium is not transcendable. One can, of course, include the culture into the decision process – and in many organisations it does get included – but in that case we can no longer speak of the organisational culture as such. Through its

---

[127] Cf. Luhmann (2000), pp. 244f.

[128] These attempts have been ridiculed by some critics as 'value engineering'. See Martin and Frost (1996), p. 602.

[129] E.g. Peters and Waterman (1982), Deal and Kennedy (1982), and Ouchi (1981).

[130] As Martin and Frost (1996), p. 602 write: 'culture quickly became the hottest product on the consulting market.'

[131] See also the criticisms on attempts to manage culture by Fitzgerald (1988).

integration in the decision process, organisational culture changes[132] and thus evades being determined *through* the decision process.[133] Organisational culture only exists in distinction to the decision process and not as part of it. Organisations can change their cultures through their decision processes, but the way in which they are changed cannot be determined by the decision processes. For the organisation, the outcome of such change efforts is determined by chance.[134]

5. Summary

In this chapter we have explained Luhmann's autopoietic theory of organisation and developed it somewhat further by applying Heider's distinction of medium and form to it.

In the first section we explained the concept of organisation as a system that reproduces itself on the basis of decisions. We started with an analysis of the concept of decision, which was shown to be paradoxical; then we explained that the concept of uncertainty absorption refers to the process of connection between decisions, while the concept of decision premise refers to the structural aspect of decisions. In the last part, we explained the double closure of organisations; both on the level of their operations and on the level of their structures.

In the second section we analysed the relation between organisation and society. For this purpose we first explained and developed the concept of medium/form. On the basis of this concept, we argued that society could be conceptualised as a form in the medium of meaning; and that society itself could be conceptualised as a medium in which the organisation constitutes a form. At the end of the section we argued that the reproduction of the organisation involved (indirectly) also the production of non-decision communications.

In the third section we analysed the relation between organisation and interaction. We started with an explanation of the concept of interaction. We then argued that organisation and interaction share society as their direct medium. On the basis of this argument, we analysed organisational interaction as a phenomenon where organisation and interaction use the same communicative elements as components for the creation of their respective operations. We distinguished two different forms: 'formal' interactions are interactions which are coupled with the organisation in such a way that the organisation reinterprets some of the interactional communications as decisions. From the perspective of the

---

[132] Similarly, Theis (1994), p. 102 argues that organisational culture is changed simply by being made explicit.

[133] The impossibility of managing organisational culture makes it, of course, very interesting again: possessing a 'successful' culture means having a strategic advantage, due to its inimitability (cf. Barney 1986).

[134] This is so in the case of causations that descend from a higher order (form) to a lower one (medium). Heider (1959), p. 11 speaks of 'mass events' or 'mass processes', the concrete effects of which are only 'accidental': '[i]t is not probable that I could produce definite molecular events by the movement of my hand, for instance, make a certain molecule move in a particular way.'

organisation, this leads to interactionally framed decision processes. 'Informal' interactions are interactions that develop on the basis of organisational decision processes, but their communications are not observed by the organisation as decisions. In the last part we examined the different ways in which organisations can condition interactions in order to use their dynamic for the reproduction of their decisions.

In the fourth section we developed a new conceptualisation of organisational culture as the communicative medium in which the organisation reproduces itself. We argued that this medium on the one hand depends on the part of society in which the organisation reproduces itself and, on the other hand is continually modified through those operations of the organisation that it makes possible. At the end of the section we discussed the idea of 'culture management', arguing that it is incompatible with our concept of culture.

Chapter 3

Organisational Identity

Introduction

Over the last few years, interest in concepts of *organisational* identity has grown among social scientists.[1] The literature is expanding rapidly. The concept of organisational identity has even found its way into textbooks.[2] However, although the idea of organisational identity has been subjected to much scrutiny and debate, definitions and conceptualisations of the topic remain essentially contested.[3]

On the basis of our theory of organisation as an autopoietic system we can offer a new understanding of organisational identity, in which other concepts of identity can be integrated. Here, identity is conceptualised as constructed by the organisation in a dynamic self-referential process. This is a 'genetic' perspective on identity that is primarily concerned with the process of production of self-description and only secondarily with its form and content.

In the first section of this chapter we will give a general overview of different concepts of organisational identity in the relevant literature. In the second section we will explore new concepts of identity based on an understanding of organisations as autopoietic systems. We will focus particularly on the concept of organisational self-description as an organisation's description of its own unity. In the third section we will differentiate between various forms of self-descriptions and in the last section we will analyse the phenomenon of multiple self-descriptions.

1. Concepts of Organisational Identity in the Literature

The literature on organisational identity can roughly be divided into three groups:[4] corporate identity, substantive identity, and reflective identity. Each of them is concerned with a different identity question. The first one addresses the question: how does the organisation present itself as a unified and distinguishable system to its different audiences? The second one poses the question: what is the unity of the

---

[1]   On the topics discussed in this chapter see Seidl (2003a).
[2]   E.g. Hatch (1997).
[3]   Cf. Albert (1998). See also the exchange of views between Cornelissen (2002a; 2002b) and Gioia and colleagues (2002a; 2002b); Haslam et al. (2003).
[4]   See also Brown (2001), Ravasi and Van Recom (2003), and Whetten and Godfrey (1998) for reviews of the literature on identity.

organisation? And what makes the organisation different from other organisations? The last one tackles the question: how does the organisation itself perceive its unity and uniqueness? In the following sections we will first look at each of the three groups of literature and the way they address these questions. This will serve as a background for developing an autopoietic concept of identity.

a.   Corporate Identity

The concept of corporate identity is mainly used in the practical discourses of marketing. It is a rather inconsistent and vague concept that has been interpreted in many different ways. However, in very general terms one could say that corporate identity refers to the presentation of the organisation to its different audiences.[5] Corporate identity

> means the sum of all the ways a company chooses to identify itself to all its publics – the community, customers, employees, the press, present and potential stockholders, security analysts, and investment bankers.[6]

In the beginning, the main focus of this approach was on visual presentation, highlighting the importance of corporate design, in the meantime, however, it has grown to include all aspects of the organisation that are observable from outside. As Olins observes:

> It is clear that corporate identity has begun to expand out of its graphic roots and embrace corporate communications, organisational behaviour and other non-design disciplines.[7]

As a marketing tool corporate identity is more of a normative than a descriptive concept. It focuses on positive ways of presenting the organisation to its audiences. Normally, the development and management of a corporate identity is seen as part of public relations.[8] The aim is to develop and manage a clear and, most importantly, consistent appearance, that makes the organisation easily recognisable, memorable and distinguishable from its competitors.[9]

---

[5]   For a good collection of essays on corporate identity, see Birkrigt and Stadler (1993). For a more recent analysis of the concept of corporate identity with links to other references, see Van Riel and Balmer (1997), and Balmer (1998; 2001).

[6]   Margulies (1977), p. 66.

[7]   Olins (1990), p. 5.

[8]   Cf. Jefkins (1989), pp. 618-620.

[9]   There have been various criticisms of the corporate-identity approach – mostly for its lack of academic rigour. Tafertshofer (1982), for example, criticised the concept as tautological: corporate identity uses elements of corporate identity to achieve corporate identity.

The concept of corporate identity shows some similarity with the (more academic) theory of impression management.[10] As in the case of corporate identity, research on impression management analyses the organisation's attempts at influencing the environment's perceptions of it.[11] The theories of impression management refer mostly to situations in which the organisation is perceived in a negative light by the general public due to unfavourable circumstances:[12] examples of this would be Dow Corning's breast implant crisis,[13] USAir's aircraft crash in Pittsburgh,[14] the explosion of the Challenger space shuttle,[15] the Exxon Valdez oil spills,[16] the negative press on General Motors from Dateline NBC,[17] or the 'Arms to Iraq' scandal.[18] In such cases organisations try to 'manipulate' the audience's perception and create a more favourable picture of themselves.[19]

When we compare the concepts of corporate identity and impression management, we can find some similarities and some differences. Both concepts refer to 'external' perceptions of the organisation and the ways in which the organisation can try to influence them positively. However, whereas the concept of corporate identity deals with the means of achieving a consistent and enduring image of the organisation over time, impression management is more concerned with the different situations in which the organisation has to be presented in a positive light.[20] The concept of corporate identity is thus rather static – focussed on long periods of stability and short intersections of change – whereas the concept of impression management is more dynamic. Combining the two approaches, one could say that while corporate identity concerns the general presentation of the organisation in the long run, impression management deals with the application of this presentation to different situations.

b. Substantive Identity

The literature on substantive identity is concerned with two basic questions. The first question is, what is the unity of the organisation, or better: what keeps the different parts of an organisation together as a unity? In particular, how are the

---

[10] Cf. e.g. Tedeschi (1981), Tedeschi and Melburg (1984), Meindl (1990), Ginzel, Kramer and Sutton (1992), Bromley (1993), Alvesson (1994), Elsbach (1994; 2003), Elsbach et al. (1998), Bolino (1999), and Arndt and Bigelow (2000).

[11] Impression management originated in the sociological work of Goffman (1959).

[12] Impression management can, however, also refer to instances in which an already positive reputation is further enhanced (cf. Dukerich and Carter 1998; Ginzel et al. 1992). See also Palmer et al. (2001) with reference to the distinction between protective and acquisitive impression management orientations.

[13] Brinson and Benoit (1996).

[14] Benoit and Czerwinski (1997).

[15] Vaughan (1986).

[16] Ginzel et al. (1992), p. 278.

[17] Hearit (1996).

[18] Brown and Jones (2000).

[19] Tedeschi (1981). Dukerich and Carter (1998) also speak of 'reputation repair behavior'.

[20] Cf. Weber (1985), p. 179.

various actions of an organisation related to each other? The integration and coordination mechanisms, which are found in shared rules, world views or values is what the literature on substantive identity focuses on. The second question, which is often more implicit, is: what distinguishes one organisation from another? The usual answer to this question is closely connected to the first question: it is the specific integration and coordination mechanisms that distinguish one organisation from another.

One of the first articles on organisational identity is that written by the German organisation theorist Edmund Heinen.[21] In his article he introduces the concept of organisational identity as an important element in the goal system of organisations. He sees in the organisational identity mechanisms that integrate the different decision makers into the organisation and coordinate their decisions. Later Reinhard[22] and Weber[23] tied this concept of organisational identity to the concept of organisational culture.[24] They defined organisational identity as shared rules, world views and values, which constitute the deep structure of the organisation.

In that early literature on the topic organisational identity is understood as an achievement of the organisation; organisations do not possess an identity by definition. Furthermore, identity is perceived as something that comes in different degrees. In this sense organisations can be unified to a greater or lesser extent – or to use Heinen's terms: integrated and coordinated to a greater or lesser extent. To create a high degree of identity is seen as an important managerial task.

In the English-speaking scientific community this concept of organisational identity was not developed very much under this terminology. However, similar ideas were suggested with concepts such as 'collective cognitive maps',[25] 'hypermaps',[26] 'organisations as shared meanings',[27] 'dominant logics',[28] 'negotiated belief structures',[29] 'core beliefs',[30] 'deep structure',[31] 'organisational minds',[32] 'collective mind',[33] or 'organisational archetypes'.[34] Behind those concepts lies the assumption that organisational members share important rules, views and values, which make the organisation a consistent system of actions and distinguish it from other organisations.

---

[21] Heinen (1981).
[22] Reinhard (1983).
[23] Weber (1985).
[24] See also Kirsch (1992), pp. 133-137 and Schreyögg (1992).
[25] Axelrod (1976).
[26] Bryant (1983).
[27] Smircich (1983).
[28] Prahalad and Bettis (1986).
[29] Walsh and Fahey (1986).
[30] Pettigrew (1985)
[31] Gersick (1991).
[32] Sandelands and Stablein (1987).
[33] Weick and Roberts (1993).
[34] Greenwood and Hinings (1993).

c. Reflective Identity

The literature on reflective identity, in contrast to literature on substantive identity, is not so much concerned with the unity and distinctiveness of the organisation per se, as with the way the organisation *perceives* its unity and distinctiveness. Albert and Whetten[35] were among the first to pose this particular question in their seminal article of the mid-eighties.[36]

Albert and Whetten suggested a reflective concept that refers to an organisation's 'beliefs' about itself, or 'claims' which it makes about itself. There are two important points in this concept of identity. First, the formal-logical aspect: as in the case of beliefs about the organisation, identity is also located on a higher logical level than the organisation itself. To illustrate this point with a metaphor, if the organisation is the territory, then the organisational identity is the map. For the concept of identity it is irrelevant whether the believed characteristics 'really exist' in the organisation; it is the belief that is important. Different individuals may even have different beliefs about the organisation.

The second important point concerns the content of identity statements.

> Organisations define who they are by creating or invoking classification schemes and locating themselves within them.[37]

However, only those classification schemes are relevant that are understood to refer to *central*, *enduring* and *distinctive* properties of the organisation. Again, let us stress that it is the *claim* that certain characteristics are central, distinctive and enduring that is important.

Dutton and colleagues[38] picked up Albert and Whetten's ideas and developed the concept of the organisation's *collective identity*; or, to put it more simply, the concept of *the* organisational identity, in contrast to *an* organisational identity. They speak of a collective identity in the case that the beliefs about the organisation are shared.[39] An organisation's collective identity, they define, 'consist[s] of the beliefs that members *share* as distinctive, central and enduring'.[40] Ashforth and Mael expressed a similar idea:

> An organisational identity is an intersubjective construct: that is, it cannot exist unless people *agree* that it exists.[41]

---

[35] Albert and Whetten (1985).
[36] On the development of this concept of identity see also Gioia (1998).
[37] Albert and Whetten (1985) p. 267.
[38] Dutton et al. (1994).
[39] There remains, however, the question of how many and which members have to share the same beliefs in order to speak of a collective identity: cf. Scott and Lane (2000), p. 43. Gioia and Thomas (1996), for example, consider only the beliefs of the top management team to be relevant.
[40] Dutton et al. (1994), p. 243 (my emphasis).
[41] Ashforth and Mael (1996), p. 28 (original emphasis).

This was an important step in the development of the theory, because from that moment onwards, organisational identity as a concept became independent of any particular member of the organisation. The unit of analysis was no longer the individual member but the organisation. Again, we have to stress that in contrast to the substantive organisational-identity approach, here we are not talking simply of shared beliefs, but of shared beliefs *about* the organisation, that is to say, shared 'maps' of the organisation.

Three further theoretical extensions were made to the original concept of organisational identity. First, a link between the theory of organisational identity and psychological theories of identity was established through Social Identity Theory (SIT).[42] According to SIT, which was mainly developed by Henry Tajfel and John Turner,[43] an individual's identity is composed of two elements: a personal identity, which refers to an individual's concepts about his/her particular idiosyncrasies, and a social identity, which refers to specific social categories that the individual uses to describe himself. As Ashforth and Mael explain:

> according to SIT, the self-concept is composed of a personal identity encompassing idiosyncratic characteristics (e.g., bodily attributes, abilities, psychological traits, interests) and a social identity encompassing salient group classifications. Social identification, therefore, is the perception of oneness with or belongingness to some human aggregate.[44]

In the case of organisations this means that the individual member uses descriptions of the organisation as part of his own self-descriptions. This theoretical framework now allows us to apply psychological identity theories to organisations, and argue that if all members use the shared concept of the organisation as part of their individual identity, then the organisation as a whole – or all the members taken together – will exhibit behaviours consistent with the psychological theories of individual identity.[45] On the basis of this argument, Brown, for example, applied the psychological theory of narcissism to organisations.[46]

Second, the concept of organisational identity has often been connected to research on sensemaking. It has been argued that the organisational identity serves the organisation's members as a lens for their observations:[47] the organisational identity is used as a cognitive scheme for interpreting organisational and environmental events.

---

[42] See the seminal article by Ashforth and Mael (1989). See also Hogg and Terry (2000).

[43] See Tajfel (1972), Tajfel and Turner (1986), Turner (1985), Turner et al. (1987), Turner and Oakes (1989), and Turner et al. (1994).

[44] Ashforth and Mael (1989), p. 21.

[45] There is, of course, again the question of how many and which members have to share the same identity characteristics. See also criticisms by Nkomo and Cox (1996), pp. 336ff.

[46] Brown (1997).

[47] E.g. Fiol (1991; 2002), Dutton and Dukerich (1991), Dutton and Penner (1993), Ashforth and Mael (1996), Elsbach and Kramer (1996), Gioia and Thomas (1996), Gustafson and Reger (1995), and Glynn (2000).

An organization's *identity* [...] filters and molds an organization's interpretation of [...] an issue.[48]

Third, the original concept of identity by Albert and Whetten has been criticised for its emphasis on perceived *endurance* as a defining characteristic. Gioia and Thomas ask: '[How] can identity be enduring if strategic change is to occur?'[49] In order to solve this problem they suggest extending the concept of identity to include both an 'existing' identity and an 'envisioned' identity. An alternative solution to this problem is offered by Gustafson and Reger,[50] who distinguish between 'abstract, intangible' and 'substantive' attributes. While the substantive attributes refer to 'what we do', the intangible attributes refer to 'why/how we do things'. Abstract attributes allow for greater flexibility, since they can embrace a wider variety of operations, the attributes themselves, however, are conceptualised as static. A further suggestion for making the concept more dynamic was again made by Gioia and his colleagues, who argue that only the 'labels' that the organisation uses to describe itself are static but the meaning of these 'labels' can change.[51]

Apart from the literature building directly on Albert's and Whetten's seminal article there is a second stream of works on reflective identity based on a narrative approach. The most important writer in this field is Barbara Czarniawska.[52] For her, organisational identity can be captured as 'autobiographical narratives', which are constantly being written and rewritten.[53] In contrast to the Albert–Whetten concept, here organisational identity is conceptualised already from the outset as a *dynamic* phenomenon.[54] While Czarniawska's take on organisational identity is clearly concerned with the way the identity of the organisation is *perceived* by the organisation – and as such can be counted amongst the 'reflective-identity' approaches – she does not, however, explicitly distinguish between different 'levels', that is to say, between the organisation as such and the description of it in the autobiographical narrative.[55]

d. Summary

Before elaborating on the concept of organisational identity in the context of Luhmann's theory of autopoietic systems we will try to systematise the different approaches described so far. In Figure 3.1 we have tried to summarise the three identity concepts.

---

[48] Dutton and Dukerich (1991), p. 520 (original emphasis).
[49] Gioia and Thomas (1996), p. 371.
[50] Gustafson and Reger (1995). Also, Whetten and Godfrey (1998), p. 162.
[51] Gioia et al. (2000). On theorising on stability and change of identity, see also Meyer et al. (2002).
[52] For another example of a narrative approach see Humphreys and Brown (2002).
[53] See Czarniawska-Joerges (1994), Czarniawska-Joerges (1996), and Czarniawska (1997).
[54] In the field of personal identity such an approach is well established. See e.g. Giddens (1991). See also Peacock and Holland (1993).
[55] See also the discussion on Czarniawska's approach in Christensen and Cheney (1994).

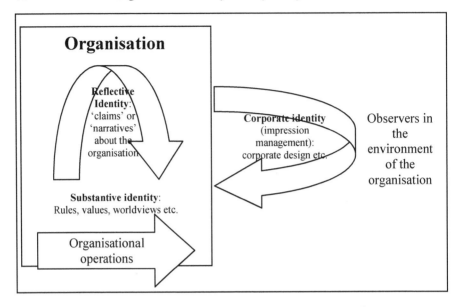

Figure 3.1 The relationship between substantive, reflective and corporate identity

Substantive identity as shared rules, values and world views is realised in the organisational structures and as such influences all organisational operations. Reflective identities as 'claims' or 'narratives' about the organisation are not directly inbuilt in the operations. They are reflections on the operations and therefore on a higher logical level. Because reflections take place within the organisation, they influence operations and might even become (part of) the substantive identity, if they take the form of shared rules, values or world views. Corporate identity as the presentation of the organisation to other observers is not directly related to organisational operations. It is aimed at generating particular positive impressions in other observers. However, in order to realise this, the organisation has to create particular organisational structures, influencing its substantive identity. The development of a corporate identity, furthermore, presupposes a sense of self, a reflective identity. At the same time, the development of a corporate identity has effects on the reflective identity.[56] All in all, it is apparent that the three approaches to organisational identity are circularly related.

---

[56] On the relation between (reflective) organisational identity and corporate identity, see also Rindova and Schultz (1998), Balmer and Wilson (1998), and Marziliano (1998).

2. Organisational Identity in the Context of Autopoiesis

The identity questions described above are also addressed in Luhmann's theory of autopoietic systems. However, due to his particular concept of organisation they are approached somewhat differently. In the first two sections of the following pages we will discuss two concepts, which, similarly to the substantive identity approaches, refer to the unity and the uniqueness of the organisation. In the third section we will present, in line with the reflective identity approaches, a concept of organisational self-description that refers to an organisation's perception of itself. In the last section we will present the concepts of reputation and image, which, similarly to the corporate identity approach, capture an organisation's unity with regard to external observers.

a. The Unity of the Organisation: Operative Closure

If we conceive of organisations as systems that consist of events, which disappear as soon as they come into existence, the question about the unity of the organisation and about the preservation of this unity over time becomes particularly interesting (this was the question raised by the substantive identity approach). In our context, the answer to this question can only be found in the mode of reproduction itself. As explained above,[57] the organisation is conceptualised as a system of decisions that reproduce each other recursively. These different decisions are not held together by anything but the recursivity of their production, in other words, by autopoiesis. In this context Luhmann writes:

[T]he unity of the [...] system cannot be anything but this self-referential closure.[58]

It makes little sense to say that an organisation has more unity or less unity (as many of the substantive-identity approaches described above do), or that it is either unified or fragmented, when we come to conceptualise the unity of an organisation as its autopoiesis. The reproduction of the organisation can only take place as an operative unity. In this sense, if the organisation is reproduced it constitutes a unity.[59]

Autopoiesis either occurs or does not – just as a biological system either is alive or is not.[60]

The 'unity' of the organisation that is constituted by its autopoiesis (operative closure) applies both to the time dimension and to the question of boundaries. In

---

[57] See Chapter 2.

[58] Luhmann (1995a), p. 408. See also Luhmann (2000), p. 304.

[59] Teubner (1987b) and Teubner (1987a) have tried to argue against this view for a 'gradualisation' of operative closure. For its application to organisations, see Kirsch and Zu Knyphausen (1991), and Kirsch (1992). On Luhmann's criticism on Teubner's argument, see Luhmann (2000), fn. 36, p. 51. Teubner (personal communication, 2/11/2000) himself agrees with Luhmann's criticisms.

[60] Luhmann (1995a), p. 266.

the time dimension different decisions at different points in time are connected through their reference to each other: earlier decisions give rise, or 'produce', later decisions; and, the other way around, later decisions are the 'product' of earlier decisions. In this sense, organisations remain 'identical' over time in that they constitute *one single reproduction process* irrespective of any structural changes – analogously to a living system.

Autopoiesis also defines clearly the boundaries of the organisation. Whatever takes part in the autopoiesis of the system belongs to the system and whatever does not take part in the autopoiesis does not. As only decisions produce decisions, the organisational boundary is defined by the distinction decision/everything else. Also very important in this respect is that an organisation can select its elements autonomously: the organisation can decide with respect to every communication whether to conceive of it as a decision of the organisation (and thus its element) or not. As Luhmann writes:

> As in all systems, the boundaries are adequately defined if problems with the boundary line or with using the difference between inside and outside can be handled by the system's own operations.[61]

Through their autopoiesis different organisations are also clearly differentiated from each other. The concept of autopoiesis does not allow for any overlap between different operative unities.[62] Thus, the autopoiesis of the organisation not only distinguishes between decision and non-decision but also between the decisions of different organisations. Only the organisation's own decisions are part of the system; other decisions belong to its environment. If there is any doubt about the status of a decision, the organisation can decide about it.

b.   The Uniqueness of the Organisation: Individuality

In Luhmann's theory organisations are not treated as different from each other only in that they are different operative unities. There is also a 'qualitative' difference between them. The concrete realisation of the autopoietic reproduction is unique in every organisation. This uniqueness he refers to as *individuality*.[63] This individuality is itself also a result of the autopoietic reproduction. Every operation has to connect to the momentary system state, which is the product of previous operations. Thus, the reproduction of the system at any moment depends on the particular development of the system in the past (history), as represented by the

---

[61] Luhmann (2000), p. 412 (my translation). To an external observer the boundary might very well look fuzzy as he or she might use a different distinction for observing it.

[62] Not even in organisational networks. See Luhmann (2000), Chapter 13, Section 7; Baecker (1998), p. 42; Wimmer (1995).

[63] The term 'individuality' is generally used in two different ways: first, individuality as indivisibility (Latin: *in-* and *dividere*). In this sense individuality is synonymous with 'operative unity'. Second, individuality as uniqueness. See Luhmann (1993d), pp. 149-258. Here we use it in the second sense.

particular momentary system state.[64] The system, in Von Foerster's terms, has historicity.[65] In order for two organisations to be identical they have to share the same history. This is extremely unlikely, as even small differences between organisational operations can lead to completely different developments precisely because of historicity.[66] Luhmann writes:

The dependence on its own history individualises the system.[67]

One can thus say that the autopoiesis of a system inevitably leads to individuality. The two concepts, however, must not be confused with each other. While the concept of 'operative closure' (autopoiesis), discussed above, refers to the level of operations, the concept of 'individuality' refers to the level of structures. Past operations of an organisation affect future operations by functioning as decision premises for them. In other words, the history of the system is given as the set of particular decision premises in the particular concrete decision situation.

So far the individuality of the organisation has been defined only formally. One might, however, also be tempted to define the concrete individuality of a concrete organisation. In other words, one might analyse the concrete structures of a system. In principle there are two different possibilities for such an endeavour: either one attempts a (more or less) comprehensive description of the multiple decision premises at one concrete moment in time (in the next moment, however, everything will be completely different again), or one focuses only on a few but important structures, namely, decision premises that are particularly stable and refer to many decision situations. In this respect, it is often the case that organisations are described by their programmes (e.g. a 'car manufacturing organisation'), their personnel (e.g. the 'medics'), their communication channels (e.g. 'hierarchical'), and the number of positions within the organisation (e.g. '3000 employees'). Alternatively, they might be described with regard to their culture, that is to say, their undecidable decision premises (e.g. a 'Japanese firm').

c. Reflective Identity of the Organisation: Organisational Self-Description

Having described how Luhmann conceptualises the unity and uniqueness of the organisation in the last two sections, in this section we shall focus on the question of reflective identity, which is conceptualised as organisational self-description.

(1) Self-observation and self-description. In the last section we argued that the organisation is realised as a unity on the basis of its autopoietic reproduction. In this sense, any organisation is a unity *by definition*. However, on the level of

---

[64] It is important to be clear on this point: the past development of the system is only relevant in so far as it results in a particular system state at the particular present moment.
[65] Von Foerster (1991).
[66] On this point, generally, see Maruyama (1963).
[67] Luhmann (2000), p. 248 (my translation).

reproduction the organisation is blind with regard to this unity. The different decisions distinguish between those operations (i.e. decisions) that belong to the organisation and those that do not (i.e. basic self-observation) – otherwise decisions would not 'know' what to connect to. However, they do not observe the different decisions as forming a unity. Organisations *can*, however, draw special distinctions that allow them to observe this unity: they can communicate about themselves as *unities*. Thus, while the *production* of the unity is a necessity of being an organisation, the *observation* of this unity by the organisation is a particular achievement of it.[68]

Thus we have to distinguish between three different, but related system/environment distinctions: first, the distinction that results from the autopoiesis of the organisation; that is to say, the factual organisation in distinction to its environment. Second, the distinction which every operation draws between that which belongs to the organisation, and which it can therefore (self-referentially) connect to, and that which does not belong to the system and which it can therefore only (other-referentially) refer to. The basic self-observation is mostly merely implicit in the communications; it becomes, however, explicit when the organisation makes a decision about whether to treat something as an element of the organisation (i.e. as a decision) or not. Third, the internal observation of the organisation as the unity of its operations: in other words, the internal reconstruction of the factual system/environment distinction. Such self-observations are permanently made all over the organisation and can have various forms: the accounting department, for example, observes the organisation in the form of financial figures.

As operations, organisational self-observations are communicative events, which have merely a momentary existence. With the disappearance of the communication about the organisation, its indication of the organisation also disappears. Organisations can, however, also create semantics or texts indicating the organisation's unity, which persist beyond the communication's momentary point of existence. The simplest form of such a text is the name of the organisation[69] – for example, 'Cambridge University'. The self-description can also be more elaborate, e.g. a formal constitution. These semantics are created for repetitive use. They do not disappear with their usage but can be actualised repetitively within different contexts. As these semantics represent the organisation's unity within the organisation we can call them the organisation's 'reflective identity', or, in Luhmann's terms, the 'organisational self-description'.[70] This is Luhmann's definition:

---

[68]   Luhmann (1995a), p. 455.
[69]   Cf. Glynn and Abzug (2002); Christensen and Cheney (1994), pp. 223-224.
[70]   There are other examples in the literature that suggest treating organisational identity as a discoursive rather than a social-psychological phenomenon, e.g. Hardy et al. (2005).

By 'self-description' we mean the production of a text or functional equivalents of a text (e.g. indexical expressions like 'we' or 'here' or a personal name) with which and through which the organisation identifies itself.[71]

[Self-descriptions] are texts of a specific kind, which first of all distinguish themselves phenomenally through their reference to the system as the unity of all its operations (= autopoietic unit of reproduction).[72]

There are two points which are central to the definition: the first point concerns the usage of the text. Texts are not self-descriptions by nature, but become self-descriptions by being used or communicated as such; that is to say, by being used by the organisation's members for referring to the organisation. The second one concerns the point of reference of the description. Self-descriptions refer to the organisation as a whole, that is to say, as the unity of all its operations. This does not mean that the text literally describes this unity, but merely that the text is understood as (or better: used as) a description of the unity. A text might refer explicitly only to a part of the organisation, but might be used to refer to the organisation as a whole.

Like everything that takes part in the autopoiesis of the organisation, self-description must also be understood as the product of organisational operations.[73] The production of self-descriptions can be explained using Spencer Brown's concept of *condensation*,[74] that is, a contraction of several distinctions into a single one: self-descriptions can be conceptualised as 'condensates' of different self-observations. The organisation observes its self-observations and extracts from them a *generalised* distinction, omitting all contextual differences (particularly regarding time and space).[75] In this respect, Luhmann writes:

Self-observations serve as the medium, the memory material, from which the forms of self-descriptions are created.[76]

With the concept of *confirmation*,[77] that is to say, the reproduction of a distinction, we can describe the way in which self-descriptions come to take part in the autopoiesis of the organisation. Texts as such are not operations and therefore do not indicate (verb!) anything at all. Only by being used – or rather, confirmed – by concrete organisational operations can they indicate the organisation. For example, a member of the organisation communicates: 'Cambridge University will

---

[71] Luhmann (2000), p. 417 (my translation).

[72] Luhmann (2000), p. 419 (my translation).

[73] Being social systems, organisations, make use of the semantics which society, particularly language, provides. The self-description is nevertheless the organisation's own product as, first, it depends on the organisation whether it is used or not, and, second, the particular meaning of the semantics is only specified through the particular organisational context.

[74] See Chapter 1, Section 3.b.

[75] Cf. Luhmann (1992a), p. 311. Similarly Brown and Jones (2000).

[76] Luhmann (2000), p. 417 (my translation). Luhmann (1987) refers to these self-observations also as a 'variety pool' for the extraction of self-descriptions.

[77] See Chapter 1, Section 3.b.

appoint a new professor'. By using the semantic form 'Cambridge University' the communication, in passing, indicates (i.e. observes) the unity of this particular organisation.

Confirmation, however, is not pure repetition of the same text.[78] Instead, self-descriptions adjust to the different contexts of the concrete communications in which they are confirmed. With every new self-observation for which they are used, they are enriched with new meaning.[79] The text is still the same, but the particular distinction it makes is constantly shifting. As Barrett and colleagues write: 'words are continuously extended beyond the boundaries of their existing applications.'[80]

Condensation and confirmation are relational concepts. They are the two sides of a form. Self-descriptions as condensates of self-observations have no 'reality' as such; they only 'exist' in the concrete instances in which they are being confirmed, that is to say, used for self-observations. This mutual implication of condensation/confirmation or self-description/self-observation expresses the necessary tension between sameness and change that is inherent in the very idea of identity. The text remains the same text but it is realised differently in different situations. We can also look at the relation between condensation and confirmation from a dynamic point of view: the confirmation of self-descriptions realises a self-observation, but at the same time self-descriptions are the result of the condensation of the very self-descriptions they give rise to.

(2)   Integrative and operative functions of organisational self-descriptions. Organisational self-descriptions provide the organisational decision processes with some kind of guidance. We can distinguish in this respect two different types of function: an integrative and an operative function.[81]

We start with the *integrative* function, which probably constitutes the self-description's central function. Organisational self-descriptions represent the organisation to the organisation. They provide the organisation with a sense of unity: on the basis of the self-description the organisation can observe its different parts as related to each other. On a very basic level the self-description is to the organisation what the body is to the psychic system: it marks the 'location' where the system takes place, it focuses its operations and prevents the organisation from 'losing' itself. 'Organisations have no body', Luhmann[82] writes, 'but they have a text.' In this sense the self-description can indicate to the single decision where to find other decisions, which to connect to, and where it is unlikely to find other

---

[78] Luhmann (1993c), p. 272, fn. 22, argues that this is a modification of Spencer Brown's concept of confirmation. One could, however, argue that it is merely a more complex form of confirmation.

[79] Luhmann (1992a), pp. 108ff., pp. 311f. See also Luhmann (2000) p. 417.

[80] Barrett et al. (1995), p. 358.

[81] In the relevant literature the distinction between integrative and operative functions has variously been discussed with regard to similar concepts, especially paradigms, myths and scripts. See, for example, Johnson (1987), particularly p. 271, Geertz (1973), particularly p. 93, Pondy (1983), and Gioia and Poole (1984).

[82] Luhmann (2000), p. 422 (my translation).

decisions. Of course, this does not mean that without self-description the organisational boundaries would be less clear (see above). The self-description merely makes it simpler for the organisation to identify its own boundaries. It makes it less often necessary to decide whether something has to be treated as a decision or not. In this sense the self-description is not a prerequisite for the organisational autopoiesis but a facilitator.

The integrative function of self-description can also be described with the metaphor of map and territory.[83] The map is a representation of the territory. As such it makes orientation in that territory possible. By looking at the map one can observe the different parts of the territory as an integrated whole even if one cannot see the different parts of the territory simultaneously. Similarly, the self-description can be seen as a map of the different organisational elements. By observing the self-description decisions get a sense of the unity of all decisions without actually connecting to them.

> In other words, the identity orientation serves in the systemic processes as a substitute for the orientation according to [its own] complexity.[84]

We now come to the *operative* function. This second function is probably less central as it can also be served to some extent by the 'normal' decision premises. One might even consider it merely a by-product of the integrative function. Luhmann himself was somewhat sceptical as to its significance.[85] We nevertheless believe it to be of importance, not least because this function has received particular attention in the general literature on organisational identity. The significance of the operative function of self-descriptions is also likely to vary from organisation to organisation. One might hypothesise that the less bureaucratic the organisation, the more likely it is to rely on the self-description's operative function, and vice versa.[86]

Organisational self-descriptions serve an operative function to the extent that they give direction to decision making and thus influence what decisions are produced. This operative aspect is manifest if self-descriptions offer themselves explicitly as selection criteria; for example, in the form of organisational goals or strategies. Such directives can be given both in positive and negative ways: they can instruct what to do or what *not* to do.[87] The operative aspect of self-descriptions is often latent. This is the case if self-descriptions merely influence the way particular situations are interpreted. Thus, instead of self-descriptions giving instructions on how to decide between alternatives, they influence what is perceived as alternatives.[88] As Ashforth and Mael write:

---

[83] With regard to the metaphor of the map, see particularly Weick (1990).

[84] Luhmann (1993a), p. 203 (my translation).

[85] Luhmann (2000), p. 421.

[86] See Kärreman and Alveson (2004) for a critical discussion on this point.

[87] Cf. Barney et al. (1998, p. 151) and Fiol (2002) on 'anti-identity'.

[88] Cf. Whetten and Godfrey (1998), pp. 116-118.

An OI [organisational identity] provides a lens for perceiving and interpreting the environment [...] An OI affects what is attended to and, therefore, what gets *noticed*.[89]

Gioia and colleagues, for example, describe how IBM's single-minded self-description as a mainframe company prevented it in the eighties from seeing investment possibilities in connection with the burgeoning PC market.[90]

Traditionally, the integrative and operative functions described above were understood to be served by the hierarchy or the top of the hierarchy. It was assumed that they could represent the organisation within the organisation. In the light of this assumption Ashforth and Mael suggest that the less hierarchical an organisation is, the more important the organisational identity becomes for providing a sense of unity.[91] Luhmann goes a step further by suggesting that it is not the dissolution of hierarchies but the inevitable failure of any attempt at a hierarchical ordering of organisational operations which makes self-descriptions necessary for providing orientation and guidance.[92]

(3)   Contingency and viability. Self-descriptions are doubly contingent: not only the self-observations, from which they were condensed, are necessarily contingent,[93] but also the condensation is contingent. To be precise, we are dealing with two sets of distinctions: first, the particular momentary self-observations; namely, distinctions drawn to indicate the organisation. Second, the observation of the concrete momentary self-observations, that is to say, distinctions drawn to indicate the distinctions that are drawn to indicate the organisation. Since condensation is itself an observation it depends on a contingent distinction. Depending on the particular distinction it uses, the condensing observation will condense observations differently. Every condensation is thus necessarily a contingent construct that could as well be different.

Self-descriptions, in this sense, cannot be said to be 'more true or less true'.[94] Most writers on organisational identity, even if they are talking of a socially constructed identity, assume – at least implicitly – that there *is* something like an *underlying* 'central, distinctive and enduring' character of the organisation, the

---

[89] Ashforth and Mael (1996), p. 46. They also use the metaphor of the 'blinker', p. 50. Dutton and Penner (1993) argue that organisational identity affects the perception of importance, legitimacy and feasibility of organisational issues and, thus, strategic agenda setting.

[90] Gioia et al. (2000), pp. 74f. In the same article (p. 77) the authors also describe the case of two further firms (one computer-peripherals manufacturer and one hearing-aid manufacturer) that opened up new possibilities for themselves by changing their self-description. Brown and Starkey (2000) argue that the organisational identity prevents learning in ways which contradict the organisational identity. On the relation of organisational identity and learning see also Fiol (2002), and Corley and Gioia (2003).

[91] Ashforth and Mael (1996), p. 20.

[92] Luhmann (2000), p. 420.

[93] Since every observation depends on the distinction it uses, see Chapter 1, Section 3.

[94] Cf. Luhmann (1997), pp. 884-885. Similarly, Christensen and Askegaard (1998).

only problem is that one cannot conceptualise it.[95] They do not acknowledge that 'centralness', 'distinctiveness' and 'enduringness' are distinctions which are introduced by an observer in order to observe organisations and not something that exists independently of the observation.

Apart from that, self-descriptions are inevitably *self-simplifications*; that is to say, they are less complex than the organisation.[96] The organisation's complexity cannot be represented in the text.[97] On the one hand, because of practical reasons, a text cannot contain as many elements and relations between elements as an organisation – this would require infinite volumes of self-descriptive texts.[98] On the other hand, there is a logical necessity for self-descriptions to be simplifications. Self-descriptions become part of the system they describe; as a consequence, the system is necessarily more complex than the self-description as it comprises the system *plus* its self-description.[99]

Although there are no 'right' or 'wrong' self-descriptions, there are differences in their viability. This viability, however, is entirely dependent on the organisation itself: a self-description is viable as long as the organisation can make use of it. Thus, in order to analyse the viability of a self-description, one has to examine it in relation to its two functions within the system.[100]

With regard to its integrative function a self-description has to display the right degree of complexity for the different operations to be able to *relate* to it and in this way see themselves in relation to the unity of the organisation. We can illustrate this with our metaphor of map and territory: maps do not reflect the entire complexity of the territory; they do not account for every single stone present there. Instead, they account only for 'significant' features, such as hills, roads, or lakes. Every single point in that territory can, however, be related to the unity of the territory if it can be related to those features that are represented in the map – e.g. between (sign for) lake and (sign for) road. Analogously, a viable organisational self-description has to account for 'significant' elements of the decision network, such as the formal hierarchy, according to which the concrete decisions can be orientated. While a map, in order to be viable, has to account for a *sufficient number* of 'features' of the territory, there is also a limit to its degree of precision. If the map becomes too detailed – in an extreme case even a copy of the territory – it loses its orientating function. Similarly, differences in degree of complexity between self-description and organisation are not only a logical inevitability, but a practical necessity. Self-descriptions have to be simple enough

---

[95] See, for example, Ashforth and Mael (1996), p. 23: 'The OI [organisational identity] may bear little relation to the "*objective*" or *impartially measured* OI' (my emphasis).

[96] Cf. Luhmann (1995a), p. 456, and Luhmann (2000), p. 418.

[97] Ashforth and Mael (1996), p. 30, make a similar point, giving, however, a slightly different explanation.

[98] Cf. Luhmann (1993b), pp. 59-76.

[99] The system, in this sense, is 'hyper-complex' (Löfgren 1977). See also Luhmann (1997), p. 876.

[100] Corley and Gioia (2004) introduced the concept of 'identity ambiguity' to describe a situation where the existing self-descriptive labels do not provide orientation and direction to the organisation (i.e. its members).

to be relatively easily and quickly memorable, accessible and comprehensible. A self-descriptive text spread out over ten volumes is, in this sense, unlikely to be suitable for providing an orientation to individual decision operations.[101]

The viability of a self-description with regard to its integrative function depends on how successfully different decisions relate to it.[102] It is not the case, however, that all decisions inevitably try to relate to a self-description; a majority of decisions are probably just orientated according to directly related decisions. In this sense, one should probably speak of the viability of a self-description in the face of *attempts* made by decisions to relate to it. In terms of the map-and-territory metaphor, the map is viable as long as attempts to relate concrete locations in the territory to points in the map are successful.[103]

With regard to their operative function, self-descriptions are viable as long as their operative implications are seen as 'unproblematic' in the particular decision situations in which they are invoked.[104] In principle there are two cases in which the operative implications can come to be seen as problematic. First, self-descriptions might have vague, ambiguous or no operative implications at all. Whether or not this is problematic depends on whether there are other (local) structures[105] that can provide decisions with selection criteria – this is probably mostly the case.[106] Second, self-descriptions might become problematic if they have conflicting operative implications for a concrete decision situation. Again, we are not concerned with any 'objective' operative implications, but only the operative implications that are observed by the particular decision situation. In other words, we are not concerned with any sort of 'objective' consistency of operative implications, but with consistency with regard to the operative implication for particular, single decision situations.[107] With regard to a particular decision on prices, for example, a self-description might suggest both a high and a

---

[101] However, the viability of a self-description always depends on the concrete circumstances. Even a very complex self-description could be viable in an organisation if, for example, it were meant for specific communications within the organisation, which were specialised in dealing with complex texts. Society, for instance, has very complex self-descriptions. See e.g. Luhmann's (1997) theory of society, which is meant for communications within the sub-system of science in the field of sociology (see Section 3.c on the 'location' of self-descriptions within the decision processes).

[102] A single failure to relate to the self-description does not necessarily lead to the self-description becoming non-viable. Organisations normally can tolerate a certain amount of inconsistency.

[103] In this respect, see Weick's (1990) anecdote of the soldiers who got lost in the Alps, but by (unknowingly) using a map of the Pyrenees orientated themselves and found their way back to the camp. Weick, however, draws a different conclusion.

[104] In terms of our metaphor, the self-description has to be able to highlight a viable path. Cf. Barry and Elmes (1997), p. 433 with regard to strategy: 'the strategist's problem is as much one of creating an inviting cartographic text as it is one of highlighting the right path.'

[105] Or additional self-descriptions. See Section 4.

[106] In fact, Luhmann (2000), p. 421, argues that other structures are normally sufficient for providing selection criteria.

[107] It is also possible that the organisation observes the consistency of structures on the basis of hypothetical decision situations.

low price and in this way lead to a conflict in this particular decision situation. Apart from that, with respect to its operative implications, a self-description might conflict with local structures in a particular decision situation. As a result of such a case either the self-description or the local structure would become unviable. If the organisational structures were strictly transitively arranged, the local structure would have to be changed, but since such transitivity is normally not given,[108] the local structure could also dominate the self-description and thus challenge its viability.

The viability of self-descriptions depends not only on each of their two functions but also on the *interplay* between them. The integrative and operative functions of a self-description appear to be circularly related: self-descriptions give rise to operations, which they then have to be able to account for and integrate into a unifying picture (Figure 3.2). In this sense, a self-description is viable if it is able to integrate the very operations it invokes;[109] a self-description becomes non-viable if the operations it gives rise to cannot be integrated. A similar idea can be found in many other writings on related topics.[110]

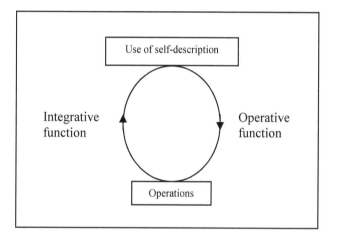

Figure 3.2 The interplay between operative and integrative functions

d.   Reputation and Image

In this section we want to present two concepts, which – similarly to those in the corporate-identity approach – conceptualise the organisation's unity with reference

---

[108] Cf. Luhmann (2000), p. 420.

[109] Or, to use Von Foerster's term: if it is an 'eigen-value'. Von Foerster (1976).

[110] Barrett et al. (1995), p. 368, for example, describe how interpretive repertoires are challenged by the interests that they invoke. Hedberg (1981) describes the interplay between myths, strategies, and actions as one in which myths lead to strategies which lead to actions which challenge the myth. See also Hedberg and Jönsson (1977).

to external observers.[111] These are the concept of reputation, which will be defined as a description of the organisation by an outside observer,[112] and the concept of image, which will be defined as an internal construction of reputation.[113]

(1)   Reputation: external descriptions.   By 'reputation' we refer to the descriptions that outside observers use to refer to the organisation.[114] These descriptions can be understood to be generated in a way analogous to that of the self-description. An external observer[115] observes the organisation as a unity. In the same way as outlined above, the observer can condense several observations of the organisation into a description of the organisation. He or she might, for example, condense his or her observations on environmental pollution, rises in profit, unsatisfied workers, etc. into a description that can 'account' for these different observations: e.g. 'ruthless profit-maker'.

Any such description, as has already been argued with regard to self-description, is contingent: first of all, it is based on contingent observations, that is to say, distinctions; second, every condensation is a contingent simplification, in the sense that other condensations are possible. Following this line of argument, our observer might make certain observations that do not fit with the description he or she has made. If, for example, he or she observed that the organisation donated all its profits to charities, the description 'ruthless profit-maker' might no longer be viable as a point of convergence for the various observations.

---

[111] This, however, is where the similarity ends!

[112] For a similar definition, see e.g. Fombrun and Shanley (1990), Dutton and Dukerich (1991), Dutton et al. (1994), Fombrun (1996), and Rindova and Fombrun (1998).

[113] For a similar definition see Dutton and Dukerich (1991). Some authors also use the term 'image' as a general term to refer to all kinds of descriptions of the organisation (including reflective identity), and speak of 'construed external image' or 'shared external image' to refer to the internal construction of external descriptions, e.g. Dutton et al. (1994), Dukerich and Carter (1998); Dukerich et al. (2002). For an overview of different definitions of image, see Gioia et al. (2000), pp. 65ff. See also Whetten and Mackey (2002) for some clarifications on the distinction between identity, image, and reputation.

[114] Christensen and Askegaard (1998) criticise the distinction between internal and external observers, and consequently the distinction between reflective identity and reputation (they refer to it as 'image'). They argue that there are no clear-cut boundaries that allow us to distinguish between inside and outside. In particular: members are only partially included in the organisation and are thus both part of the organisation and of the environment. This criticism is justified if one defines organisational identity with regard to psychic systems (i.e. the members' shared descriptions of the organisation), as most writers do. If, however, one defines identity with regard to an autopoietically closed social system, as we do, the boundaries between inside and outside are necessarily clear-cut and a clear distinction between reflective identity and reputation can be made. Of course, this is not to deny the possibility that the organisation might use the same words to describe itself as the external observers would; however, these words will have a different meaning to the organisation (cf. Seidl 2004). Similarly to the authors cited above, Scott and Lane (2000), do not distinguish between internal and external observers but instead, between top managers and stakeholders.

[115] Another social system or a psychic system, e.g. the psychic system of a member of the organisation.

In the environment of an organisation there are many observers, using different distinctions to observe the organisation. Hence, every observer has a different sequence of observations, which he or she condenses differently. A business consultant will observe the organisation differently and condense a different description of it from a housewife or an environmentalist group. Even different academics describe the same organisation differently. On the basis of the principle-agent theory, the organisation may be described as a particular bundle of contracts,[116] whereas on the basis of a biographical perspective, it may be described as a particular product of its history.[117] On the basis of a transaction-cost perspective, it may be described as a hierarchical network of relations, in contrast to a market network.[118] Moreover, even a single observer might possess several (compatible or conflicting) descriptions of the organisation. With regard to the multiplicity of different descriptions, some writers suggest conceptualising reputation as some sort of synthesis of all descriptions.[119] This stance, however, seems problematic as one would have to indicate an observer who synthesises them. Instead, we had better speak of reputations in the plural.[120]

(2)   Image: internal construction of external descriptions.   For the organisation its reputations are not directly accessible, since they are not part of the organisational communications. They belong to the environment.[121] For the organisation the observers and their descriptions do not exist, unless it uses specific distinctions to observe them. This does not mean that the observers do not exist as such, but that for the organisation they are not accessible as observers. Through the perturbations that these 'real' observers cause in the organisational communications the organisation might, however, construct an observer, in the same way that the external observer constructs the organisation in his observations. Thus, the organisation produces a description of an external observer, on the basis of which it assumes that it is being observed.[122] One example of such an internally

---

[116] Jensen and Mecklin (1976).

[117] E.g. Kimberly (1987).

[118] E.g. Williamson (1975).

[119] E.g. Fombrun (1996).

[120] Similarly, Bromley (1993), Carter and Deephouse (1998), Dukerich and Carter (1998), and Schultz et al. (2000).

[121] The strict distinction between internal and external descriptions of the organisation has been criticised by several authors as 'inadequate'. See, e.g. Coupland and Brown (2004); also Scott and Lane (2000); Cheney and Christensen (2001). These critics argue that there is no clear boundary between organisation and environment, which would allow for such a distinction. On the basis of our autopoietic conceptualisation of organisation, however, there is a clear boundary (see above). For that reason we still believe that the distinction is useful.

[122] Language provides organisations with plenty of terms for constructing external observers, e.g. competitors, business consultants, academics, markets. More elaborate 'guidelines' for constructing external observers can be found, for example, in the stakeholder approach (Freeman 1984). In the end, however, it is the organisation itself that determines whether and how such concepts are used.

constructed observer is '*the* customer' or 'the public'. Both terms refer to several persons, who are *constructed* by the organisation as *one* observer.[123]

Having distinguished other observers in its environment, the organisation can (re)construct[124] their descriptions of the organisation. That is to say, the organisation (re)constructs the way it is described by external observers (who are themselves a construct of the organisation). Such a constructed internal description is what we refer to as *image*. An organisation might distinguish several external observers and, on that basis, (re)construct several external descriptions of itself. In this case the organisation has many *images*.

(3)   The relationship between reputation, image and self-description. The concepts of reputation, image and self-description all refer to descriptions of the organisation, but by different observers. In the following pages we will analyse the relationship between them (Figure 3.3). In order to avoid making the analysis unnecessarily complicated we will only look at the relation between a single reputation, a single image, and a single self-description (the case of multiple descriptions is based on the same principle).

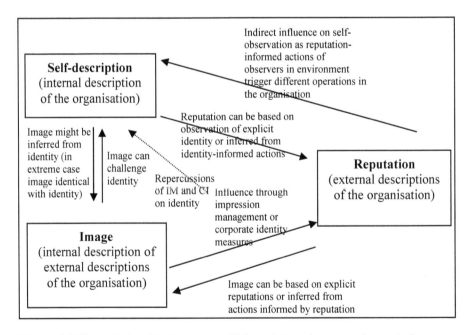

Figure 3.3 The relationship between self-description, image and reputation

---

[123] Cf. Luhmann (2000), p. 239.
[124] We put 're-' in brackets because the internal construction is related to an internal construction of an observer.

• *Reputation and image.* The relation between reputation and image can be described as a relation between an observation of the first-order and an observation of the second-order. Systems in the environment observe and describe the organisation (first-order observation) and the organisation observes them observing it (second-order observation). However, as the organisation itself needs distinctions in order to observe other observers, its observation is its own creation; that is to say, it is not identical with the original description. The organisation itself, however, is probably for the most part unaware of the distinction between image and reputation.[125] In reacting to its image the organisation assumes itself to be reacting to the reputation.

There are two ways in which the reputation can influence the image. First, the reputation might be explicitly communicated, in which case the organisation can observe it and construct its image accordingly.[126] It is important to note, however, that by being directly observed, external descriptions are not 'copied' into the organisation as an image. Even for the purposes of observing 'directly' the organisation has to choose a distinction according to which it observes, and thus cannot but *construct* the image.[127] Second, the organisation can infer the outsiders' descriptions by observing their behaviour towards the organisation. For example, if an external system is perceived to behave in a friendly way, the organisation can infer a positive image of itself.[128]

Image has normally no direct influence on reputation. On the basis of its image, however, the organisation might undertake specific operations in order to influence its reputation, such as impression management or corporate-identity measures.[129]

• *Self-description and image.* Self-description and image are particularly close to each other as they are both descriptions of the organisation, and are held within the organisation. The only difference is that image has merely an indirect reference to the organisation, as it refers to an outside observer describing the organisation. As both constructs are so close, it is a particular achievement of an organisation to keep them apart. Many organisations might, in fact, not distinguish between the

---

[125] Unless the organisation reflects on it.

[126] Elsbach and Kramer (1996), for example, described how business schools observed their reputation in the form of rankings. The authors, however, do not distinguish clearly between reputation and image.

[127] Dukerich and Carter (1998), p. 21, for example, are not very clear on this point when they speak of the 'accuracy' of perceptions of reputation.

[128] Dukerich and Carter (1998) distinguish three sources of 'reputation cues': media, direct communication by interest groups, and solicited information about outsiders.

[129] These measures can influence not only the reputation, but also the self-description. If the organisation presents itself to external audiences in a very favourable light, the organisation itself might start to believe its own 'slogans' and start to make use of them in its self-description: cf. Gioia et al. (2000), p. 70. In this respect, Christensen (1995) and Christensen and Askegaard (1998) also speak of 'autocommunication'. Elsbach and Glynn (1996) argue that organisations have greater chances of influencing their reputation in a desired way if they believe in their own 'PR'.

two and instead assume that external observers describe the organisation in the same way as they do themselves.

However, if an organisation can distinguish between self-description and image, then it can and most probably will compare them. In other words, the distinction between self-description and image can become the subject of communications. Since both refer to the same organisation, the organisation will expect some sort of consistency between them. This is a question of viability. In a strict sense, the self-description of the organisation would also have to be able to account for the image, as this is part of the organisation. Manifest contradictions between self-description and image will have to be explained. If they are not, the image can constitute a challenge to the self-description.[130] Often the organisation will explain contradictions simply as a result of the external observers' lack of 'adequate' information about the organisation.[131] Elsbach and Kramer, for example, report how American universities justified the inconsistency between their self-descriptions on the one hand, and how they saw themselves described by the magazine *Business Week* on the other, by claiming that *Business Week* had used the wrong distinctions for observing them.[132] In such cases, the organisation could try to influence the environment's observation through impression management or corporate-identity measures.[133] Contradictions between self-description and image can also be intentional.[134] That is to say, the organisation might want to deceive external observers about (what it sees as) its 'true' self – perhaps even using impression management or corporate-identity measures for that purpose.[135]

It is not only the self-description that is influenced by the image, but also the other way around. Since the self-description as a point of convergence for different observations directs organisational operations, it also influences the ways in which the environment is observed. In this context, Dukerich and Carter argue that identity serves as a lens that affects how reputation cues from the environment are observed.[136] From this it follows that organisations will be conditioned by their self-description in the construction of their image.

• *Self-description and reputation.* Self-description and reputation are both descriptions of the organisation, but they belong to different systems and are therefore not directly comparable: the organisation has no direct access to its

---

[130] Cf. Dutton and Dukerich (1991), Gioa et al. (2000), Chreim (2002), and Foreman and Whetten (2002).

[131] It could also blame the contradiction on it own lack of information about external opinions, claiming that the image does not reflect the reputation.

[132] Elsbach and Kramer (1996). The authors, however, did not clearly distinguish between image and reputation.

[133] Cf. Dukerich and Carter (1998).

[134] Note that in this case the organisation wants the self-description and *reputation* not to match. However, because it conceives of the image as a direct reflection of the reputation, the discrepancy between self-description and reputation is translated into the discrepancy between self-description and image.

[135] See also Christensen (1995), who argues that marketing can serve as such a 'buffer'.

[136] Dukerich and Carter (1998).

reputation and the outside observers have no direct access to the self-description. Nevertheless, self-description and reputation can exert an influence on each other.[137]

The influence of reputation on the self-description is mostly indirect; namely, via the image.[138] That is to say, reputation influences the image in the described way, and the self-description might be influenced through a comparison between image and self-description. Apart from that, reputation can also influence the self-description indirectly, in that the behaviour of external systems informed by the reputation might trigger certain operations within the organisation (e.g. reflection), which influence the self-description.

There are three ways in which the self-description can influence reputation. First, directly; through impression management or corporate-identity measures that are based on a comparison between self-description and image. That is to say, if the self-description incorporates a particular image that is to be achieved, the organisation can try to influence actively the systems in the environment.[139] Second, the self-description, if explicit, can be observed by systems in the environment and their descriptions of the organisation can be based on it. Third, reputation can be influenced indirectly, if the self-description gives rise to particular behaviours that can be observed by external observers and thus challenge their descriptions of the organisation.

3. Forms of Self-Description

In this section we will take a closer look at the variety of available self-descriptions and examine their functioning in the organisational reproduction.

a. Simple Distinction vs. Double Distinction

Generally, there are two ways in which self-descriptions can describe the unity of the organisation: either through implicit or explicit reference to its environment. Organisations can describe the unity of the organisation either directly, by indicating the *organisation* in distinction to its environment, or indirectly, by indicating the *distinction* between the organisation and its environment.

If one analyses the two forms of self-description one finds that in the first case one is faced with a simple distinction, while in the second case one is faced with a

---

[137] On the relation between reputation and self-description (identity), see also Rindova and Fombrun (1998), who argue that organisations have incentives to monitor their reputations and align their self-descriptions. See also Albert and Whetten (1985), p. 269 who argue that a significant discrepancy between the organisation's identity and 'the way outsiders view it' (reputation) might impair the organisation's 'health' and lead to lower effectiveness. See also Chreim (2002), and Hatch and Schultz (2002).

[138] However, if image and self-description were conflated, the influence from reputation would be direct.

[139] Fombrun and Shanley (1990), for example, describe how firms attempt to influence their stakeholders' assessments by signalling their positive characteristics.

double distinction. In the first case the self-description refers to the unity directly by indicating the organisation (marked state) in contrast to its environment (unmarked state). The environment is contained within an unwritten cross. That is to say, the unity of the organisation is described in the *context* of its environment, but there is no explicit reference to the environment (Figure 3.4).

Figure 3.4 Self-description as simple distinction

In the second case the self-description indicates the unity of the organisation indirectly by indicating the distinction between the organisation and its environment (marked state), in contrast to other possible distinctions (unmarked state). That is to say, the distinction between organisation and environment is contained on the inside of the observational distinction. The implicit context of the observation is alternative distinctions, that is to say, alternative relations between system and environment (Figure 3.5).

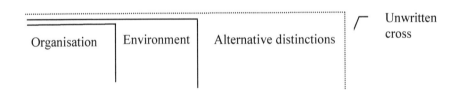

Figure 3.5 Self-description as double distinction

Although both ways of indication are suitable for serving the two functions of the self-description, they have different implications for the particular *way* these functions are served. In the first case, decisions will be integrated with regard to a unified whole in contrast to everything else and decisions will be invoked in the face of this unity. Since the self-description includes the environment only as an unmarked state, it cannot observe it; the focus is entirely on the unity itself. Thus, the environment's influence on the organisation and vice versa cannot be seen. From this perspective, the aspect of *separation* in the concept of distinction is emphasised: the organisation is understood as separated from its environment.

In the second case, decisions will be integrated and new ones invoked with regard to the *relation* between the organisation and its environment.[140] The orientation is thus not only according to the unity of the organisation but according to the unity of the organisation vis-à-vis its environment. In this way the environment's constitutive role for the organisation is appreciated; the mutual influence between organisation and environment is explicitly recognised.[141] In other words, organisational decisions can be assessed with regard to their effect on the organisation's relation to its environment. While in the first case the emphasis was on the aspect of separation between the two sides of a distinction, in this case it is on the *relation* between the distinguished sides; that is to say, on the unity of the distinction.[142] Connected to this different focus is a different sensitivity to environmental events. While in the first case the self-description tends to reduce the organisation's responsiveness towards its environment, in the second case the self-description tends to enhance it.[143]

b. Dimensions of Self-Descriptions

Self-descriptions can also be distinguished according to the (primary) dimension of meaning in which they are formed. Although the three dimensions of meaning generally appear in combination, they can be analysed separately. Apart from that, self-descriptions are normally dominated by one dimension.

(1) Fact dimension. The fact dimension of meaning is defined by the distinction this/other. With regards to operations this implies a distinction between different *attributions*, e.g. an operation is attributed to this organisation or to another one, or an operation is attributed to this or another programme.[144] In this sense, the fact dimension of self-descriptions concerns the boundaries according to which the attribution of operations can be orientated.

---

[140] Luhmann (in his later writings) refers to an orientation according to the unity of the difference system/environment as 'rationality'. See Luhmann (1993f), Luhmann (1995a), pp. 437ff., Luhmann (1997), pp. 171ff., and Luhmann (1998b). See also Schulze-Bönig and Unverferth (1986).

[141] This does not imply that the description of this relation is anything other than an organisational construct; the organisation has as little access to the environment or to itself as it does to the relation between organisation and environment.

[142] Note that every distinction (border, boundary etc.) distinguishes but also connects its two sides. In the terms of Spencer Brown (1979), p. 1: 'Distinction is perfect continence.'

[143] Morgan's distinction between 'egocentricism' and 'systemic wisdom' with regard to an organisation's understanding of itself runs along similar lines. See Morgan (1997), pp. 258ff. Organisations are egocentric if they orientate themselves according to their own unity and they possess wisdom if they conceive of themselves as integrated into their environment.

[144] Luhmann (1995a), pp. 83-84.

Generally, there are two kinds of boundaries to which a self-description can refer: external and internal boundaries.[145] In the first case the self-description describes a boundary that distinguishes what is attributed to the organisation from what is attributed to the environment.[146] In the second case it describes internal boundaries according to which attributions to different parts of the organisation are regulated.[147,148]

There are several ways of describing external boundaries. One way of describing the border between organisation and environment is to refer to some physical location, such as a building, address etc. The organisational operations are seen as a unity due to their taking place at the same physical location. A similar representation of the boundary between self and other can be found in the literature on personal identity. Here, it is the body that serves as a signpost for the organisation of self-references.[149] However, in contrast to psychic operations, communications are not strictly connected to any physical locations. Organisational meetings, for example, might be held in a pub instead of the office.[150] A similar way of describing the external boundary is by reference to the members of the organisation. This form of self-description might be particularly prominent in very small organisations where members know each other very well. This self-description, however, becomes problematic if membership changes frequently. A common form of self-description for firms is by reference to their products or services. An organisation might describe itself as a car manufacturer or an airline, for example. Or the self-description might refer to the production process, describing core competences, for instance.[151] In these cases, all organisational operations are described as a unity through their connection to the product, service or production process.

Analogously to external boundaries, self-descriptions can also refer to boundaries within the organisation. In this sense the self-description can describe boundaries between different departments, for instance. Such descriptions can refer

---

[145] The internal differentiation is closely related to the distinction of system and environment and can be seen as a reflection of it. See Luhmann (1995a), pp. 18-19.

[146] Ortmann and Sydow (1999), for example, see the description of the organisational boundary as the main function of the organisational self-description.

[147] Independently of the description of a boundary, the organisation distinguishes between system and environment or between different programmes within the organisation on the operative level.

[148] Describing either internal or external boundaries of the organisation is not directly correlated with the form of simple and double distinctions, as explained above. In this sense, the external boundaries can be described as the bounds of the organisation or as a connection between the organisation and its environment. Equally, the internal differentiation can be described as differentiation within the bounds of the organisation or as a differentiation pertinent to the organisation/environment relation.

[149] Cf. Luhmann (2000), p. 422.

[150] Down and Taylor (2000).

[151] Prahalad and Hamel (1990). See, however, also Glynn (2000), who argues that the identity affects how the organisation perceives its core competencies.

either to physical boundaries in the form of different buildings or office spaces, or to occupational differences (e.g. 'marketing' and 'production').

(2)   Social dimension. The social dimension of meaning concerns the relation between different observers, or different perspectives. It is defined through the distinction ego/alter.[152] With regard to self-descriptions we can distinguish two relevant realms: the distinction between different observers within the organisation and the distinction between the perspective of the organisation and other observers in its environment.

With regard to the relation between different observers within the organisation a self-description might refer to the particular forms of coordination of its members. In this way the organisation might describe itself through formal structures of relations between its members. This might take the form of an organisational chart. Similarly, a specific form of decision making might be described as 'participatory' or 'dictatorial'. The co-operation between different members might be described as 'competitive' or 'co-operative'.[153]

In relation to its environment the organisation describes itself in the social dimension with reference to other social or psychic systems, which have their own perspectives, needs, etc. That is to say, the environment presents itself to the organisation as a conglomeration of *alter egos*. A semantic term that can be used to address the relation between the organisation and its social environment is 'function'.[154] The organisation might describe the function that it serves for the societal system of which it is part: 'main employer of the region', for example. The semantic 'function' combines the internal perspective of the organisation with the external perspective of other systems.[155] The operations of the organisation are related to needs, wishes etc. of *alter egos* in the environment. However, since the organisation has no access to its environment, the organisation can only account for the perspectives of other observers in the form of its own constructs. Thus, 'function' is a construct of the organisation that does not have to reflect any 'real' relation between organisation and environment.

Another important semantic term in the social dimension – especially for business organisations – is 'competition'. The organisation describes itself as a competitor in a specific market segment. For this purpose (for reasons similar to those explained above), the organisation has to define other organisations in its environment as systems with specific interests and perspectives, which 'compete' in a defined domain with the interests and needs of the focal organisation. Pepsico, for example, describes itself with reference to its competition with Coca-Cola.

---

[152] Luhmann (1995a), p. 80.

[153] Note that these descriptions are constructions and do not have to resemble any 'reality' as such.

[154] This form of self-description seems to be particularly prominent in non-profit-organisations.

[155] In this sense it constitutes a double distinction in the above sense.

Again, as in the case of the concept of 'societal function', the concept of 'competition' combines environmental and organisational perspectives.[156]

(3)   Time dimension. The time dimension is constituted through the distinction before/after.[157] Accordingly, self-descriptions in the time dimension describe the relation between events at different points of time. We can distinguish self-descriptions with two different perspectives: past development and future development.

With regard to past development, self-descriptions construct histories. This form of self-description has particular prominence in the literature on personal identity.[158] The important point here is that narrated histories are different from the 'real' events. In order to make this point clear, Peacock and Holland suggest in their research on personal identity that we speak of 'stories' instead of 'histories', 'because this does not connote that the narration is true, that the events narrated necessarily happened, or that it matters whether they did.'[159] However, as Czarniawska-Joerges points out, there has to be some claim to facticity.[160] Thus, the story must claim to refer to actual events, otherwise it undermines its own legitimacy as a self-description. In organisations we can find such self-descriptions in both written and informally narrated forms.[161]

The second form of identity in the time dimension is self-description with regard to the future. This can take the form of plans or goals that are to be achieved. Self-descriptions with a future perspective are particularly important; for example, in project organisations, i.e. organisations that are set up to accomplish a particular project. Finishing the project serves as the *raison d'être* for the organisation. Similarly, campaigns or political parties are often organised around a future state that is to be achieved – for instance, the campaign against landmines. Here we can distinguish between two possible forms: self-descriptions can either focus on a future (theoretically achievable) state – for instance, the banning of landmines – or they can adopt a future perspective that is not focussed on an achievable state – for example, increasing living standards around the world. While in the first case the organisation conceives of its own end (i.e. when the future state has been reached),[162] in the second case it conceives of a future with an open end.

For organisations that are faced with frequent and quick changes the time dimension, especially with a focus on the past, might be particularly suitable for

---

[156] Several other writers have analysed the identity construction with reference to a competitor, but with partly different explanations for it. Cf. Messick and Mackie (1989), Porac and Thomas (1994), and Ashforth and Mael (1996), p. 25.

[157] Luhmann (1995a), pp. 77-78.

[158] Written autobiographies are of particular interest in this respect. See e.g. Giddens (1991).

[159] Peacock and Holland (1993); cf. Goleman (1985), and Adams (1990).

[160] Czarniawska-Joerges (1996), p. 160.

[161] Cf. Ashforth and Mael (1996), p. 36.

[162] This does not mean that the organisation will be necessarily dissolved when that state is reached. The organisation can always claim that the state has not really been reached yet, or 'just' change its self-description and set a new objective.

constructing a viable self-description.[163] If the range of products, physical locations, members, and competitors change very often and quickly, self-descriptions dominated by the fact or social dimension might not be very viable. In view of such fragmentation a self-description dominated by the time dimension might provide a good foundation in which the fact dimension and social dimension can be integrated.[164]

c. The Integration of Self-Descriptions in the Decision Network

As a further way of analysing and distinguishing different self-descriptions we can examine their integration with regard to the organisational communication channels. To be more precise, we can examine at what location and in what way self-descriptions are communicated.

(1) Explicit self-descriptions. Self-descriptions are explicit if the self-descriptive text is explicitly communicated, either in oral or in written form. Often organisations have specific documents in which the self-description is written down; for example, mission statements, strategy or policy papers. The location of self-descriptions with respect to communication channels is crucial to the influence that self-descriptions have on decision processes.[165]

First, explicit self-descriptions may be 'located' at the top of a hierarchical communication network.[166] In other words, they are only communicated at the top but not at lower levels of the hierarchy.[167] In modern business organisations such self-descriptions can frequently be found under the name of 'organisational strategies' or 'organisational policies'. Due to the hierarchical separation of different levels of decision making, the self-description cannot relate directly to most of the individual decisions. Instead, the self-description 'in-forms' directly only those decisions that are made at the level directly below it. In their turn, these decisions give rise to further decisions and so on. The further down within the decision hierarchy, the less the influence of the original self-description. Because of the hierarchical structure, however, the self-description (theoretically) exerts an indirect but systematic influence on all decisions, as long as they are integrated into the hierarchy.

Although self-descriptions that are located at the top of the hierarchy may have a systematic influence on all decisions, they cannot ensure consistency between different decisions within the organisation or even consistency with regard to the

---

[163] Cf. Ashforth and Mael (1996), p. 58, fn. 2.

[164] One can find similar arguments in the sociological literature on personal identities in (post)modern times, e.g. Giddens (1991).

[165] On communication channels, see Chapter 2, Section 1.c.

[166] Although not all organisations are strictly hierarchically organised, some sort of hierarchy, as Baecker (1999b), pp. 198ff. argues, can always be found.

[167] In such cases the self-description might not even be known at lower levels of the hierarchy.

self-description itself.[168] As many studies have shown, the hierarchical organisation of decision networks leads to a systematic corruption of the original meaning of a communication: this is a consequence of a shift between means and ends.[169]

Second, explicit self-descriptions can be 'located' in one place within the organisation, but outside the formal decision hierarchy.[170] Mission statements provide the best example of self-descriptions that are integrated in that way. Mission statements are written documents in which the organisation describes itself.[171] They normally have no formally binding status even if they contain clear instructions for the organisation's decision making. The influence of such self-descriptions on the decision process is not systematic but sporadic; that is to say, the location of the self-description does not automatically ensure that any decision process is 'in-formed' by it.[172] While in the first case the hierarchy enforces the recognition of the self-description in the concrete decision situations, this does not happen in the second case. Different decisions *can* consider the self-description as an orientation but they do not have to. In this sense, the self-description constitutes a possible but not a necessary orientation. Because the self-description is not structurally enforced, it might be entirely ignored.[173] This actually seems to be the fate of many self-descriptions at such a location.[174] The chance of self-descriptions in such positions being invoked probably increases in situations where local structures fail to provide enough of an orientation, as, for example during restructuring.[175]

---

[168] We are not referring to some sort of 'objective' consistency between structures, but to the influence on particular decision situations. Structures are consistent as long as in the concrete decision situation their expectations with regard to the decision are not perceived as contradictory.

[169] Cf. Merton (1957), pp. 199-200, Selznick (1943), Blau (1956), pp. 93ff., Sills (1957), pp. 62ff., and Luhmann (1976), pp. 307ff.

[170] E.g. codes of ethics or newsletters. See Rindova and Schultz (1998), p. 49.

[171] The literature on mission statements is extensive. For a review of some of the literature see Bart and Baetz (1998).

[172] Access to such self-description might either be restricted, as in the above case, or open, in which case decisions throughout the organisation might be directly informed by it.

[173] For a general analysis of the 'problem' of not hierarchically integrated 'knowledge' being ignored, see Baecker (1999b), pp. 68ff.

[174] There is, however, no empirical study that has analysed directly the influence of self-descriptions on different decision situations. The available studies analyse at most the correlation between the existence of a mission statement (i.e. a self-description in such a position) and the firm's performance. The findings with regard to this correlation could be said to support to some extent our claim that self-descriptions at such locations have no systematic influence on the decision processes. Wilson (1992), Klemm et al. (1991), and David (1989), for example, find no clear correlation, while Bart and Baetz (1998), and Campbell and Yeung (1991) find merely some (weak) correlation.

[175] Ghoshall and Bartlett (1994), for example, describe how a manufacturing firm used a mission statement as a means of orientation during the restructuring of the firm. The firm got so used to invoking the mission statement that even after the restructuring had taken place the mission statement was regularly referred to.

Third, explicit self-descriptions can be distributed throughout the communication channel and influence decisions in various decision situations directly. In this case, self-descriptions are not 'located' at one point within the communication channels but are carried through to the individual decision situation. What is particularly important here is that the self-description is memorised in a different way. While in the last two cases self-descriptions were ideally preserved in the form of a written document to which one could refer, here they are stored in the individual psychic systems.[176] In the different decision situations, the self-description is very close at hand and so tends to be invoked very often. In an extreme case, all decisions invoke explicitly the self-description.

An example of such a form of self-description is a 'vision'.[177] Similarly to organisational goals, visions describe the organisation in the form of desired projections into the future. However, while goals tend to divert attention to the prevention of missing them and to the necessity of dividing the goal into sub-goals, visions have the advantage of focussing attention directly on the desired future state itself.[178] For the individual decision situation this means that the desired future state itself can serve *directly at the point of decision* as orientation, rather than indirectly through a derived construct. Although visions are not binding, it is often claimed that their short, direct, and positive form makes them so attractive as a form of orientation that they tend to spread comparatively easily throughout the organisation.[179]

Fourth, self-descriptions can also be neutral with respect to the communication channels. That is to say, whatever the concrete location with regard to the decision processes, the self-description does not make a difference to them. The neutrality of the self-description can be due to the self-description being too general or without any content at all. In both cases the self-description can merely serve the rudimentary function of a pure indication of the organisation. With respect to this rudimentary function all self-descriptions are functionally equivalent; switching from one self-description to another does not affect the decision process. One can often find such self-descriptions in the form of slogans.[180] Other examples of self-descriptions without content are indexical expressions such as 'we', 'the organisation XYZ', 'here'.[181]

---

[176] This does not contradict the assumption of the operative closure of social and psychic systems. On the basis of its thought-operations, the psychic system can memorise communications on behalf of the social system, even if these communications have a different meaning for the psychic system than for the social system. See Luhmann (1995a), Chapter 6.

[177] On visions, see e.g. Peters (1987), pp. 400ff., Westley and Mintzberg (1989), and Collins and Porras (1991).

[178] Baecker (1993a), p. 215.

[179] Ibid.

[180] Cf. Luhmann (1995a), pp. 431-432 on slogans.

[181] Cf. Cheney (1983) and Fiol (2002).

(2)   Implicit self-descriptions.   Self-descriptions do not have to be explicitly communicated: they can also be merely implied in the decision situation.[182] In this case, the self-description is invoked, but not explicitly referred to.[183] Implicit self-descriptions presuppose a great degree of familiarity with the self-description, as ego has to presuppose that alter not only knows about the self-description but can also associate it automatically with the decision situation. At the same time, this means that implicit self-descriptions will have to be used fairly regularly. First, only regular use can ensure the necessary familiarity, and second, because of that very familiarity, every decision will be expected to make use of the self-description: familiarity and expectation of use reinforce each other.

While the implicitness of self-descriptions means a high frequency of use, their reach within the organisation can be limited. The use of the self-description does not have to extend to the entire organisation; it can be limited to particular areas within the organisation. In this sense, the self-description might, for example, be familiar and used among senior managers or on the shop floor, but not elsewhere in the organisation.

Frequency of use might not only be a precondition and consequence of implicit self-descriptions, but also lead to explicit self-descriptions becoming implicit. If explicit self-descriptions are used very frequently they might become so familiar that the reference to the self-description is taken for granted. If ego and alter expect of each other to expect of each other an *automatic* reference to the self-description, the reference need not be made explicitly anymore. We can refer to this phenomenon as *internalisation*.

4.   Multiple Self-Descriptions

Empirically one can often find that organisations possess not only one but multiple self-descriptions. We can distinguish two cases: succession and co-existence of different self-descriptions.[184] In the first case, an organisation uses specific identity semantics for a certain time only, after which it constructs a new one.[185] As there exists only one 'valid' self-description at any one time,[186] there is no competition (with regard to the organisation's reproduction) between the various self-descriptions – autopoiesis only takes place in the respective present. In the second

---

[182] Ashforth and Mael (1996), p. 29 argue that self-descriptions are normally implicit and only under exceptional circumstances (e.g. crises) become explicit. See also Albert and Whetten (1985).

[183] This does not exclude the possibility that the self-description is also explicitly formulated somewhere else in the organisation.

[184] We speak of different self-descriptions in contrast to different components of *one* self-description, if the self-descriptions do not directly refer to or imply each other.

[185] Dutton and Dukerich (1991), for example, describe the succession of self-descriptions in the case of the New York Port Authority. Albert and Whetten (1985) describe the substitution of a normative for a utilitarian self-description and vice versa.

[186] Apart from the transitional period, where one might find a co-existence of self-descriptions (discussed as the second case).

case, several self-descriptions are simultaneously involved in the organisation's reproduction. In *this* respect (i.e. their concrete effect on the autopoiesis[187]) we can distinguish substitutable, complementary or conflicting relations between them.[188]

First, we want to look at the case where different semantics are substitutable for each other – that is to say, where their meaning is similarly confined: a change from one type of semantics to another does not make a difference to the organisation. In other words, self-descriptions are synonymous. It is like having two maps of a territory that use different signs and symbols but refer to the same characteristics of the territory. An example for such substitutable self-descriptions is the indexical expression 'we' with regard to the name of the organisation.[189] The existence of several self-descriptions can be manifest or latent. By reflecting on its self-descriptions, the organisation becomes aware of the coexistence of several self-descriptions; i.e. the co-existence becomes manifest. Initially, this constitutes a problem for the organisation, as it is faced with two (or more) 'selves'. The problem can be solved, however, if the organisation considers – or perhaps even declares – both sets of semantics to be equivalent. In terms of the metaphor of map and territory, the existence of two maps seems to indicate two different territories; however, by comparing the maps one might judge that both refer to the same territory and also to the same characteristics of that territory.

The second relation between self-descriptions that we want to look at can be described as complementarity, with regard to its effects on the organisation's reproduction. This second relation is comparable to a situation where one has both a geographical and a political map of a territory. Analogously, self-descriptions can describe the organisation from different 'perspectives': for example, organisations can have several semantics dominated by different dimensions of meaning. Another possibility is that an organisation has different self-descriptions for different communicative contexts.[190] Horvath and Glynn[191] give the example of a healthcare co-operative whose two self-descriptions 'family' and 'business'

---

[187] We only look at the relation of self-descriptions with regard to their concrete implications for the organisation's reproduction and not at their relation as such, as the specific meaning of self-descriptions is only established through the concrete context in which they are being used. In this sense, for example, two self-descriptions that are used in different parts of the organisation are not considered conflicting, as they affect different operations. The literature is generally not very clear on the point of who observes the relation between structures.

[188] Albert and Whetten (1985), p. 267, speak of 'compatible, complementary, unrelated, or even contradictory' statements of identity.

[189] However, it is important to note that the organisation could distinguish between the meanings of the semantics, in which case the change from one set of semantics to another would make a difference for the organisation.

[190] Cf. Gioia (1998), pp. 21-22. However, they are complementary only as long as the self-descriptions are not (directly or indirectly mediated through intermediate chains of decisions) applied to one and the same decision situation. Cf. Albert and Whetten (1985), pp. 287-290.

[191] Horvath and Glynn (1993), cited in Ashforth and Mael (1996).

functioned in that way. Ashforth and Mael[192] give the example of a state university that would refer to its 'teaching effectiveness' when compared with other state universities, and to issues of relative funding when compared with private universities. Corley[193] describes the differentiation of organisational identities according to the organisational hierarchy: while at higher levels of the hierarchy the identity is defined in the light of the organisation's strategy, on lower levels it is related to its culture.

The existence of several self-descriptions is often latent and only becomes manifest if the organisation reflects actively on the self-descriptions. Once manifest, the organisation might try to establish a unity between the different semantics. This could mean that the organisation authorises different semantics in their specific contexts as referring to the same unity of organisation. In this case, one could say that the different self-descriptions become elements of *one* complex self-description.

One way of ensuring the consistent use of different semantics is the construction of a meta-semantics to which the other semantics have to refer.[194] To come back to our metaphor, both maps could, for example, be related to the name of a country, one as a political map and the other as a geographical map of it. This means that consistency in the uses of different semantics is guaranteed through the construction of a consistent arrangement of semantics. In this way, the organisation possesses a set of semantics to refer to the unity of different self-descriptions, through which it can make sure that all self-descriptions refer to the same unity of the system. This meta-semantics, then, can either be reserved exclusively for organising the different identity semantics, or it can be used itself semantically to describe the organisation. In the first case, the meta-semantics is just used for organising the unity of the different identity semantics and does not itself refer to the unity of the organisation. In the second case, it is the primary self-description, of which the other identity semantics are just sub-semantics. In other words, the sub-semantics are just derivatives of the meta-semantics.

Business-management or business-policy books often refer to such hierarchies of self-descriptions. Miller and Dess, for example, describe what they call a hierarchy of 'strategic intentions'.

> [This hierarchy ranges] from (1) a broad *vision* of what the organization should be, to (2) the organization's mission, to (3) specific *goals* that are operationalized as various (4) strategic *objectives*. The elements of this hierarchy set forth the ideals and ideas that serve to unify the energy and the forces scattered throughout an organization.[195]

The most interesting case is that where there are several coexistent identity semantics with conflicting effects on the organisation's reproduction. The self-

---

[192] Ashforth and Mael (1996), p. 25.
[193] Corley (2004).
[194] Cf. Pratt and Foreman (2000), p. 34.
[195] Miller and Dess (1996), p. 6 (original emphasis). The example of Miller and Dess is used here only as an illustration; we do not share their normative claims.

descriptions – either directly or indirectly mediated through chains of decisions – serve as conflicting decision premises in concrete decision situations.[196] That is to say, the self-descriptions present the concrete decision situations with structural preconditions which, instead of simplifying the situation, make the decision practically impossible without disregarding at least one of them.[197] Westley and Vredenburg[198] described the case of a zoo that possessed two conflicting self-descriptions: the zoo as 'park', highlighting educational and entertainment purposes, and the zoo as 'ark', highlighting conservation purposes. The self-descriptions had conflicting implications for operational and strategic decisions. As 'park', for example, the zoo would expose the animals as much as possible to the eyes of the visitors, while as 'ark' it would try to keep visitors away in order to create a suitable atmosphere for breeding. A similar identity conflict can be found in Glynn's study of the Atlanta Symphony Orchestra.[199] In this case, there was a conflict between an aesthetic and an economic identity, which had different implications on the way resources were to be spent. Glynn writes:

> Claims on the aesthetic identity evoked resource claims consonant with artistry (e.g., expanding the size of the orchestra, tenuring more musicians, investing in more complex musical pieces, touring worldwide, hiring guest conductors etc.); claims on the economic identity argued for a pecuniary strategy of resource deployment (e.g., cutting costs, increasing ticket prices, raising funds, growing the endowment, limiting the number of costly orchestra performances, etc.).[200]

The conflict between different self-descriptions can be latent or manifest. In the first case, the organisation experiences disruptions in its reproduction due to structural conflicts, but is not aware of them being caused by the self-descriptions.[201] That is to say, it is aware of conflicting expectations with regard to a concrete decision situation, but does not attribute the conflict to the relation between the self-descriptions. It might instead attribute it to the idiosyncracies of the concrete decision situation or to conflicts between other, local structures. In the second case, the organisation – with or without[202] experiencing conflicts in concrete decision situations – observes the relation between them as conflicting. As tends to be the case, here too the awareness of multiple self-descriptions will

---

[196] In this sense, self-descriptions, which are complementary due to being used in different contexts or parts of the organisation, might become conflicting if they are suddenly applied to the same decision situation.

[197] One could also say that the decision situation becomes entropic, in that the order provided by one self-description is dissolved by another.

[198] Westley and Vredenburg (1996).

[199] Glynn (2000). For other examples, see also Golden-Biddle and Rao (1997), and Albert and Whetten (1985).

[200] Glynn (2000), p. 293.

[201] The organisation might not even be aware of possessing more than one self-description.

[202] In this case the organisation observes *hypothetical* decision situations in which there might be conflicts.

prompt attempts at 'managing'[203] the relation between them in such a way as to prevent fragmentation.[204]

One way of dealing with manifest contradictions can be found in an article by Osborn and Ashforth,[205] where they analyse the tension between the self-descriptions of a nuclear power plant – as 'safe provider' and as 'efficient provider'. The organisation explicitly tried to align the two self-descriptions by declaring them to be synonymous. This is a case of 'glossing over' – suppressing, that is, the awareness of the conflict without really affecting the relation between the self-descriptions.[206] The conflict becomes latent. Conflicting self-descriptions, furthermore, can be stabilised through meta-semantics, which justify the coexistence of conflicting self-descriptions – an example of this would be 'fruitful tension'. As explained above, meta-semantics can either form a new set of identity semantics, with the other semantics classified as 'sub-semantics', or be reserved exclusively for the coordination of conflicting semantics.[207] Alternatively, organisations might try to restrict the use of conflicting self-descriptions to different contexts, as described above.[208] Another response to a reflection on contradictory self-descriptions is to decide between the semantics by legitimising only one of them, with the other semantics being declared invalid.[209] In some cases such a reflection might also lead to a new self-description in the form of a synthesis of the existing self-descriptions.[210]

5. Summary

In this chapter we have presented a new understanding of organisational identity, based on the organisation theory presented in Chapter 2. We first reviewed the literature on organisational identity, distinguishing three major approaches: *corporate identity* refers to the way an organisation presents itself to external observers, *substantive identity* refers to integration and coordination mechanisms, which provide the organisation with a distinctive unity, and *reflective identity* refers to organisation's perception of itself.

In the second section we presented different concepts of organisational identity in line with Luhmann's autopoietic theory of organisation. Analogously to the substantive-identity approach, we first examined the unity and distinctiveness of an organisation, which can be captured in the two concepts of operative closure and individuality. Analogously to the reflective identity approach, we then examined

---

[203] Pratt and Foreman (2000); Phillips and Hardy (1997).

[204] Luhmann (1993d), p. 225 sees the integration of the multitude of different self-descriptions into a consistent unity as the main problem of the modern individual. See also Giddens (1991).

[205] Osborn and Ashforth (1990).

[206] Ashforth and Mael (1996), and Westley and Vredenburg (1996), p. 155.

[207] In Pratt's and Foreman's (2000) classification: 'aggregation'.

[208] In Pratt's and Foreman's (2000) classification: 'compartmentalisation'.

[209] In Pratt's and Foreman's (2000) classification: 'deletion'.

[210] In Pratt's and Foreman's (2000) classification: 'integration'.

the way organisations refer to their own unity. We argued that organisations condense self-descriptions from their various self-observations, which represent the organisation's unity to itself. Such self-descriptions serve two functions: they provide an orientation for the different organisational operations (integrative function) and give direction to them (operative function). Furthermore, we argued that self-descriptions are contingent, in the sense that there are many alternative ways of describing the organisation. These different possible self-descriptions can be distinguished according to their viability; that is to say, according to their ability to serve their two functions. Finally, as in the corporate identity approach, we focussed on the external observers' perceptions of the organisation. By the concept of 'reputation' we referred to external observers' descriptions of the organisation and by 'image' to an organisation's reconstruction of its reputation(s).

In the third section we differentiated different forms of organisational self-description. We first distinguished between self-descriptions in the form of simple and double distinctions. While the former indicate the organisation directly in distinction to its environment, the latter indicate the organisation by indicating the distinction between the organisation and its environment. We then distinguished different self-descriptions according to the three dimensions of meaning: self-descriptions focussed on the fact dimension, on the social dimension, and on the time dimension. At the end of the section we analysed self-descriptions according to their integration within the decision network. We distinguished particularly between explicit and implicit self-descriptions.

In the fourth section we examined the phenomenon of multiple self-descriptions co-existing in an organisation. We distinguished between substitutive, complementary and conflicting relations between self-descriptions, and discussed different organisational strategies for dealing with them.

Chapter 4

The Logic of Self-Transformation

Introduction

In the remainder of this book we will explore the possibilities of intentional identity change – so-called 'self-transformation'. An exploration of this kind of change seems particularly interesting as it demonstrates the degree of an organisation's control over itself. In this chapter we will analyse the logic of self-transformation, which will serve as a basis for the exploration of mechanisms of self-transformation in the next one.

In the first section we will explore the concept of change in general and differentiate self-transformation as one particular type from other types of change. In the second section we will analyse the 'paradox of self-transformation'. In the third section we will analyse the logical implications of this paradox for the organisation's reproduction. Finally, in the last section we will identify organisational mechanisms for dealing with this paradox.

1. Self-Transformation and the Concept of Change

a. Complexity and Change

In order to discuss organisational change we have to deal with the concept of complexity. This concept is necessary for understanding how a system that is operationally closed – in the sense that it cannot receive new elements from its environment – can change. The argument is that systems can only change into forms that already exist in the system as *possible* forms.

We have to start our discussion with the definition of the term 'complexity'. The complexity of organisations is often discussed in the organisation literature without a clear definition of the concept.[1] Mostly, the term 'complexity' is contrasted with the term 'simplicity'. The underlying distinction is that between a whole and its parts. A unity, in this sense, is complex if it is composed of several parts and simple if it cannot be further decomposed.[2] As Luhmann writes:

---

[1] Luhmann (1980), column 1064; Luhmann (1991b), pp. 204-220.
[2] Luhmann (1992a), p. 364; Luhmann (1993b), p. 60.

Traditionally, the term *complexity* could be defined through a distinction, one side of which contained *the complex* and the other *the simple*. The distinction marks mutually exclusive terms: something has to be either simple or complex.[3]

This definition, however, proves to be inconsistent, since all 'simple' phenomena can be shown to be themselves composed of parts and thus complex. As Luhmann writes:

> Especially from physics we learn that there are no *simple* phenomena; everything that is taken as an element (atoms, particles, quarks) is just a temporary limit of further decomposition [...][4]

Because all 'simple' phenomena are themselves complex, the two terms cannot be mutually exclusive. The distinction complex/simple contains complexity on both sides, and thus does not help define complexity.

Instead of basing the concept of complexity on the distinction between a whole and its parts (i.e. simple parts making up a complex whole), Luhmann suggests basing it on the distinction between element and relation. Something is considered complex if there are more possible relations between its elements than can be realised. For example, a system is complex if it cannot relate every element to every other element. Since the number of possible relations increases geometrically with the number of elements, even systems with a small number of elements are unable to realise all possible relations.[5] As a consequence, the system is forced to make selections amongst the possible relations. Luhmann suggests defining complexity with reference to this *necessity* of selection:

> [W]e will call an interconnected collection of elements 'complex' when, because of immanent constraints in the elements' connective capacity, it is no longer possible at any moment to connect every element with every other element.[6]

That is to say, complexity refers to the phenomenon where there are more elements than can be related to each other. In this sense, the system has a higher potential than it can actualise. Hence, instead of defining complexity in distinction to simplicity, Luhmann suggests treating complexity itself as a distinction: the distinction between complete and selective relationing between elements.[7]

---

[3]   Luhmann (1993b), p. 61 (my translation; emphasis added).

[4]   Ibid. (my translation; emphasis added).

[5]   Complete relationing between elements is an exception. It can only be found in extreme circumstances; for example, in crystals, which are extremely compact and completely inflexible, or in the opposite case of gases, which are completely amorphous and have to be organised from outside. See Baecker (1998), p. 26; Atlan (1979).

[6]   Luhmann (1995a), p. 24. See also Baecker (forthcoming, a).

[7]   The distinction between complete and selective relationing between the elements of a system corresponds directly to the difference between medium and form (see Chapter 2, Section 2). A medium is an 'open multitude of possible connections' between elements which are defined as elements through this possibility of connection. Within this medium a form is the selective actualisation of the possible connections. In this sense, the medium

At every concrete moment, however, the organisation cannot make a selection from the entirety of possibilities.[8] The complexity of the system (as the difference between all possibilities and the selection of some of them) would overburden the momentary points of decision and the reproduction of the system would be in danger.[9] In order to ensure the continued reproduction of the system, the organisation has to *reduce* the complexity facing the concrete decision situations. In other words, there has to be a pre-selection of possibilities before the selection of the concrete decision can take place. The complexity has to be reduced so that the concrete selection can be made easier, creating what Baecker calls 'simple complexity'.[10] This reduction of possibilities is the function of structures.[11] Structures[12] reduce the possibilities from which the momentary decisions can be chosen. In the case of organisations, decision premises reduce the complexity of the system, that is to say, the set of possibilities for particular decisions. A hierarchical communication structure, for example, reduces the possibilities for decision communications to those between subordinate and superior.

With regard to the reduction of complexity we can distinguish three different types of possibilities for a system. First, there are the general possibilities, which are defined by the autopoiesis of the system. Contained within this set of possibilities is everything that can contribute to the autopoiesis of the system. Formally, this refers to all possible relations between the elements of a system. As the number of possible elements in organisations – as in all meaning-constituted systems – is unlimited, we can speak of an infinite number of possibilities.[13] Structures divide these general possibilities into two subsets: a subset of possibilities that are directly available for the organisational reproduction, and a subset of (for the time-being) unavailable possibilities. The unavailability of possibilities does not, however, mean that they are impossible, only that they cannot for the moment, or can only with difficulty, be actualised (Figure 4.1).

---

describes complete relationing between the elements of a system, in contrast to the form that describes the selected relations. From moment to moment the organisation shifts the distinction of medium and form as new relations between decisions are chosen.

[8] We can speak of a selection of possibilities in general, instead of a selection of possible connections, as the selection of relations is at the same time a selection of elements.

[9] From the perspective of the system as a whole, the selection of possibilities in the concrete decision situation would be the result of pure chance (i.e. there would be no systematic relation between the particular selection and other selections within the organisation). This would constitute a situation of entropy. See Luhmann (1995a), p. 49. The complexity of the system would constitute 'unorganised complexity' in the sense of Weaver (1948) and La Porte (1975).

[10] Baecker (1998).

[11] With regard to organisations, see Luhmann (1980), column 1065.

[12] See Chapter 1, Section 2.e on structures in social systems in general, and Chapter 2, Sections 1.c and 1.d on organisational structures in particular.

[13] Note: this does not mean that *everything* is possible!

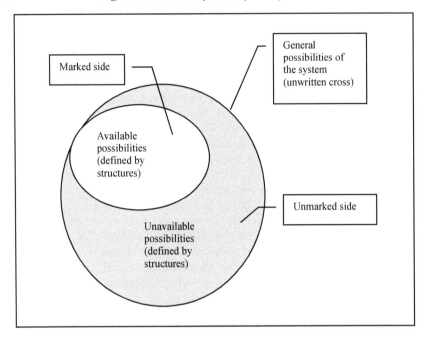

Figure 4.1 The possibilities of the system[14]

In the terms of Spencer Brown, structures can be explained as distinction and indication: structures draw a *distinction* within the possibilities of the system, which creates two different sets of possibilities, and they *indicate* one of the sets as the 'available' possibilities.

We can now take a closer look at the concept of change. At every particular moment in time the organisation realises a particular form, as it selects some of the generally possible connections it possesses. This particular form changes from moment to moment as new selections are made. One possibility would be to conceptualise this transition from one system state[15] to the next as organisational change. In this sense, the organisation would be in a constant state of change.[16] Such a concept of change, however, is not very helpful in our context, as it does not add anything beyond the concept of autopoiesis itself. Instead Luhmann

---

[14] We decided to use circles, instead of Spencer Brown's 'cross', here, as the circle illustrates the infinity of possibilities very well.

[15] In the sense of 'information value' (cf. Baecker 1999a).

[16] Luhmann (1995a), p. 345 argues that one cannot speak of change with regard to the elements of social systems, as they have no duration. As communicative events disappear with their appearance, they cannot change. However, if one looked at the system as a whole and at its momentary system state, which is defined by its concrete elements and their relations, one could, in fact, speak of change, as the system changes its system state (i.e. information value) from moment to moment.

suggests we tie the concept of change to the concept of structures.[17] Change, in this sense, is a change of structures (including the creation of new structures[18]). Organisational change thus means that a different 'set' of the organisational possibilities becomes available. The distinction between directly available and unavailable possibilities is shifted (Figure 4.2).

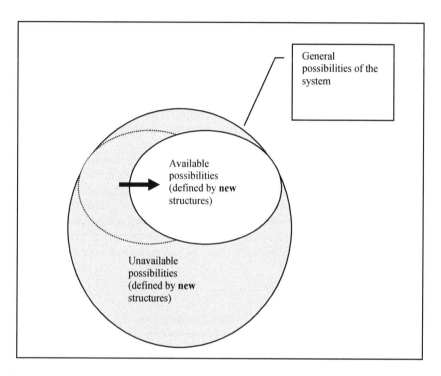

Figure 4.2 Change as a shift between available and unavailable possibilities

b.   The Concept of Self-transformation

After these remarks on organisational change in general, in the following pages we will concentrate on self-transformation as one particular type of change. Etzioni developed a very useful concept of self-transformation in connection with his studies on modern societies. He suggested the concept of self-transformation to describe cases where a system changes what he calls 'self-image'. In this sense, societies capable of performing self-transformation could be said to possess '(self-) transformability'. He writes:

---

[17]   Luhmann (1995a), p. 345. On organisational change, see Luhmann (2000), p. 331.
[18]   Luhmann (1995a), p. 352.

A societal unit has *transformability* if it is able to set – in response to external challenges, in anticipation of them, or as a result of internal developments – a new self-image which includes a new kind and level of homeostasis and ultrastability, and is able to change parts and their combination as well as its boundaries to create a new unit. This is […] an ability to design and move toward a *new* system *even if the old one has not become unstable.*[19]

If we look at the concept carefully we find two distinctions, which differentiate self-transformation from other forms of change. First, the change refers to a change of a particular kind of structure: the 'self-image' We can translate this in our context to the change of self-description – in contrast to other forms of structural change. Similarly,[20] Brunsson and Olsen distinguish between a change that accords with the institutional identity of an organisation and changes in the institutional identity itself.[21] In the relevant literature this is variously described as 'second-order change' in contrast to 'first-order change',[22] 'paradigmatic' in contrast to normal change,[23] 'quantum change' in contrast to incremental change,[24] or 'double-loop learning' in contrast to 'single-loop learning'.[25]

Second, the concept of self-transformation refers to an 'intentional' change of the self-description. The system itself *chooses* to change its self-description.[26] In other words, the organisation *decides* on a new self-description. Formally, the decision on the self-description can be represented as a double distinction: a primary distinction distinguishing alternative self-descriptions (including the old one) from the rest of the world, and a secondary distinction distinguishing the chosen (new) self-description from the excluded alternatives (Figure 4.3).

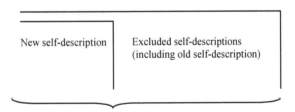

Decision on new self-description

Figure 4.3 The form of the decision on a new self-description

---

[19] Etzioni (1971), p. 121 (original emphasis).
[20] Rajagopalan and Spreitzer (1996) argue that this classification of two different types of change can be found in all 'cognitive lens' studies of change.
[21] Brunsson and Olsen (1993), p. 5.
[22] Watzlawick et al. (1974); Bartunek (1984).
[23] Kuhn (1962).
[24] Greenwood and Hinings (1993).
[25] Argyris (1976), Argyris and Schön (1978). Similarly, Bateson (1972) with his distinction between 'Proto-' and 'Deutero-Learning'.
[26] On intentional identity change, see also Fiol (2002), and Corley and Gioia (2004). Corley and Gioia (2004), however, point out that intentional identity change is often accompanied by unintentional change.

What this analysis makes clear is that the concept of self-transformation presupposes the system's 'awareness' of the existence of several possible self-descriptions, i.e. of the contingency of any self-description. In this sense, a 'blind' shift from one self-description to another would not qualify as self-transformation.[27] In summary, self-transformation, as we have re-described it, is defined as a change of the self-description based on an explicit decision.[28]

2.   The Decision to Change the Self-Description

In this section we want to take a closer look at the form of self-transformation. Our particular focus is on the decision to change the self-description, which will be shown to be paradoxical. Not only is the concept of decision generally paradoxical – as it refers to the unity of the distinction between chosen and excluded alternatives or between open and fixed contingency[29] – but also the relation of this particular decision to the organisation constitutes a paradox. We will argue that this second paradox lies at the heart of self-transformation. A thorough analysis of this concept is thus a precondition for an exploration of the possibilities of self-transformation.

a.   The Paradox of the Decision to Change the Self-Description

The role of paradoxes in organisational change in general has been widely acknowledged. Czarniawska writes in this respect:

> Paradoxes, until recently the villains of organizational drama, constitute its dynamics and, even more important, accounts for its transformations. Without paradox, change would not be possible.[30]

Similarly Ford and Backoff assert:

> Paradoxes are important because they reflect the underlying tensions that generate and energize organizational change.[31]

Quinn and Cameron have edited an entire book on the role of paradox for organisational transformation,[32] and also March and Olsen,[33] and Brunsson and

---

[27]   In this respect, Albert and Whetten (1985) speak of unintentional 'identity shifts'.

[28]   Note that this is not to say that self-transformation is a decision to change the self-description. The reason for that is that the decision on a new structure does not mean that the structure will automatically become effective. For our exploration of mechanisms of self-transformation this is an important point. See Chapter 5.

[29]   See Chapter 2, Section 1.a.

[30]   Czarniawska (1997), p. 97; see also Czarniawska (forthcoming).

[31]   Ford and Backoff (1988), p. 82.

[32]   Quinn and Cameron (1988).

[33]   March and Olsen (1976).

Olsen[34] emphasise the importance of paradox for change. Zu Knyphausen even argues that paradox is so central to change that only theories that can deal with paradox are capable of analysing change. Most theories, he claims, are severely limited in their usefulness, if not totally inadequate, for analysing organisational change, as they are based on a strictly two-valued logic, which obscures paradoxes.[35] While change in general can be understood as a paradoxical phenomenon, here we will concentrate particularly on the paradox of self-transformation. To that end, we will have to take another look at the form of self-transformation, which itself is paradoxically constituted.

There are three important paradoxical aspects in the formal concept of self-description, which we need to analyse. First, every self-description is part of what it describes. Self-descriptions are realised in concrete operations of the system and as such are part of the system they describe. Luhmann writes:

> [...] The description and the described are not two separate and only externally connected phenomena, but in the case of a self-description, the description is always part of what it describes [...].[36]

Thus, as part of the system they describe, self-descriptions also have to describe themselves; and they also have to describe their descriptions of themselves and so on. In this sense, self-descriptions constitute formally a paradox: a self-description equals the self-description *plus* a description of the self-description.

Second (and as a result of the first point), self-descriptions change the system they describe by being part of the system. A change of self-description, in this sense, means a change of the system. Thus, viable self-descriptions cannot refer to the system as it is, but have to refer to the system as it *becomes* through the self-description.

Third, organisational self-descriptions as descriptions of the organisation's unity (logically) refer to all parts of the organisation. Consequently, the organisation by definition does not possess any positions from where to observe the self-description, which are not themselves included in the self-description. For the self-description this means that it cannot substantiate itself with regard to any criteria outside itself: any potential criterion for substantiation is necessarily part of what it describes – otherwise the self-description would not qualify as a self-description. In other words the self-description itself has to define the criteria according to which it is to be observed. Thus, the only form of substantiation is *self*-substantiation. In this respect, Luhmann writes:

> Self-descriptions [...] can only be substantiated in a circular manner; if they try to interrupt their circular substantiation through externalisation, then this happens precisely as a component of the text, as part of the realisation of the self-description.[37]

---

[34] Brunsson and Olsen (1993).
[35] Zu Knyphausen (1988) *passim*; similarly, but less polemically, Chia (1999).
[36] Luhmann (1997), p. 884 (my translation; footnote omitted).
[37] Luhmann (1997), p. 890 (my translation).

This does not mean that every self-description is necessarily substantiated through reference to other criteria. On the contrary, self-descriptions will be mostly communicated without any substantiation as nobody will question them; they are understood as necessities as they stand. They are normally used to substantiate other decisions or structures, but they themselves need not be substantiated. In this sense they are very similar to values.[38]

We now have the necessary background for analysing the paradox of self-transformation. The crucial point is that self-transformation – as defined above – must be based on a *decision* to change the self-description. This means that the contingency of a self-description necessarily becomes salient: the possibility of alternative self-descriptions has to be communicated in order for the decision to appear as a decision. Thus, while before the self-transformation the organisation might have taken the established self-description as given and thus be unaware of its paradoxical form, the decision to change it necessarily makes the organisation aware of the contingency of any self-description. For example, an organisation that described itself as a 'theatre' might see this self-description as the only possible one until it decides to change the self-description to, say, 'firm'.

With the contingency of a self-description becoming manifest, substantiation becomes necessary. For a decision to be made with regard to a new self-description, it becomes necessary that the chosen self-description be substantiated. The new self-description has to be substantiated as the 'right' selection. As explained above, however, the problem is that no substantiation from outside the self-description can be found; only self-substantiation is possible. If we look at the decision situation, different self-descriptions can define different criteria according to which they themselves are 'better' than alternative self-descriptions. Thus, any self-description, according to its own criteria, might appear as the 'right' selection. However, apart from those conflicting criteria there is no higher level from which the different criteria could be analysed. In our example above, the self-description 'theatre' might substantiate itself with reference to the value of art, and the self-description 'firm' might substantiate itself with reference to the value of profit. However, there are no independent criteria according to which the value of art can be compared with the value of profit – apart from the self-descriptions themselves (the self-description 'theatre' substantiates the criterion 'value of art' and the self-description 'firm' the criterion 'value of capital'). In this sense, the selection of the criterion for selecting the self-description depends on the selection of the self-description and vice versa. Or, more succinctly: the selection of the self-description depends on the selection of the self-description.

We can describe this situation as self-observation. Self-observations (together with their selection criteria) observe the self-observations. In Spencer Brown's terms this constitutes a re-entry. This re-entry can also be understood as an

---

[38] On values, see Luhmann (1996) and Luhmann (2000), p. 244. Von Krogh and Roos (1995), p. 123 argue that, in this case, self-descriptions function as 'paradigmatic warrants' in Toulmin's sense.

oscillation between self-descriptions (Figure 4.4), and in our example above, as an oscillation between the self-descriptions 'theatre' and 'firm'.[39]

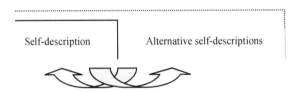

| Self-description | Alternative self-descriptions |

Figure 4.4 The decision to change the self-description as an oscillation between alternative self-descriptions

The organisation is thus faced with a situation in which selection is logically impossible as no criteria for making the selection exist. In Yves Barel's words: 'On doit et on ne peut choisir. C'est la quintessence du paradoxe.'[40] Instead of one of the two sides being selected, the organisation oscillates between the two sides. Logically, the oscillation continues forever. Practically, however, the oscillation can be terminated.[41] In order to conceptualise possibilities for terminating the oscillation we have to introduce a further concept: chance.

Chance does not imply a negation of causality. That is to say, it does not mean that an event is not determined by other events. Instead, chance should be defined in relation to structures. We can speak of chance, if an event is not *structurally* connected to earlier or later events. Luhmann defines chance as follows:

> [C]hance does not mean the complete lack of conditions and causes, but the lack of coordination between events and a system's structures [...].[42]

This concept can be directly applied to our specific context. We have a situation in which one of the alternative self-descriptions has to be selected, but the organisation does not possess any specific criteria, or specific structures, on which the selection could be based. Thus, whatever the outcome of the decision situation, – that is, whatever the decision (event) – it is uncoordinated with the system's

---

[39] For an empirical example of such an oscillation, see Aschenbach (1996), who analysed the self-transformation of the Siemens AG in the years between 1987 and 1989.

[40] Barel (1989), p. 282.

[41] Carefully analysed, the paradox of self-transformation not only implies the impossibility of terminating the oscillation, but also the impossibility of commencing it, i.e. of creating the decision situation. Here, however, we will concentrate on the problem of termination, as it constitutes a problem *for the organisational reproduction.* Commencement, in contrast, does not. In the case that no decision situation is created, the organisation will just continue reproducing itself on the basis of the established self-description. On the creation of the decision situation see also Chapter 5.

[42] Luhmann (1995a), p. 120. See also Luhmann (1997), pp. 448ff., Luhmann (1992a), pp. 465ff., 563ff.

structures. In this sense, with regard to the system, the concrete decision is the result of chance.[43]

Thus, the paradoxical form of the decision situation does not mean that no selection is possible *in practice*, merely that strictly *logically* it is impossible, as no selection in *strict* coordination with the system's structures is possible. In the concrete situation, the decision might in fact even be based on some (local) decision premises, but the selection of the decision premise itself is not coordinated with the overall system's structures. In the above example the self-description 'theatre' might be selected based on the personnel: the director of the organisation happens to be an actor and not a businessman. However, the (latent[44]) selection of the reference to the existing personnel (and not, for example, to the existing decision programmes) as decision premise for this particular situation is itself not coordinated with the overall system's structures. In other words, it is by chance that this particular decision premise is drawn on.

This whole process can be described as an interruption of the circular logic of the situation, or as a restriction of self-reference. Logically, we have a circle in which self-descriptions imply structures which imply self-descriptions. Practically, the first link is interrupted: it is logically implied but not explicitly communicated. In this sense, the structure itself is either not explicitly substantiated, or it is substantiated through another structure, which itself is not substantiated.

In the following, we want to take a look at the function of the paradoxical form of our decision situation for the organisation. We have described the situation as one lacking in structures, according to which the selection between alternative self-descriptions could be decided; all alternative self-descriptions have an equal possibility of being selected. Thus, any concrete selection between the self-descriptions is a chance selection, that is to say, not determined by the system's structures. In this sense, one can say that the particular decision situation is 'free' of the determinism of the system's own structures. If we conceptualise 'structure' as the restriction of the availability of possibilities, as suggested above, such situations can be understood as situations in which unavailable possibilities become available.[45]

In every decision situation there is some element of chance: no decision premise completely determines the decision, otherwise the decision would not be a decision.[46] Nevertheless, in the case of decisions on the self-description, the chance element is particularly significant for two reasons. First, in contrast to most decision situations, *all* potential premises for this decision are logically dissolved,

---

[43] Kuhn (1962) describes a similar phenomenon with his concept of 'paradigm debate' as a choice between competing scientific paradigms. Similarly to our situation described above, there exist no scientific criteria according to which one paradigm can be chosen over another. As a consequence, the choice between paradigms can only be made on the basis of non-scientific criteria, e.g. aesthetics. That is to say, *from a scientific point of view* the selection is attributed to chance.

[44] If not latent, the selection might be substantiated through another structure whose selection as a decision premise then remains latent.

[45] Luhmann (1997), p. 450.

[46] See Chapter 1, Section 1.

so the decision rests entirely on chance. Second, the decision (logically[47]) determines the structures, and thus the availability of possibilities, for the *entire* system. As different self-descriptions represent different availabilities of possibilities for the system, the decision between self-descriptions ultimately constitutes a decision between different availabilities of possibilities for the system (Figure 4.5).

Thus, if we consider both that the different possibilities of the system become available through selecting different self-descriptions, and that the selection of a self-description is itself not determined by the organisational structures, this decision situation constitutes a situation in which – in principle – *all* possibilities become available to the system.[48] In this situation, all structural restrictions are removed. This constitutes the limit case of entropy,[49] in which all operations are equally possible: the reproduction of the system depends on pure chance. As we will discuss in Chapter 5 below, this does not mean, of course, that the organisation can also *realise* the switch to *any* self-description. Rather, if a new self-description is decided on, this decision has to pass a very restrictive evolutionary selection mechanism.

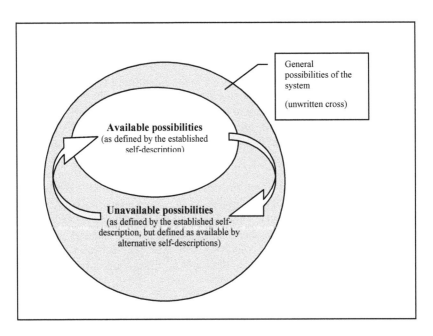

Figure 4.5 The oscillation between alternative self-descriptions as a situation in which (logically) all possibilities become available

---

[47] Logically, decisions on structures necessarily lead to structures; practically, however, decision and decision premise are only loosely coupled. See Chapter 5.

[48] Similarly Kirsch (1992), Zu Knyphausen (1988), Zu Knyphausen (1992), and Zu Knyphausen (1991) describe how new possibilities become available through the 'liquification' of established structures.

[49] On the definition of entropy see Luhmann (1995a), p. 49.

b. Change of the Self-Description vs. Change of the Interpretation of the Self-Description

We have argued that in the case of organisations self-descriptions materialise as texts. On the basis of such an understanding there are essentially two ways in which self-descriptions can be changed. First, the organisation can change the text itself, by selecting a different text; or, second, it can keep the text but select a new interpretation of it.[50] In the following we will compare these two forms of self-transformation.

Self-transformations that involve the change of the self-descriptive text are based on oscillations between different texts. On both sides of the oscillation we find different self-descriptive texts. The result of the oscillation is the selection of a new self-descriptive text. That is to say, the old and the new self-description are two *different* texts. In the case of a new interpretation of an existing self-descriptive text, the oscillation will not take place between different texts, but between different interpretations of the same texts. The oscillation ends with the selection of a new interpretation of the text, but the 'text as such' is the same. In order to understand this oscillation we have to analyse its underlying form; that is to say, the form of the meaning of a self-description.

The meaning of a text is constituted by its reference to other elements of meaning or, to put it in other words, it depends on its con-text.[51] Thus, with different contexts the meaning of the text changes. For organisational self-descriptions this means that with every new confirmation – that is to say, every time it is communicated – the meaning of the self-description adjusts to the particular situation.[52] In other words, the meaning of the text is constantly shifting.[53] We have argued that for a self-description to be applicable to different contexts, a certain flexibility with regard to its meaning is necessary. However, the degree to which texts are flexible with regard to different meanings varies considerably.[54] In the extreme, a text can mean virtually anything.

When formally analysed, the meaning of a self-description can be presented as an arrangement of distinctions. The meaning of the self-descriptive text constitutes a difference, on the marked side of which we find the self-descriptive text, while on its unmarked side we find other elements of meaning (Figure 4.6).

---

[50] Similarly Gioia et al. (2000) and Corley and Gioia (2004). The latter point out that intentional identity change is mostly associated with a change of labels, while unintentional identity change is mostly associated with a change in the interpretation of the existing labels.

[51] See Chapter 1, Section 2.d.

[52] See Chapter 3, Section 2.b(1).

[53] Cf. Derrida's (1968) concept of *différance*. See also Jabri (2004) on the constant identity shift due to shifting interpretations.

[54] Particularly interesting in this respect are metaphorical self-descriptions (cf. Seidl 2003b).

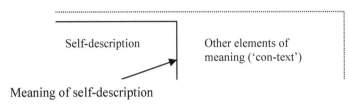

Meaning of self-description

Figure 4.6 The meaning of a self-descriptive text

As the other elements of meaning are contained on the unmarked side of the distinction the self-descriptive text cannot observe them, and thus has no 'control' over them.

The organisation can try to stabilise the meaning of the self-descriptive text by coupling it to 'secondary' texts. In other words, in addition to the self-description the organisation generates 'secondary' texts, which provide an interpretation of the self-description. After that, the meaning of the self-description will still shift with different contexts, but only as much as the secondary texts shift with it.

We can analyse this constellation formally: what we have here is an arrangement of distinctions. The marked side of the distinction contains the ('basic') self-description in distinction to the secondary text, while the unmarked side contains the other elements of meaning that the distinction between 'basic' self-description and secondary text refers to (Figure 4.7).

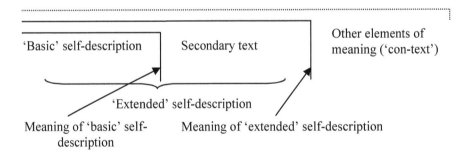

Figure 4.7 Stabilisation of meaning of a self-descriptive text through secondary texts

What we see here is that the meaning of the self-description is defined through the reference to a secondary text. The meaning of this *distinction*, then, is defined by the unmarked side; that is to say, by other elements of meaning. If the relation between ('basic') self-descriptive text and secondary text is firmly established, the secondary text becomes part of the self-description. In other words, the 'basic' self-descriptive text and the secondary text are stabilised as a unity. In this sense, we can speak of an 'extended' self-description. The self-description thus contains two elements: a basic description of the organisation and the interpretative text.

The two cases differ considerably with regard to their stability: without secondary texts, self-descriptive texts shift directly with their contexts; with secondary texts, the 'basic' self-descriptive text shifts only indirectly, as only the *distinction* between basic text and secondary text is affected by the context. The 'extended' self-description as a whole, however, shifts in the same way as the text without a secondary text.

In principle there are two ways in which secondary texts can stabilise self-descriptive texts: they can define the text either positively or negatively. That is to say, they can say either what the text is supposed to mean, or what the text is supposed not to mean. Secondary texts, which offer themselves as exact synonyms (positive) or exact opposites (negative) of the self-description, are particularly important, because they are simple and easy to remember.[55] Exact opposites are also called 'contrasting designators' or 'antonyms'.[56] If we take, for example, the word 'efficient', we can add a secondary text that will be treated as a synonym – such as 'profitable' or 'fast' – or we can add a secondary text that will be treated as its opposite, such as 'unprofitable' or 'slow'.[57]

Secondary texts need not be explicitly communicated together with the 'basic' self-description: they might just be implied. In other words, the secondary text might not be explicit, but it *could* be made explicit on request. In this sense, secondary texts are contained on the unmarked side of the 'basic' self-description, but with regard to the entire ('extended') self-description they are on the marked side, that is to say: they are manifest and not latent.

This analysis of the meaning of self-descriptions can be tied to our earlier discussion on the reduction of complexity. While the 'basic' self-description *draws* the distinction between available and unavailable possibilities, the secondary text defines *where* (more or less) exactly this distinction is to be drawn. If no secondary text exists, the self-description will vary with regard to where exactly it will distinguish between possibilities. In our example above, the self-description 'efficient', which was contrasted with 'slow', will make available those possibilities that can be associated with something like *fast*. Were 'efficient' contrasted with 'unprofitable', it would make available all those possibilities that can be associated with something like *profitable*, and make all other possibilities unavailable.

We can now take a closer look at self-transformation that is based on a change in the way the self-descriptive text is interpreted. In order to speak of self-transformation, in contrast to a mere transformation, a *decision* has to be made on

---

[55] It is important to note that these are not secondary texts that *are* synonyms or opposites, but are only *presented* as such.

[56] Cf. Holmes (1987). Exact opposites can serve as binary codes, e.g. true/false, good/bad (cf. Luhmann 1987).

[57] Note that the 'plain' negative (here: 'inefficient'; i.e. not efficient), cannot serve as a stabilising contrasting designator, since it shifts in the same way as the self-description itself.

the change of meaning. In principle, we can distinguish between self-transformations where secondary texts exist, and self-transformations where they do not. In the first case, the decision situation will lead to the organisation becoming aware of the existence of alternative secondary texts that change the meaning of the 'basic' self-description and thus realise a different distinction between available and unavailable possibilities. The organisation will oscillate between different distinctions, which all contain the same 'basic' self-description on the one side but different secondary texts on the other (Figure 4.8).[58] In the above example the oscillation would take place between efficient/slow and efficient/unprofitable.

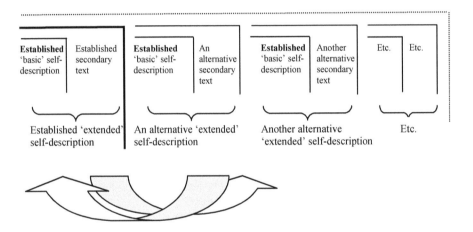

Figure 4.8 Decision situation with alternative meanings of a self-description

If a self-transformation is to take place, the oscillation has to come to an end with the selection of an extended self-description that includes a different secondary text.[59]

In the second case, where no secondary text is established, the decision situation will make the organisation aware of the instability of its self-description's meaning. Or the organisation might realise that it had interpreted the self-description in a particular way in the past, although it had not stabilised it with regard to any particular secondary text. In other words, although there had been a

---

[58] One could also imagine that reflections on the self-description combine oscillations between the different meanings of a self-descriptive text, as well as between the different self-descriptive texts.

[59] Although in a different context, Holmes (1987) provides an example of how the meaning of a primary semantics can be changed, when the secondary semantics is replaced. Holmes describes how the term 'competition', which was at the centre of liberal ideas in the 17th and 18th centuries, was changed by anti-liberal scholars through a change of its antonym: the original antonym of 'monopoly' was replace with 'brotherly love', which gave the originally positive semantics a negative meaning. See also Holmes (1993), Holmes (1989), and Luhmann (1997), p. 891.

relation to other elements of meaning within the organisation, this relation had not been manifest for the organisation and as such did not constitute an extension of the self-description. In such a case, reflecting on the meaning of the self-description will lead to an extension of the self-description, as a secondary text is included.[60]

The oscillation between different secondary texts constitutes the same 'unresolvable indeterminacy'[61] as the oscillation between different self-descriptive texts. There are no external criteria for deciding between different meanings. The basic text itself might be drawn on as substantiation for a particular secondary text, but since the stability of the basic text depends on the secondary text it cannot serve as stable point of reference. As there is no external position from which the different secondary texts could be observed, the oscillation, again, can only be resolved by chance.

In comparison with a self-transformation involving a change of the entire self-description, a change of meaning might be more easily accomplished within the organisation. While a new text for the organisation seems to imply a new, different system, a change in the meaning of a text, which itself is retained throughout the process of self-transformation, can 'symbolise' the continuity of the system in spite of self-transformation.[62] In some cases, the 'basic' self-description might be so central and deeply integrated within the organisation that a change of the text itself would lead to a dissolution of the organisation. In such cases, an exchange of secondary texts is the most likely form of self-transformation.[63]

3.   Paradox and the Risk of Paralysis

Having argued above that the concept of self-transformation, *formally* analysed, constitutes a paradox, we will now explore the *practical* implications of this paradox for the organisation's reproduction.

If we conceptualise the autopoiesis of the organisation as the processing of distinctions (i.e. the double distinctions of decisions),[64] a paradox can be conceptualised as a distinction whose indication oscillates between its two sides. As ensuing distinctions can generally connect only to indicated sides, in the case of paradoxes, connection is *logically* impossible. In other words, paradoxes logically

---

[60]   Unless the oscillation is disrupted before a selection has been made.

[61]   Spencer Brown (1979).

[62]   We repeat: it is important to distinguish clearly between the continuation of the autopoiesis and the stability of structures. Structural change does not imply a change of the autopoiesis. Even after the self-transformation has taken place, it is the same system. For the system itself, however, since the self-description represents the system (i.e. its autopoietic unity) to itself, a different self-description *appears* to imply a different system (autopoietic unity).

[63]   Cf. Luhmann (1997), p. 891.

[64]   Cf. Seidl and Becker (2006).

lead to a paralysis in the production of further distinctions.[65] In practice,[66] there are two possibilities for resolving such paralysing situations: either one side of the distinction is *arbitrarily* chosen as a point of connection (i.e. by chance), or the distinction is cancelled and another, earlier distinction becomes the point of connection instead. Thus, in order to prevent paralysis in such cases, organisations have to ensure that these solutions are 'close at hand':[67] either an arbitrary selection of one side (i.e. chance), or a switch to another distinction, or a combination of both.

In the next two sections we will first examine the organisational paradoxes at the operative and structural levels and their associated risks of paralysis more generally, then focus on the risks associated with the self-transformation paradox in the last section.

a.   The Paradox of Decision and the Risk of Paralysis

Self-transformations are not the only paradoxical forms in organisation. On the contrary, as discussed above[68] every single operation is paradoxical. This seems to imply that the reproduction of the system is logically impossible. However, organisations possess mechanisms that enable them to deparadoxify paradoxes and so prevent paralysis. In the following, we will analyse these mechanisms and discuss their applicability to the paradox of self-transformation.

Every decision is a paradox *by definition*:[69] in the fact dimension it communicates both that there are and that there are not alternatives; that is to say, it oscillates between selected and excluded alternatives. In the time dimension it communicates both that the selection has been made and that it has not been made; that is to say, it oscillates between open and fixed contingency. The logical consequence of no side having been clearly indicated is that no further communications can connect to them. Thus, logically, every decision would inevitably paralyse the production of further communications. Practically, however, the organisation 'deparadoxifies' the paradox of decision by selecting 'arbitrarily' one side of the communicated distinction as the point of connection (i.e. our first solution): in the fact dimension the chosen alternative serves as a decision premise for further decisions, and in the time dimension the contingency is treated as fixed; that is to say, the uncertainty is absorbed.[70]

For the *organisation* the selection of one side of the oscillating distinctions is not arbitrary. As organisations operate on the basis of decisions they cannot but select the one side of the distinction as the point of connection for further decisions.[71]

---

[65] Czarniawska (1997), p. 97, comes to a similar conclusion when she writes: 'Paradoxes, when revealed, paralyse routinized action'. See also Czarniawska (forthcoming), and Fiol (2002).

[66] Note that these are not logical-mathematical operations.

[67] Cf. Czarniawska (1997), p. 176; Luhmann (1986).

[68] Chapter 2, Section 1.a.

[69] See Chapter 2, Section 1.a.

[70] We can also say that the organisation puts a restriction on self-reference into the decision communication.

[71] Cf. Luhmann (2000), p. 145; Kieserling (1999), pp. 352f.

In other words, if organisations treat something as an element (i.e. as a decision), the side that will serve as a point of connection is automatically determined. Consequently, for the organisation a decision does not appear as a paradox: ensuing decisions do not observe the paradox that is constitutive of earlier decisions.[72]

So far we have analysed the paradox of decisions as a communication paradox and identified communicative mechanisms that make it possible to communicate *both* sides of a distinction, while at the same time ensuring that only *one* side functions as a point of connection. That is to say, we have been looking at the relation between decisions. In the following we want to focus on the decision situation itself (i.e. on the production of a decision), and analyse how the organisation determines *which* alternative is selected. For this purpose we have to look at a situation in which earlier decisions serving as decision premises define the set of alternatives, from which one alternative has to be selected. The contingency of the situation is open in that all alternatives are equally possible candidates for selection. It is important to note that the decision premises do not determine the selection, otherwise the decision would already have been made. We have a paradoxical situation where a selection has to be made but no selection criteria exist; that is to say, an undecidable decision situation. As Von Foerster writes, this undecidability is constitutive for decisions:

Only *those* questions that are in principle undecidable, *we* can decide.[73]

Thus, decision situations lead *logically* to a paralysis. In practice, however, the organisation possesses mechanisms which ensure that one alternative is chosen. The main mechanism is the organisation's structural coupling to psychic systems. In the decision situation the organisation opens itself up to (chance) influences from the psychic systems of its members. In other words, the organisation makes sure that in every decision situation (for the organisation) chance influences from the psychic systems are close at hand to determine which alternative is selected (our first solution). Particularly important in this respect is the structuring of decision processes according to positions (i.e. the combination of programmes, personnel and communication channels). By assigning decision situations to particular positions (and thus to particular members) the organisation makes sure that a psychic system is close at hand to 'produce' perturbations in the organisation that result in the selection of one alternative over the others.[74]

In the case that no suitable perturbation is produced by psychic systems, according to which the decision could be decided, organisations possess secondary mechanisms that enable the organisation to step out of the paralysing decision

---

[72] Communicatively, the paradox in the decision communication is deparadoxified through an *attribution* to an organisational member. In this sense, the member is perceived as selecting the side of the decision communication that serves as a connection. See Luhmann (2000), pp. 136, 147, on the shift from decision to decider.

[73] Von Foerster (1992), p. 14 (original emphasis).

[74] This does not contradict the principle of operative closure: only the organisation can determine in what way influences from a psychic system are made use of in the organisation.

situation (our second solution). Most important in this respect is the hierarchical organisation of positions. Whenever a decision is caught up in a paralysing oscillation (i.e. cannot be decided), the next higher position is offered as the position from which the reproduction can be continued. That is to say, the communication can jump from the paralysed decision situation to a decision situation in the next higher position. In this position it may be decided to change the decision premises of the original decision, in order to facilitate the decision process. Alternatively, it may be decided not to decide the original decision at all.[75]

b. *Structural Paradoxes and the Risk of Paralysis*

Having analysed paradoxes at the operative level, we now want to look at structural paradoxes. Structural paradoxes are paradoxes that result from conflicting structures. However, structures are never conflicting per se, but only with regard to operations.[76] In other words, structural paradoxes manifest themselves in concrete operations. Let us analyse the form of such paradoxes. Decision premises define the decision situation. That is to say, they define the alternatives between which the decision has to decide, and draw the primary distinction between the alternatives and the rest of the world.[77] In this sense, we can speak of structural paradoxes, if decision premises define paradoxical parameters for particular decision situations. This could either mean that the decision situation both is and is not a decision situation or that the alternatives both are and are not alternatives. In the first case, for example, a member may be required to make a particular decision, despite not being formally competent to do so. In the second case, for example, a decision may have to be made between the two alternatives A and B and between the two alternatives X and Y by selecting only one of them. As a consequence, it is logically impossible to make the decision. The logical result is paralysis.

Practically, there are, again, two solutions to the paralysis. The first one is the arbitrary selection of one side of the primary distinction. In the case of a decision situation oscillating between being a decision situation and not being one, it could be arbitrarily either accepted or rejected as decision situation. In our example from above, the decision might just be made (ignoring the lack of formal competence) or the decision situation might be rejected by pointing out the lack of formal competence. In the second case a decision of either set of alternatives is arbitrarily made. In our above example, a decision either between A and B, or between X and Y is made. As in the case of the paradox of decisions in general, here too the organisation facilitates arbitrary selection between decision situations by assigning decision situations to particular positions. In that way, a coupling to psychic systems is achieved, which can trigger the necessary chance events.

---

[75] The switch to higher levels for dealing with paradoxes has been analysed by many writers, e.g. Czarniawska (1997).

[76] In contrast to what structuralist theories argue.

[77] See Chapter 2, Sections 1.c, 1.d.

The second solution to the paralysis is stepping out of the paralysed decision situation. In this case too, the most important mechanism is the hierarchical organisation of positions. When a decision situation is paralysed, the organisation offers the next higher position as a point from where the reproduction can be continued. Again, a switch to the next higher position can only be suggested, but not enforced.[78] From this higher position, the paralysed decision situation can be observed (second-order observation[79]) and possibly 'reframed'.[80] In other words, new decision premises can be decided in order to remove the paradox from the paradoxical decision situation.

c. The Paradox of Self-Transformation and the Risk of Paralysis

So far we have analysed organisational paradoxes on both the operative and the structural level. We have identified several organisational mechanisms that prevent the organisation from getting paralysed by these paradoxes. In the following, we will concentrate on the paradox of self-transformation and examine the particular risk it poses. We will argue that in the case of this paradox, the standard mechanisms for solving paradoxical decision situations do not apply.

With regard to the risk of paralysis, decisions on self-descriptions stand out against other decisions, primarily because of the degree to which other organisational decisions are affected by them. As self-descriptions directly or indirectly refer to *all* operations of the system,[81] a paralysis of the decision on the self-description could paralyse the entire organisation. For other decisions that try to relate to the organisational self-description, a paradoxical decision situation is produced: the definition of their decision situation oscillates together with the oscillation of the decision on the self-description. Here we can conclude that the paradox of self-transformation poses a particular risk to the organisation.[82]

As with all paralysing paradoxes, there are two solutions to the situation: the arbitrary selection of one side of the distinction, or switching to another distinction. With regard to the first solution, we have identified as a standard mechanism the assignment of decisions to positions, and through that a structural coupling to psychic systems. In the case of a decision on the self-description, however, this mechanism is ineffective, because, logically, the assignment of the decision to particular positions depends itself on the decision. Furthermore, as every organisational structure depends logically on the self-description, the organisation cannot define ways in which chance influences from the psychic systems could be used to decide the decision.

---

[78] Empirically, one can observe that the switch to a higher position often does not take place because of a fear of loss of independence with regard to other positions.
[79] Czarniawska (1997), p. 175.
[80] Ford and Backoff (1988), p. 89.
[81] Cf. Luhmann (1995a), p. 460.
[82] Similarly Corley and Gioia (2004), p. 199 write: 'Perhaps the organizational change with the most potential for disruption is a change of identity.' See also Fiol (2002) on the paradox of self-transformation (however a slightly different one) and its potential for paralysis.

With regard to the second solution, we have identified as a standard mechanism the hierarchical order of positions. In the case of the decision on the self-description, however, this second mechanism is also ineffective for two reasons: first, the hierarchical structuring of positions itself depends logically on the self-description, and as such oscillates with the decision on the self-description. Second, even if moved to a higher position, the paralysis would not be solved: the initial decision situation cannot be 'reframed' by the higher position as the higher position is in the same situation as the lower position; nor can the higher position offer any alternative decision situations, from where the reproduction of the organisation could be continued, as every decision situation depends logically on the self-description.

To conclude, decisions on self-descriptions pose a severe threat to the reproduction of the organisation. Not only are the standard mechanisms for solving the paralysis associated with the paradox of self-transformation virtually ineffective, but the paralysis has the potential of affecting the entire organisation. However, since there are many empirical cases of successfully completed self-transformations, there must be other means for preventing their paralysing effects. We will look into this in the next sections.

4. Loose Coupling, Episode and Interactionally Framed Decision Processes

Dealing with the paradox of self-transformation entails two (closely related) preconditions: first, the organisation has to restrict the circular reference between *self-description* and *decision* on the self-description. Second, the organisation has to provide an alternative orientation for this decision. With regard to the first point, we can find two concepts described in the relevant literature: loose coupling and episodes. Both are means of restricting references between the elements or structures of a system. In the next two sections we will explain briefly the two concepts and discuss their relevance to our paradox of self-transformation. In the third section we will bring these two concepts together with the concept of interactionally framed decision processes. We will argue that by coupling decision processes to interaction systems, the organisation can create episodes that are only loosely coupled to the rest of the organisation. In addition to that, this coupling can also help the organisation meet the second requirement for dealing with self-transformations: the organisation can use the dynamics of the interaction systems as a means of orientation with regard to its decision processes.

a. The Concept of Loose Coupling

The concept of loose coupling was introduced and developed by Karl Weick.[83] It is often mistakenly understood to refer to the relationship among parts of a system that are independent of each other, in contrast to tight coupling, which is taken to

---

[83] Weick (1976; 1979; 1982a; 1982b; 1986; 1989; 1995); Orton and Weick (1990). Weick himself refers to two earlier sources that use the term 'loose coupling': Glassman (1973) and March and Olsen (1975).

refer to the relationship among parts of a system that are interdependent. Orton and Weick,[84] however, emphasise the importance of treating the concept of loose coupling as a 'dialectical' one; that is to say, as a concept that 'combine[s] the contradictory concepts of connection and autonomy'.[85] Hence, loose coupling does not mean that different parts of a system are independent of each other but only that they are independent in certain respects.[86]

Glassman, as the first person to use this concept, suggested that we refer to 'loose coupling' if two systems or parts of a system have only few variables in common, or if the variables they share are relatively weak compared to others;[87] that is to say, if systems or certain parts of a system are independent of each other with regard to most, or the most important variables, but coupled with regard to other variables. This conceptualisation, however, might be misleading, as it gives a rather static picture in which the points of connection are predefined. Weick's concept of loose coupling, in contrast, seems to suggest some degree of uncertainty and unpredictability with regard to the points of coupling. In other words, here the influence of the loosely coupled parts on each other is not structurally predetermined. The system leaves the possibilities for connecting different parts open, to be determined in the concrete situation.

The notion of unpredictability and uncertainty with regard to the connections between certain parts might be better explained when examined in the context of Heider's distinction between medium and form.[88] Above, we distinguished medium from form, taking medium to refer to the open possibilities of connections between the elements, while form referred to the determined possibilities of connections. In our specific context, loose coupling between certain parts of a system means that there is a multitude of possibilities for connecting different parts of a system, but none of the possible connections has been selected yet. Different parts are *coupled* because there are possible *connections*, but they are only *loosely* coupled because the couplings are possible, but not (yet) determined. In contrast, the different parts of a system can be seen as tightly coupled, if the connections between those parts are not only possible but have already been selected.

There are two consequences of loose coupling that are of particular interest to us. The first concerns the effect of a breakdown in one part of a loosely coupled system on other parts. Weick writes:

---

[84] Orton and Weick (1990).

[85] Orton and Weick (1990), p. 216.

[86] Orton and Weick (1990), p. 204 write: 'The fact that these elements are linked and preserve some degree of determinacy is captured by the word *coupled* in the phrase *loosely coupled*. The fact that these elements are also subject to spontaneous changes and preserve some degree of independence and indeterminacy is captured by the modifying word *loosely*' (original emphasis).

[87] Glassman (1973), p. 83.

[88] See Chapter 2, Section 2. Weick himself draws on Heider to explain his concept of loose coupling; e.g. Weick (1976), p. 6.

[I]f there is a breakdown in one portion of a loosely coupled system then this breakdown is sealed off and does not affect other portions of the [system].[89]

The second important consequence, which is closely related to the first one, concerns the relative independence of processes going on at the same time in different parts of a system. Since the connections between loosely coupled parts are not rigidly determined – that is to say, since the reference between the structures of different parts is restricted – the system can have processes in one part continue relatively undisturbed from processes in other parts. Furthermore, different parts can develop different structures, which do not have to be integrated with regard to each other.[90]

We can now discuss the significance of the concept of loose coupling for the paradox of self-transformation. It was argued above that decisions on the self-description could be decided if they were based on decision criteria (decision premises) that did not themselves depend on the self-description (first solution). The standard mechanism for this solution, however, proved ineffective as the mechanism itself depended on the decision. It is exactly at this point that the concept of loose coupling becomes interesting. If the decision on the self-description were 'located' within a loosely coupled part of the organisation whose reference to the organisational self-description was restricted in such a way, that its structures were not substantiated by the self-description, the decision premises would not be perceived as being dependent on the decision. Thus, the self-referential loop would be interrupted and would not paralyse the decision. In this sense, the decision on the self-description would appear as an 'ordinary' decision.

Loose coupling is of significance also in the case that the decision on the self-description becomes paralysed. First, loose coupling can prevent the paralysis from affecting other parts of the organisation. Processes in other parts of the organisation can continue reproducing the organisation by using the established self-descriptions. Second, these other parts might just close down the paralysed part if they see that the paralysis cannot be solved otherwise (second solution).

In the following section we will look into the concept of episode, which is closely related to that of loose coupling. One may even treat it as a specific form of loose coupling – loose coupling in the time dimension.

b.   The Concept of Episode

Luhmann conceptualises episodes as sequences of operations that are marked by a beginning and an end.[91] However, while every sequence can be said to start at some point and end at another point, the essential characteristic of the episode is that the distinction between beginning and end is not (only) used by an external observer to observe the sequence, but by the operations of the sequence itself. In

---

[89]   Weick (1976), p. 7.
[90]   Cf. Meyer and Rowan (1977); Thompson (1967).
[91]   On the topics discussed in this section see Hendry and Seidl (2003).

other words the distinction beginning/end serves as a structure for the included operations.[92]

As the distinction beginning/end is central to the concept of episode, we have to analyse it more closely. Within Spencer Brown's formal-logical calculus, beginning and end have to be treated as the two sides of one distinction. Both sides refer to each other and are only meaningful in relation to each other.[93] Formally the distinction beginning/end constitutes a second-order distinction, that is to say, a distinction that presupposes another distinction: the distinction before/after. In this way the distinction beginning/end is composed of two before/after distinctions – before and after it has started and before and after it has finished.[94] As the distinction before/after is the formal definition of an event[95] (an event is what makes the difference between before and after) we can also conceptualise an episode as the distinction between a start event and an end event.

Beginning and end serve as an orientation for the operations taking place between them. The difference between a start event and an end event serves the operations in between as their basic structure. That is to say, the operations of the episode are selected on the basis of their contribution to getting from the start event to the end event. As such they form a teleological process.[96]

An important point for the conceptualisation of the end event is that, although the events taking place within the episode refer to an end, the end does not have to be defined in advance; the operations are focused simply on *an* end. That is to say, the concrete criteria for what can serve as an end of an episode can be established and revised during the episode.

There are basically two forms of finalisation: goal-orientation and time-limitation. Although they are to some extent connected, here they can be treated separately. In the form of goal-orientation all operations within an episode are focussed on the achievement of a specified goal. When the goal is achieved, the episode is expected to come to an end. But even if the system cannot achieve the goal the episode can be terminated by the realisation of the impossibility of achieving it. As Luhmann writes:

> [T]he termination [can] be based on the achievement of the goal or on the realisation of the unattainability of the goal. Terminability (periodicity) is in any case guaranteed and is not dependent on success.[97]

---

[92] Luhmann (1990a), and Hendry and Seidl (2003). On the concept of episode see also Kirsch et al. (1979), pp. 233ff., Kirsch (1988), pp. 163ff., and Kirsch (1991), pp. 131ff. Kirsch and colleagues, however, are not entirely clear whether the episode is just a construction of the researcher or whether it is a structure of the organisational process itself.

[93] Luhmann (1990a), p. 14.

[94] Luhmann (1990a), p. 15.

[95] Cf. Luhmann (2000), p. 45; Luhmann (1990a), p. 16.

[96] Luhmann (1990a), p. 21.

[97] Luhmann (1992a), p. 582 (my translation); see also p. 486, fn. 206, and Luhmann (1990a), pp. 21-22.

The second form of finalisation is time-limitation. Independently of any goal orientation, there can be a time limit to the communications in the episode. The end of the episode in this case is simply marked by a date.[98] The two rules for termination can also be combined; that is to say, the communications can be focussed both on the achievement of a goal and on a time limit. The combination of the two rules can serve both as an additional assurance for the termination of the episode and as additional intensification for the achievement of a particular goal.

In our context, a particularly interesting feature of the episode is the certainty that the sequence of operations defined by the episode will come to an end at some point; that the process will not go on indefinitely. In this respect, Luhmann writes:

> If there are criteria for termination, one can start something without thereby binding energy in the long term. One can undertake much more, if one knows that and how one can end it.[99]

Another important point concerns the relation between an episode and the rest of the organisation. Here we have to ask: what is taking place at the beginning and end of the episode? In other words: what is there inside the episode that is different from what there is outside of it? It is not enough to say simply that the operations are different. That would be a truism, as any concrete communication is unique and thus different from any other.[100] Instead, Luhmann argues that it is structures that change at the beginning and end.[101] Beginning and end in this sense are points of structural change: at the beginning (some of) the system's structures are replaced with particular structures of the episode[102] and at the end the episode's structures are changed back into the system's structures. We could also say: the episode is a means of temporarily *suspending* (some of[103]) the organisation's structures and replacing them with alternative ones. With regard to the suspended structures, the operations inside the episode become merely loosely coupled to those outside.

As the switch from the system's structures to the episode's structures does not take place within the episode but at its border, the switch itself is not directly observed by the operations of the episode.[104] This means that, within the episode, the structures of the episode are not substantiated through a reference to those

---

[98] Luhmann (1990a), p. 22. Time-limitation can take different forms, from defining a single episode to a planned sequence of episodes. See Luhmann (1997), p. 818.

[99] Luhmann (1992a), p. 582 (my translation).

[100] Luhmann (1995), p. 345.

[101] Luhmann (1990a), p. 14.

[102] At the same time the episode is only defined through this change in structures.

[103] The concept of episode does not say anything about the number or types of structures that have been suspended. In order to speak of an episode it is merely necessary that at least *one* structure is temporarily changed.

[104] At most, the episode can reconstruct the distinction between the system's structures and its own structures, according to its own structures – a re-entry. The situation is analogous to that of the system that has no access to the distinction system/environment. Cf. Luhmann (1990a), pp. 19ff., who argues that the episode cannot observe its own beginning and end, but can only reconstruct them internally. See also Luhmann (1997), p. 816.

structures of the greater system that have been switched, even though the initiation of the episode may have been based on them. We could also say that the references by the episode's operations to the structures of the greater system are restricted.[105]

With their ability to restrict references between their inside and their outside, episodes provide a means of dealing with the paradox of self-transformation. By suspending the reference to the existing self-description, the episode could provide a frame for deciding the self-description that itself did not depend on the self-description. Thus, the self-referential loop would be interrupted and the risk of paralysis would be reduced. The decision on the self-description would appear like any other decision.

The episode is also of interest in the case where the decision on the self-description becomes paralysed. As an episode can guarantee its own end, it can also guarantee an end to a paralysed decision process within it. By ending the episode, the organisation automatically jumps back to the structures and decision situations before the episode. While the standard mechanism in the case of paralysis suggested a jump to higher positions, the episode suggests a jump *out* of the episode. Thus, if no decision on the self-description can be made, the established self-description will remain valid.

c. The Interactionally Framed Decision Process

In the following we want to look at one particular way in which organisations can create episodes in, and loose coupling between, their decision processes: *structural coupling to interactions*. There are certainly also other forms of episodic and loosely coupled decision processes; however, with regard to our paradox of self-transformation, interactionally framed decision processes seem particularly significant.[106]

Although interactions themselves cannot take part in the autopoiesis of the organisation,[107] they can be 'instrumentalised' to create specific structural effects in the organisation. For that purpose the organisation has to couple its decision processes to the communication processes of the interaction. This can be achieved through conditioning decision processes in such a way that they use interactional communications as the medium for reproducing their decisions. In other words, the decision processes are conditioned to observe the interactional communication processes and re-interpret them as decision processes.[108] To give a simple example, the organisation might just decide to organise a strategy workshop in which to decide some important issues.

The coupling of a decision process to an interaction presupposes that the interaction produces communications that are compatible with a reinterpretation by

---

[105] Cf. Luhmann (1995a), p. 407.

[106] Apart from that, many studies, especially in the field of strategy, have observed that the most important organisational discourses take place in interactional contexts e.g. Barry and Elmes (1997), pp. 435f., Mintzberg (1980), Kirsch (1992), and Hendry and Seidl (2003).

[107] See Chapter 2, Section 3.

[108] See Chapter 2, Section 3.b.

the organisation as decisions. Since organisation and interaction are different types of systems, compatibility cannot be automatically assumed. Instead, it is necessary that the interaction selects its operations on the basis of their compatibility with the way they will be reinterpreted as decisions. In concrete terms this means that the interaction has to observe the organisation, particularly the organisational structures, and use these structures – interactionally reconstructed – as structures for its own reproduction. If we look at the relation between interaction and organisation we find a mutual restriction: the interactional operations are restricted (i.e. structured) by the (interactionally reconstructed) structures of the organisation, and the organisation is restricted by the interactionally pre-formed communications, which serve as a medium for its own reproduction. As a result of this mutual reference organisational and interactional reproduction (may) run parallel to each other.

This type of coupling has significant structural effects on the organisation in that it creates loose coupling and episodes. We will start with the first. Generally, interactions create boundaries around themselves, distinguishing interactional communications from other communications. They include all communications between participants and exclude all communications from or between other persons. Neither can external communications take part in the interactional communications, nor can the interactional communications take part in external communications. As interactions are operatively closed they determine themselves what effect the environment can have on them. In other words, interactions and their (communicative) environment are only *loosely coupled*.[109]

Through the coupling of a decision process to an interaction, the differentiation between interaction and environment carries over into the relation between the interactionally framed decision process and its organisational context. If the interactionally framed decision process is exclusively based on interactional communications, the decision communications are restricted to those members who participate in the interaction. In this sense, the interactionally framed decision process cannot produce decisions in which the participants of the interaction are not involved. Equally, other decisions in which other persons are involved cannot contribute decisions to the interactionally framed decision process. Thus, interactionally and non-interactionally framed decisions are clearly separated from each other.

Coupling decisions to interactions also leads to the creation of *episodes* in the decision processes, as we shall see. Generally, interactions are episodes in the reproduction of society.[110] Like all episodes, they have a clear beginning, when persons meet and the interactional communications start, and they have a clear end, when these communications end. The distinction between beginning and end serves as a structure for the interactional communications. Even if at the beginning of the episode no concrete end is determined yet, it is nevertheless clear from the beginning that the interaction will come to an end at some point (interactions cannot go on forever – and the interactional communication is *aware* of that fact).

---

[109] See Chapter 2, Section 3.
[110] Luhmann (1995a), pp. 406f.; Luhmann (1997), pp. 818f.

Through the coupling of a decision process to an interaction the episodic structure of the interaction necessarily also affects the decision process. If a decision process is strictly coupled to a particular interaction, the process cannot start before the interaction has started, nor can it continue after the interaction has ended. In this sense, the beginning and end of the interaction serve as ultimate points in between which the interactionally framed decision process can take place. This does not mean that the beginning and end of the interactionally framed decision process have to coincide with the beginning and end of the interaction – they are just their ultimate possible points. The decision process might start later and end earlier. The interactionally framed decision process starts with the first interactional communication *that is reinterpreted as a decision*. In this sense, a meeting for the organisation starts with the formal opening of the meeting, which often takes place a considerable time after the interaction has started; and it might end with the formal closing of the meeting, which often takes place a considerable time before the interactional communications stop.

For the interactionally framed decision processes their beginning and end are not merely arbitrary temporal boundaries, but are also observed in, and used as a structure for, the decision process. In other words, the decisions within the interactionally framed decision process are 'aware' that they are based on an episodic medium and as such have started at some point and will end at another. Let us examine these two points.

We have argued above that the beginning and end of an episode can be conceptualised as the points at which structures are changed: at the beginning the structures of the greater system are exchanged for the particular structures of the episode and at the end the structures are changed back to their original form. In the case of interactionally framed decision processes the switch is from the general organisational structures to a reference to the interaction. That is to say, the beginning of the interaction marks a switch from an orientation according to the general organisational decision premises to an orientation according to the (instruction for an orientation according to the) interaction. New operations are selected on the basis of whether they can or cannot be reconstructed from the communications of the particular interaction, rather than on the basis of whether they do or do not comply with, for instance, a decision programme.

While this switch of orientation at the beginning and end of the interactionally framed decision process does not mean that the decisions inside cannot refer to any decision premises outside, there is certainly some restriction on the references. It ultimately depends on the interaction, which external references become available to the coupled decisions. In this sense, if the interaction does not refer to the organisational self-description, neither can the coupled decisions refer to it.

We may now examine the relevance of the interactionally framed decision process to the two requirements for dealing with the paradox of self-transformation: interruption of self-reference and provision of an alternative orientation. First, if a decision on the self-description is included in a (loosely coupled, episodic) interactionally framed decision process that does not perceive the organisational self-description as referring to itself, the paradox of the decision on the self-description will not be apparent. That is to say, to the extent that the interactionally framed decision process perceives itself as distinct from the organisation as a whole, it can observe the organisation *as if* from outside (externalisation).[111] In this case, the interactionally framed decision process can decide on the organisational self-description as though it referred to something *beyond itself*. In that way, the decision situation and the content of the decision will not appear to be dependent on each other. The decision situation is clearly defined and can be decided like any other decision. For the organisation in general, as it has no control over the interactionally framed decision process, the decision on the self-description (and the premises on which it is based) is a chance selection (solution one).[112]

Even if the decision on the organisational self-description cannot be decided, for example, because the reference to the self-description is not 'sufficiently' interrupted, the rest of the organisation will not be affected by the paralysis. As the interactional communications are closed to other communications, the rest of the organisation is not affected by the paralysed decision situation and can carry on reproducing decisions based on the established self-description. As decisions on new self-descriptions often take a very long time – normally a sequence of interactions will be dealing with the decision – it is important that the rest of the organisation is not paralysed during that time even in cases where the decision can eventually be decided.[113]

In the reverse case, where the paradox of self-transformation causes paralysis in the non-interactionally framed decision processes, the organisation could initiate an interaction for deciding the decision, knowing that the chances of the paralysis being resolved there are considerably higher. This move into an interactional framing is very similar to the move onto a higher level of the hierarchy of positions. Normally, the organisation would jump to higher levels if it had difficulty deciding decisions. However, if either no higher position exists, or if the decision situation cannot be located at any position in the first place, the organisation might initiate an interaction.[114] The shift into an interactional context in the case of paralysed situations might, in fact, come more 'naturally' to the organisation, as it does not depend on any particular structural preconditions: interactions can be started from anywhere at any point. The hierarchy of positions, in contrast, has to be specified in advance, in order for the organisation to be able to use it in the way described.

In addition to the restriction of self-reference, the coupling of the decision process to the interaction also helps the organisation meet the second requirement for dealing with the self-transformation paradox. Restricting the reference between

---

[111] On externalisation through internal boundaries see also Luhmann (1997), pp. 818ff.; Luhmann (1993a), p. 205; Spencer Brown (1979), p. 105.

[112] On the unpredictability of interactionally framed decisions see also Schwartzman (1987), pp. 285ff.

[113] Cf. Wimmer (1999), p. 170.

[114] That organisations switch into an interactional context in the case of incomprehensible situations has been suggested by several authors, e.g. Schwartzman (1986), Schwartzman (1989), Weick (1995), p. 187, and Kirsch (1992), p. 278.

decision process and self-description makes it possible to decide the self-description as if from outside, but at the same time leaves the decision process without orientation. As a consequence, the decision process is in danger of becoming disorientated, which yet again could result in paralysis. In this situation, the interaction can provide a *substitutive orientation*. In other words, the interactions can provide guidance to the decision situation, where such guidance cannot be provided by the organisation itself. Since the interaction system, as an operatively closed system, possesses its own sources of orientation (in particular the perceived presence of its participants), the *organisational* paradox of self-transformation does not affect the dynamic of the interactional communication processes. Thus, even when the organisational reproduction gets stalled, the organisational interaction can continue reproducing itself. By coupling itself to an interaction the organisation can make use of this dynamic for the production of its own decisions. In other words, the decision process lets itself be pressed ahead by the dynamic of the interaction.[115]

5. Summary

In this chapter we have analysed the logical aspect of a change of the self-description. In the first section we started with an explanation of the concept of complexity on which we have to base our understanding of the concept of change. Borrowing from Etzioni's theory of societal change we defined self-transformation as a change of the self-description based on a decision to do so.

In the second section we first analysed the form of the decision to change the self-description, arguing that it constituted a paradox (the paradox of self-transformation), as the decision on the self-description logically depends on the outcome of the decision. We argued that, as a consequence of the paradox, the choice of a new self-description could only be based on chance. We also examined the case of self-transformation being based on a change of the *interpretation* of the established self-description.

In the third section we analysed the consequences of paradoxes on the reproduction of the organisation. We argued that paradoxes lead logically to a paralysis of the organisation but, in practice, the paralysis can be prevented by making use of chance. We discussed both operative and structural paradoxes with regard to organisational mechanisms for handling them. At the end of the section we argued that standard mechanisms for dealing with paradoxes do not apply to the paradox of self-transformation. Empirically, however, self-transformations seem to be possible; consequently, there have to be specific mechanisms for preventing their potentially paralysing effects.

In the fourth section we identified loose coupling and episodes as mechanisms of that kind. We explained loose coupling as the *relative independence* between different parts of a system, and episodes as *temporary suspensions* of a system's structures. We argued that both concepts are means of restricting self-reference,

---

[115] Cf. Kieserling's (1999), pp. 368-369.; Seidl (forthcoming b).

which can be instrumentalised to deparadoxify the paradox of self-transformation. Apart from increasing the chances of a decision on the self-description being decided, the two concepts can also explain how paralysis in the case of failed decision attempts can be resolved. We argued that organisations create such episodes and loose couplings by coupling decision processes to interaction systems, which results in interactionally framed decision processes. In this way, the organisation not only disrupts the circular logic of self-transformation, but it also makes use of the interaction's dynamics for its decision process.

Chapter 5

An Evolutionary Model of Self-Transformation

Introduction

In the last chapter we analysed the logic of self-transformation. We argued that self-transformation is based on a paradoxical decision, which can only be decided by chance. On the basis of this argument we will next ask the question: how is it possible that new self-descriptions, which are compatible with or viable within the organisation's reproduction, come about *by chance*. Or, to highlight the underlying paradox: how can one explain the *probability* of such an *improbability*. This question can be answered using Luhmann's general theory of evolution:[1,2] we will argue that a decision on a new self-description does not automatically lead to the self-description being used as decision premise by the organisation. Instead, decisions on self-descriptions first pass through a selection mechanism before they are implemented.

In the first section we will present Luhmann's general theory of evolution, which is abstracted from its biological roots. This will serve as the foundation for developing an evolutionary model of self-transformation in the three further sections. Each section will deal with one of the three evolutionary mechanisms of variation, selection, and retention.

1. Luhmann's General Theory of Evolution

The theory of evolution was originally developed for explaining biological phenomena. As in the case of the theory of autopoiesis, here too we are dealing with a theory that originated in a different discipline and refers to a clearly different domain.[3] Consequently, if we wish to make use of it in our specific

---

[1] For Luhmann, the basis of the concept of evolution is the unfolding of 'the paradox of the probability of the improbable'. See Luhmann (1997), pp. 413f.; Luhmann (1995a), pp. 433f. On this point, see also Campbell (1969), p. 73.

[2] In organisation studies the concept of evolution (in its various interpretations) is frequently drawn upon. Most influential in this respect are the works by Nelson and Winter (1982) and Hannan and Freeman (1989). On the history of evolutionary thinking in the social sciences – economics in particular – see Hodgson (1993).

[3] Unless we take a sociobiological view of the social as does, for example, Maturana (1980c; 1988).

context we have to indicate clearly in what way the theory is transferred from one domain to the other. One way would be to use the (biological) theory of evolution merely metaphorically. While such a strategy is reasonably unproblematic, and for the purpose of many studies sufficiently 'precise', applying this strategy here would cause the theory to lose most of its potential. For that reason, here we will follow Luhmann, who 'translates' the concept of evolution into a concept on the transdisciplinary systems level.[4,5] From there, it can be re-specified so that it can fit the different disciplines and sub-disciplines represented by different types of systems.[6] In other words, Luhmann suggests that we first *abstract* the originally biological theory of evolution from its biological roots to a general theory of evolution, and only then apply the abstracted theory to concrete types of systems, by describing in what way the different elements of the general theory of evolution materialise in the respective systems.[7]

Luhmann's general theory of evolution takes as its point of departure the distinction between three evolutionary functions: variation, selection and retention (or in Luhmann's terminology: re-stabilisation). These three functions can be defined without reference to any specific domain or type of system. The function of variation refers to the creation of a variant; that is to say, the creation of a *'candidate'* or *'proposal'* for change (variation does not constitute change in itself; that would already count as evolution).[8] The function of selection refers to the act of accepting or rejecting the variant; or rather, the 'proposed' change. The function of re-stabilisation refers to the stabilisation of the evolving unit after selection has taken place: in the case of acceptance the variant has to be integrated into the unit, while in the case of rejection the unit has to be buffered against the rejected variant.

As we can see, the three functions cannot be described independently of each other. They are only meaningful with reference to each other. We can express the correspondence between these functions as three distinctions: variation/selection, selection/re-stabilisation and re-stabilisation/variation.[9] The first distinction states: 'variation' is variation with regard to an ensuing selection and, the other way

---

[4]   Luhmann in a first step developed a general concept of evolution independently of his systems theory, which he integrated into his general systems theory only in a second step. See Luhmann (1992a), pp. 549-561, and Luhmann (1997), pp. 431-456. See also Baecker (forthcoming b).

[5]   For other general theories of evolution, see particularly Campbell (1969), Dawkins (1983), Dennett (1995).

[6]   Cf. Luhmann (1997), pp. 451ff., Luhmann (1992a), pp. 549ff. In this case, Luhmann's method for constructing his theory is the same as in the case of his theory of autopoiesis. See Chapter 1, Section 2.a.

[7]   Consequently, in the case of repeated failure to describe the concrete realisation of the elements of the general theory of evolution for a particular type of system, the theory of evolution would have to be understood as not applying to that particular type. This would be so, for example, in the case of interactions. See Luhmann (1998a), p. 365; Kieserling (1999), p. 59.

[8]   Luhmann (1997), p. 451.

[9]   Luhmann (1992a), p. 558.

around, 'selection' is a selection of a preceding variation. The second distinction states: a 'selection' is a selection with regard to ensuing re-stabilisation and, the other way around, 're-stabilisation' is re-stabilisation with regard to a preceding selection. The third distinction states: 're-stabilisation' is re-stabilisation with regard to the ensuing variation of what is being stabilised and, the other way around, 'variation' is the variation of what has been stabilised before.[10]

The three distinctions, however, do not only express a correspondence between their respective sides. They also – and this is a crucial point – express a separation between them. Mechanisms for variation do not also serve as mechanisms for selection; mechanisms for selection do not also serve as mechanisms for re-stabilisation; and mechanisms for re-stabilisation do not also serve as mechanisms for variation. In other words, the corresponding sides are not coordinated: a particular variation does not imply a particular selection; a particular selection does not imply a particular re-stabilisation; and a particular re-stabilisation does not imply a particular variation.[11] The relation between the corresponding sides of a difference can be described as chance. One can also speak of a 'chance coordination'.[12] Luhmann explains:

> [This] means that, from the point of view of the system, it is a matter of chance whether variations lead to positive or negative selections, and, furthermore, it is a matter of chance whether and how these selections, which use their own criteria, can be stabilised in the system.[13]

To summarise: in order to use the concept of evolution one must be able, first, to indicate mechanisms that serve these three functions and second, to indicate in what way the mechanisms are separated from each other. It is particularly this second point that is central to any theory of evolution, as Luhmann writes:

> One can speak of evolution theory, if this problem [the interruption of interdependency between the three evolutionary mechanisms] is accepted as a research programme.[14]

---

[10] Cf. Luhmann (1997), p. 451; Luhmann (1992a), pp. 557f.

[11] This emphasis on the *distinction* between the three evolutionary functions marks an important re-interpretation of older theories of evolution. See Luhmann (1992a), p. 558.

[12] Luhmann (1998a), p. 363.

[13] Luhmann (1997), pp. 501f. (my translation). See also Luhmann (1992a), p. 558. This does not exclude (what is particularly relevant for meaning constituted systems) that particular functions are served in anticipation of other functions. For example, a variation is proposed in expectation of its being accepted, or a selection is motivated by its chances for re-stabilisation. The important point is that, first, the differences are nevertheless retained, second, variations must not automatically result in positive selections, and third, selections must not automatically result in successful re-stabilisation. The interdependencies between the three functions have to be interrupted. See Luhmann (1992a), pp. 559f. See also Luhmann (1997), p. 475.

[14] Luhmann (1992a), p. 559 (my translation). Luhmann (1997), p. 498 speaks of the 'separation problem'.

Luhmann integrates the concept of evolution into his systems theory by assigning the three evolutionary functions to three different levels within the system: element, structure and system:[15]

Variation takes place at the level of *elements*. A variant is an element that deviates from the given structures. In the case of social systems variation refers to a deviation of a communicative event from expectations – in other words, to the production of unexpected, surprising communications. In the case of organisations in particular, variation refers to decisions that deviate from organisational decision premises.[16]

Selection takes place at the level of *structures*. The selection concerns the structural value of a variation. A positive selection of the variation takes place if the deviant element leads to a new structure. Negative selection takes place if the deviant element is rejected with regard to its potential to condense to a structure or, put simply, if the established structures are retained. In the case of social systems, a variation is positively selected if it leads to new expectations, and it is negatively selected if the established expectations do not change. In the case of organisations in particular, a deviant decision is positively selected if it leads to a change in the decision premises and it is negatively selected, if the existing decision premises remain unchanged.[17]

Re-stabilisation concerns the continuation of the autopoiesis of the evolving *system*. It refers to mechanisms which ensure that the autopoiesis continues after a (positive or negative) selection has taken place. Re-stabilisation is necessary because the consequences of (positive or negative) selection for the system as a whole are not themselves criteria for the selection. That is to say, the selection does not automatically lead to stability.[18] After a positive selection the new structures have to be integrated into the network of given structures; after a negative selection the established structures have to be stabilised despite the rejection of variation. In both cases – positive and negative selection – the complexity of the system as a whole increases, and the system has to react to this with re-stabilisation. Re-

---

[15] By comparison, in living systems the different evolutionary functions were traditionally assigned to different systems that stand in a hierarchical relation of enclosure: variation referred to genetic mutations of the individual cell, selection referred to the survival of the individual organism, and re-stabilisation (retention) referred to the reproduction and stabilisation of the genetically modified population within its environment. See Luhmann (2000), p. 352.

[16] Luhmann (1992a), p. 560; Luhmann (1997), p. 454; Luhmann (2000), p. 352.

[17] Luhmann (1998), p. 364; Luhmann (1997), p. 454; Luhmann (2000), p. 352.

[18] Only if one assumes there to be a 'natural' selection, i.e. selection through the environment, which leads to an 'optimal fit', or 'equilibrium between system and environment', is re-stabilisation unnecessary as a separate function, since stability already serves as a selection criterion. In this sense, Campbell (1960; 1969), for example, combines the two functions and speaks of 'selective retention'. Nowadays, however, such a view is rarely held. Currently, it is systems that are *far from equilibrium* that is mainly of interest to evolution theorists. See Luhmann (1997), pp. 485f.

stabilisation thus concerns (primarily[19]) the system/environment distinction. In the case of social systems, changed expectations have to be integrated within the existing expectations or, if the unexpected communication is rejected, the system has to be stabilised with regard to the knowledge that a possibility has not been realised. In the case of organisations in particular, re-stabilisation after a positive selection refers to the integration of changed decision premises into the context of the existing decision premises; or, after a negative selection, to the stabilisation of the existing decision premises despite the rejection of a possibly 'better' alternative.[20]

Let us summarise: Luhmann abstracts the concept of evolution from its biological roots and integrates it into his systems theory. He thereby assigns the three evolutionary functions to different levels of the system. The *separation* of the different functions is accounted for by the separation of the different levels of the system: elements are not also structures and structures are not also systems.[21]

2. Variation and the Interactionally Framed Decision Process

Having presented Luhmann's general theory of evolution, we will now examine the mechanisms of variation in the organisation. In accordance with our main focus, we will not look at structural change in general but only at one particular kind of structural change: self-transformation.[22]

We have to start with the basics. Variation is a recursive concept, in that it presupposes something from which it deviates.[23] We can thus ask very generally: in the case of self-transformation, what deviates from what? The second part of the question is clear: it is a deviation from the established self-description. The first part of the question is more tricky: it is not a new self-description – if it were, the self-transformation would be already completed – but only a '*proposal*' for a new self-description: the *decision* on the new self-description. The decision on the self-description is *not* the self-description: it is an operation rather than a structure.

As a variant, the decision on a new self-description has a peculiarity: the variant is explicitly communicated as a variant.[24] Normally, a deviating operation takes place without being 'aware' of its function as a variant. In the case of the decision on a new self-description, however, the variation communicates explicitly its potential structural value. The decision communicates its deviation from the

---

[19] Secondarily it also concerns the internal differentiation of the system. Cf. Luhmann (1997), p. 455.

[20] Luhmann (1997), pp. 454f., 485f.; Luhmann (1992a), pp. 560f., 586; Luhmann (1998), p. 364; Luhmann (2000), pp. 352ff.

[21] Luhmann (1992a), p. 561.

[22] For a general analysis of structural changes in organisations according to Luhmann's general concept of evolution, see Luhmann (2000), Chapter 11.

[23] Luhmann (1997), p. 461.

[24] Such an intentional form of variation, according to Luhmann (1997, pp. 462-463) constitutes an exception. In contrast to selection, variation is normally not explicitly communicated as such.

established self-description: it has decided *against* the established self-description, and it communicates the structural value of this deviation. That is to say, it offers a new self-description. Thus, in our case, variation is explicitly focussed on selection. As a consequence, the chances of positive selection can be taken into account in the production of the variation, at least to some extent.[25] We will come back to this point in the next section.

We have argued above that the risk of paralysis, as associated with decisions on self-description, can be dealt with by containing the decision situation within an interactionally framed decision process. If our argument is correct, we should be able to identify a mechanism of variation which comes into effect particularly in interactional contexts. That is to say, the mechanism of variation would have to explain not only why decisions on new self-descriptions are produced, but also why such decision situations arise particularly within interactions.

Our thesis is that the main mechanism of variation can be found in the 'exposure' of the organisation to the *interactional memory* in the interactionally framed decision processes. We argue that the interactional memory, under certain circumstances, re-introduces uncertainty that has been absorbed before; in other words, that it causes previously decided decision premises to be discussed openly again. In order to unfold this argument, however, first we have to take a closer look at Luhmann's concept of memory.

Drawing on Von Foerster, Luhmann conceptualises memory as a *function* that regulates remembering and forgetting. In every concrete situation memory determines what past operations to refer to and in what way to refer to them; in this way it defines the 'reality' of the situation.[26] With regard to the organisation, this means that memory selects possible references to previous decisions. In the course of their reproduction, organisations usually forget the original decision situation and remember only the chosen alternative, as it is the only point of interest for connecting decisions. In other words, a decision is normally remembered in the form of the decision premise as which it serves for ensuing decisions. When the decision situation is forgotten, the original uncertainty on which the decision had been based is also forgotten. Only in exceptional cases can this be prevented, so that the contextual factors of a decision are not forgotten – for example, if the validity of the decision is only conditional.[27]

In contrast to the organisation, organisational interactions tend to remember also the contextual factors of decisions. The interaction often remembers factors such as the course of a decision process, the reasons for which certain decision situations have arisen, the decision's different alternatives, the arguments for and against it, its supporters and opponents, and so on. One could say that the

---

[25] Cf. Luhmann (1992a), p. 559. This, however, does not mean that a positive selection could be guaranteed in any way; it can only be made more likely. See also Luhmann (2000), pp. 353f.

[26] Von Foerster (1949); Luhmann (2000), pp. 192ff.; Luhmann (1997), pp. 576ff. In contrast to traditional conceptualisation, here memory does not simply refer to 'stored information'. See Walsch and Ungson (1991), p. 61.

[27] Luhmann (2000), p. 193.

interaction remembers the constitutive uncertainty of a decision while the organisation forgets it. In this respect, Kieserling speaks of 'de-coupling' (although 'loose coupling' might be a more appropriate term) between interactional and organisational memories. He writes:

> The memory of the organisation remembers only decisions and forgets everything else. In contrast, the memory of the interaction and of its participants is conditioned in a completely different way. They might remember the process more than the result and the defeated more than the finally victorious candidates.[28]

By coupling decision processes to interactions, the interactional memory becomes available also to the organisation. In the interactionally framed decision process, the organisation can be made 'aware' of the uncertainty that has been absorbed by previous decisions.[29] This awareness, then, might prompt reflections on whether the decisions and the decision premises they gave rise to were and still are 'right'. As a consequence, a decision on confirmation or rejection of the decision premise might be called for. In this way, the uncertainty of the original decision re-enters the organisation.

Interactionally framed decision processes do not, of course, re-introduce the uncertainty of every single decision, nor do they decide on every decision premise again. As the organisation's reproduction depends on uncertainty absorption, the re-introduction of all uncertainty would paralyse the entire decision process.[30] Through its coupling to the organisation, the interaction is restricted with regard to re-introducing uncertainty; the interaction is 'aware' that by questioning every single decision premise, the organisation would be unable to re-construct decisions from their communications and that, ultimately, the coupling would be dissolved. Hence, when interactions are involved in interactionally framed decision processes their memory for the most part has to be inhibited.

There are, however, certain circumstances under which this inhibition of the interactional memory is removed, in which the re-introduction of uncertainty is stimulated. A very important 'trigger', in this respect, is the experience of structural inconsistencies created by the existing self-descriptions. In these cases, the interaction might start questioning the self-description and communicate about alternatives more or less automatically. For the decision process this means that a decision on the validity of the self-description is likely to be called for, which

---

[28] Kieserling (1999) pp. 385f. (my translation). Kieserling refers to the organisational and interactional memory also as 'official' and 'unofficial' memory. See also Luhmann (2000), p. 154.

[29] This is only the case, because the interactionally framed decision process is structurally coupled to the interaction.

[30] A re-entry of the uncertainty of *every* single decision is what the so-called 'total learning model' seems to propagate, as in e.g. Senge (1990), and Pedler, Boydell, and Burgeone (1991). However, as can be easily shown, this would lead to a paralysis, as the functioning of the organisation depends on uncertainty absorption, so the reintroduction of uncertainty has to be balanced. Cf. Schreyögg and Noss (1994; 1995), Noss and Schreyögg (1997), Baecker (1994), pp. 150f., and Baecker (2000).

creates the possibility for a deviating decision; that is to say, for a decision on a new self-description.[31]

The experiences of inconsistencies, and consequently the occasions for initiating decisions on the self-description, are intensified by the idiosyncrasies of the structures of the interactionally framed decision process. Due to their particular structures, interactionally framed decision processes tend to observe the organisational reality differently from the way the rest of the organisation does. This has implications with regard to the frequency with which such variations take place. By using different distinctions for observing the organisational reality, interactionally framed decision processes might observe inconsistencies between organisational structures even when the organisation perceives itself to be 'running smoothly'. This intensification of variation through the structural difference between organisation and interactionally framed decision process is multiplied by the number of organisational interactions and the structural differences *between* them. First, from a purely quantitative point of view, the more organisational interactions take place, the more occasions there are for such decision situations to arise.[32] Second, from a qualitative point of view, as interactions differ structurally from each other they are likely to observe different inconsistencies between organisational structures and so have different reasons for initiating such decision situations. This does not necessarily increase the number of reflections but it increases the likelihood of reflections taking place at all. The structural difference between organisational interactions also increases the diversity of results of such decisions. In other words, the probability of different self-descriptions being chosen increases with the diversity of contexts in which the decision on the self-description is decided.

Apart from these more or less spontaneous decisions on the self-description, there are other ones, which are actively initiated by the organisation. That is to say, the organisation can initiate organisational interactions for the purpose of reflecting on the self-description. Although the organisation has no direct access to what takes place in the interaction, it can at least condition the interaction in such a way that reflections become likely.[33] Such conditioning can take place in all three dimensions of meaning: first, reflection on the self-description might be given as an explicit topic; that is to say, put on the agenda of the interaction (fact dimension). Second, the participants might be selected according to the likelihood of their questioning the self-description – for example, outspoken critics of the organisation might be included (social dimension). Third, a consensus on the self-description might be given as a goal – and thus an end – of the interaction (time

---

[31] In comparison, outside the interactional context, where alternatives are not so readily available, self-descriptions are unlikely to be questioned even in the case of experienced inconsistencies. Instead, the organisation tends to change local structures so that the inconsistency disappears or at least becomes less salient.

[32] This is not to say that every organisational interaction is equally likely to initiate such reflections.

[33] On the conditioning of organisational interactions through the organisation see Chapter 2, Section 3.c.

dimension). In the relevant literature, such organisational interactions[34] have variously been described as 'change arenas',[35] 'decision arenas',[36] 'discussion arenas',[37] 'strategic conversations',[38] 'strategic episodes',[39] and 'strategic planning committees'.[40]

There are several reasons why an organisation may initiate such interactionally framed decision processes for the purpose of reflecting on the self-description. The most obvious reason is the experience of a crisis, when an organisation experiences an inconsistency between 'important' structures; in particular, inconsistencies involving the self-description.[41,42] An inconsistency might be experienced between organisational self-description and image, for example – that is to say, between the way the organisation perceives itself and the way it assumes that it is being perceived by its environment.[43] Functionally equivalent to the experience of actual crises is the anticipation of crises.[44] The organisation might anticipate crises in the future, while it observes its environment develop in a way that is likely to become inconsistent with its present structures. In these cases, the organisation might initiate interactions in order to reflect on the established self-description against the backdrop of future developments.

Apart from such more 'formal' interactions or meetings, one can find a host of 'informal' interactions in which the self-description is discussed.[45] For example, some members of an organisation may have a 'chat' about the organisational self-description at their lunch break, or at a chance meeting in the corridor. Such interactions typically develop at the 'fringes' of the organisation. In contrast to 'formal' organisational interactions, such interactions observe the organisation and

---

[34] However, mostly without an explicit concept of interaction.

[35] Rüegg-Stürm (1998b). See also Buschor (1996), pp. 161ff.

[36] Kirsch (1992), pp. 273ff.

[37] Zu Knyphausen-Aufsess (1995), p. 344.

[38] Von Krogh and Roos (1996).

[39] Hendry and Seidl (2003) and Aschenbach (1996), pp. 59ff.

[40] Johnson (1987).

[41] See Chapter 4, Section 3.b. In the relevant literature, the role of perceived inconsistencies for initiating a search for alternatives has received considerable attention. See e.g. Brunsson and Olsen (1993), Bartunek (1984), Johnson (1987), Grinyer and Spender (1979), Nelson and Winter (1982), Kirsch (1996), pp. 73-79, Kirsch (1991), pp. 536ff., Kirsch et al. (1979), and Aschenbach (1996), pp. 67ff.

[42] Fundamental structural inconsistencies are often also experienced in connection with a change of personnel, in particular chief executives or directors. The role of changes in personnel in triggering self-transformations has been widely recognised in the relevant literature. See e.g. Johnson (1987), Grinyer and Spender (1979), Mintzberg (1978), Slatter (1984), and Schein (1985).

[43] See Chapter 3, Section 2.d. Dutton and Dukerich (1991), for example, describe a case in which inconsistencies between the (reflective) identity and the image led to questioning and ultimately changing the established identity. See also Corley and Gioia (2004).

[44] Kirsch (1996), pp. 76ff.

[45] On 'formal' and 'informal' interactions see Chapter 2, Section 3.b. For an analogous argument, with regard to the role of para-scientific or pseudo-scientific findings for the evolution of the societal sub-system science, see Luhmann (1997), pp. 573f.

are conditioned by it, however, the organisation does not recognise them as part of itself. That is to say, their communications are not reinterpreted as organisational decisions. It is only under exceptional circumstances that the organisational decision communication will refer to these interactional communications. These interactions can observe the established organisational self-description and compare it with alternative self-descriptions. That is to say, they can come up with alternative self-descriptions that to them seem more appropriate.

There are two ways in which such deviant communications of informal interactions can play a role for the variation mechanism. First, the alternative self-descriptions that the 'informal' interactions communicate about can be remembered in 'formal' interactions (recollected by those who took part in those interactions, that is), and through this, influence indirectly the interactionally framed decision process.[46] Second, 'informal' interactions might establish themselves as official parts within the organisation; they can fight for recognition by the organisation and try to have their communications interpreted as decisions. Lobbying groups within organisations would be an example of this.

Within the interactionally framed decision process a first 'pre-selection' of the variation takes place. If a new self-description has been decided, it has to be viable within the interactional decision context; that is to say, it has to be compatible with other decisions within the interactionally framed decision process. In this sense, a new self-description might be decided in the interactionally framed decision process but be rejected in the course of that decision process due to conflicts with other decision premises. We can say that new self-descriptions have to be first and foremost convincing within the interactionally framed decision process, before they can become serious candidates for selection through the organisation. As Luhmann writes:

> The stability of the improbable in the interaction [analogously here: the interactionally framed decision process] is an indispensable precondition of its introduction into evolution (just as mutations must be stable at the cellular level). Here an initial sorting occurs. It supplies the first evidence of possibility.[47]

As the interactionally framed decision process is episodic and only loosely coupled to the rest of the organisation, the failure of new self-descriptions within an interactionally framed decision process does not harm the organisation.[48] The interactional context can therefore be 'used' for experiments. If the experiment

---

[46] Cf. Kieserling (1999), p. 381 on the preparation of topics for meetings in 'informal' interactions.

[47] Luhmann (1995a), p. 435. Luhmann's original text refers to the relation between interaction and society; however, on the basis of the above arguments, the same can be said about the relation between interactionally framed decision process and organisation. Similarly, Weick (1977) argues that variations have to be stable enough to wait for selection to take place.

[48] In the same way as a paralysis of the interaction does not harm the organisation.

fails, the interactionally framed decision process is simply terminated, and an alternative one might be initiated instead.[49]

Thus, with regard to the decision on the self-description, the episodic structure and the loose coupling of the interactionally framed decision process not only prevent the paradox of self-transformation from causing paralysis, but also create a testing ground for the 'proposed' new self-description.

3. Selection and the Differentiation between Organisation and Interactionally Framed Decision Process

In order for us to speak of evolution, a variation must not automatically imply a particular (either positive or negative) selection: the decision on a new self-description does not automatically mean that this new self-description becomes effective. In other words, mechanisms of variation must be distinguishable from mechanisms of selection. In our particular context, this means that we have to indicate specific mechanisms of selection through which the decisions on new self-descriptions have to pass before they can serve as new self-descriptions.

On a general level of organisational evolution Luhmann speaks of 'loose coupling' between decision and decided decision premise. Decisions do not simply become (decided) decision premises for other decisions, nor can any particular decision be derived directly from its decision premises. The 'logical, mathematical, technical connection between decision and decision premise'[50] is interrupted. Instead, any link between decision and decision premise has to be understood as the result of an interplay of various mechanisms, which work independently from the particular decision. Hence, from the perspective of a deviant decision it is a matter of chance *whether* it will come to be used as a decision premise and, if so, as *what* decision premise it will be interpreted.

While there is generally only a loose coupling between decisions and the use of these decisions as (decided) decision premises, in the case of the decision on a new self-description there is an additional 'separation' between the two: to the extent that these decisions take place within interactionally framed decision processes, the differentiation between the interactional framing and the rest of the organisation

---

[49] Luhmann writes about the role of interactions for society, which, analogously, applies to the relation between interactionally framed decision process and organisation: 'In the domain of social systems [here: organisations], it is easier to occupy relatively improbable positions because risks are spread over interaction systems [analogously: interactionally framed decision processes]. Interaction systems [analogously: interactionally framed decision processes] must come to an end, and thus one can use them for experimentation. [...] Initially only the autopoiesis [analogously: reproduction] of the interaction [analogously: interactionally framed decision process] not that of the society [analogously: organisation], [is] at play.' Luhmann (1995a), pp. 434f. Similar views can also be found elsewhere. Rüegg-Stürm (1998b), for example, speaks in a comparable context of a 'laboratory' [*Experimentierwerkstatt*], in which new ideas can be tested before the organisation is exposed to them. See also Buschor (1996).

[50] Luhmann (2000), p. 354.

serves as selection mechanism. The new self-description is accepted or rejected at the transition from the interactional decision process to the organisation as a whole. In other words, a decision on a new self-description that has proved viable within the interactionally framed decision process is positively selected, if it comes to be used also outside the particular interaction; that is to say, if it diffuses within the organisation at large. The decision is negatively selected if it does not cross the interactional boundaries; that is to say, if it does not diffuse within the organisation at large.[51]

In concrete terms, evolutionary selection results from the fact that the structures of the interactionally framed decision processes differ from the structures of the organisation as a whole. Alternative self-descriptions that are viable within the interactional context might very well be – are even likely to be – incompatible with the structures of the organisation in general. In other words, the difference between the structures serves as a filter that selects what variations can diffuse into the organisation at large.

We can distinguish between manifest and latent (or controlled and uncontrolled) selection.[52] These two forms of selection can be understood as two stages of selection: only after a positive latent selection can the manifest selection take place. The first threshold any alternative self-description has to pass is to get *noticed* outside the interaction, that is to say, to become the object of communications also outside the interactional decision process. Thus, the latent selection takes the form of repetition/non-repetition, or of remembering/forgetting of variations.[53] Many variations go unnoticed and simply disappear in an uncontrolled manner. With the disappearance of the interactionally framed decision process, variations are simply forgotten.

The number of variations that are eliminated in this way can hardly be overestimated.[54] For the organisation this latent selection has a very important function: it reduces the amount of information the organisation has to handle, and thus ensures that the organisation's information-processing capacity is not exhausted. Variations that have been forgotten do not take up decision capacity, and the selection of remembering and forgetting as such does not have to be decided. As Luhmann writes: 'The system disburdens itself through forgetting.'[55]

Whether or not interactionally framed decision processes are noticed and remembered by the organisation at large depends on various factors. Often these

---

[51] Analogously, Luhmann (1997), p. 478 argues that the differentiation between interaction and society serves as a selection mechanism in societal evolution.
[52] Luhmann (1992a), p. 577. See also Luhmann (2000), p. 352. Here, however, he does not call it explicitly 'manifest' and 'latent' selection.
[53] According to Rudolf Stichweh (personal correspondence), in a strict sense, it is incorrect to speak of a selection *mechanism* with regard to a latent selection, as there are no specific operations to perform such a selection (i.e. there are no specific acts of positive or negative selection). Luhmann is somewhat imprecise with regard to this point: Luhmann (1992a), p. 577.
[54] Cf. Luhmann (1992a), p. 577 with regard to evolutionary selection in the case of the function system of science.
[55] Luhmann (2000), p. 352 (my translation).

decisions are simply forgotten because they are not written down and are thus dependent on the memory of the individual participants. Or, if written down, they might just be filed and not looked at any more. A variation's chance of getting noticed by the organisation as a whole probably depends, among other factors, on three things: first, the degree of attention it receives within the interactionally framed decision process. Second, on the degree to which it is comprehensible from the perspective of the usual decision praxis outside the interactionally framed decision process; in other words, on the degree to which concrete operations outside the interactionally framed decision process can connect to it. Third, on the degree of attention the particular interactionally framed decision process in general receives.

Manifest selection takes place if variations are explicitly accepted or rejected by the organisation, or, in our particular case, if alternative self-descriptions are explicitly accepted or rejected by the organisation as new self-descriptions. To give an example, an explicit acceptance may take the form of a decision to implement the new self-description; that is to say, to align other structures of the organisation with the new self-description. Here, it is the *decision* to align that serves as an explicit selection, not the alignment as such. Proposed new self-descriptions can be explicitly rejected – for example, through a decision not to implement the new self-description.[56] Some justification for rejecting earlier decisions can almost always be found, e.g. formal mistakes in the decision-making process, important data not having been taken into account for the decision, or a change of circumstances.[57] Instead of rejecting the new self-description, the organisation could also decide to postpone the selection by deciding to discuss the self-description once more. In this case, either a further interactionally framed decision process is initiated or the issue is simply postponed and then forgotten (latent selection).

One of the most important mechanisms of manifest selection is the structuring of the organisation according to positions. As explained above,[58] the organisation coordinates its three types of decision premises (programme, personnel, and communication channels) through positions: every position is occupied by a particular person, has a particular task, and is located somewhere in the communication network. The position itself, however, is not a decision premise. It is merely a point of intersection between the decision premises. Abstracted from its programme, personnel and communication channels, the position does not have any information value, it is just an 'empty space' – one might say, in fact, that it

---

[56] When a decision is rejected through another decision, it is not that the earlier decision is 'changed', as one tends to say. Decisions are events, which have no temporality and cannot be changed as such – there is no time in which they could be changed. See Luhmann (1992b), p. 169, and Luhmann (2000), p. 65. However, what can be changed is the structural effect of a decision. Later decisions can decide not (or no longer) to use an earlier decision as a decision premise.

[57] Sometimes even the entire organisational interaction (together with all its decisions) can be rejected as 'illegitimate'.

[58] See Chapter 2, Section 1.c.

does not exist.[59] For the organisation, positions serve as schemata according to which it observes the *relation* of its decision premises to each other.

Not only existing decision premises but also changes in decision premises are observed according to the schema of position. Every new decision premise that has been decided upon is observed with regard to the changes it implies for different positions: the task of a position might be changed, the person occupying the position might be changed, or the integration of the position in the communication network might change. However, not all three decision premises of a position can be changed simultaneously, since, in that case, the position would no longer be recognisable as the same position: at least one decision premise has to remain unchanged for the position to 'hold onto'. These unchanged decision premises also determine how the new decision premises are observed with regard to the particular position.[60] In this way, it is these unchanged decision premises that limit also what other decision premises are possible.[61] For example, a university's decision to develop a new course (i.e. a new decision programme) will be analysed from the perspective of the affected positions, with regard to whether and how it can be combined with the persons occupying the respective positions (e.g. 'are those persons capable of teaching the course?') and whether and how the course fits in the internal communication structures (e.g. 'is the course part of the right department?').

As all new structures, new self-descriptions have to be compatible with the particular historical state that the system is in. The organisation cannot recreate itself from scratch.[62] Instead, it has to rely on its existing structures for implementing the new structures. A new self-description therefore has to be compatible with the given positions. It will be assessed with regard to the changes it implies for different positions. However, since these positions only exist as long as there are decision premises that intersect in them, the new self-description could not be assessed if it implied changing *all* decision premises of all positions. In that case, there would not be any (established) positions left, with regard to which the new self-description could be observed. To take an extreme example, if an organisation changed its self-description from 'technical university' to 'music orchestra' this new self-description would most probably be incompatible with the given positions. In the various positions, the lecturers would have to be replaced by musicians, the teaching and research duties by music playing, and the various departments by various groups of musicians. In that way, none of the positions would be able to change, as they would all disappear with the change. Because of that, the new self-description would have almost no chance of being positively selected.

The chances of a new self-description being selected are also likely to vary from position to position. Usually there will be some positions that are able to accommodate the new self-description, retaining at least one of their decision premises, while others will not. This means that from different positions new self-

---

[59] Luhmann (2000), p. 233. Luhmann (2000), p. 234, speaks of positions as 'kenogramms'. See also Luhmann (1976), p. 141.
[60] Luhmann (1975), p. 42.
[61] Luhmann (1992b), p. 178.
[62] Unless under catastrophic conditions. See Kirsch (1992), pp. 136f.

descriptions are likely to be evaluated differently. And it is also from the perspective of those different positions that the decision on the acceptance or rejection of the new self-description will be made: some positions might accept it while others might reject it.[63] It is also possible that some higher positions decide between acceptance and rejection on the basis of their evaluation of the self-description's compatibility with lower positions.

As a result of different positions evaluating the new self-description differently, the organisation might continue to reproduce itself on the basis of multiple self-descriptions as some positions adhere to the old and some to the new self-description. Alternatively, those positions that are not able to accommodate the new self-description might be erased by higher positions and new positions might be opened instead. A third possibility is that higher positions which have rejected the new self-description, prevent lower positions from accepting it.

There are several mechanisms that increase the probability that a variation is (positively) selected.[64] With regard to latent selection, for example, there are mechanisms which influence, first, the degree of attention for a variation within the interactionally framed decision process; second, the degree of comprehensibility of the variation; and third, the degree of attention the interactionally framed decision process receives. In the first case, by initiating interactions for the sole purpose of deciding on the self-description, the decision situation and its result are likely to receive a high degree of attention within the meeting. In the second case, variant self-descriptions can be supported by additional semantics, which explain their concrete consequences for the organisation at large; these may also include elaborations of how concrete operations can connect to them. Such elaborations (to be written down; for example, in the form of a protocol) might be required by the organisation. In the third case, the attention a meeting receives from the organisation can be influenced through the 'level' at which it is positioned. In this sense, if an interaction takes place in the upper reaches of an organisation or if it involves the top management team, it tends to get more attention than – by contrast – interactions between shop-floor workers.

There are also several reinforcing mechanisms with regard to manifest selections. We will give just a few examples here: one way of raising the chances of variations being positively selected is for the organisation to create a context for the interactionally framed decision process that resembles (as much as possible) the organisation as a whole. The more similar the structures are, the greater the chance that variations which were acceptable in the interactionally framed decision process, will also be acceptable outside of it.[65] Instead of trying to model the interactionally framed decision process on the organisation at large, the organisation can also try to make these decision processes particularly responsive

---

[63] Which positions accept or reject a new self-description also depends on the access to the new self-description. See Chapter 3, Section 3.c.

[64] See also Hendry and Seidl (2003).

[65] Cf. Luhmann (1995a), p. 435 with regard to the relation between interaction and society. See also Rüegg-Stürm (1998b), p. 58.

to the organisation; that is to say, the 'trans-interactional'[66] perspective of the interactionally framed decision process can be enforced. By including members from diverse parts of the organisation, the interactionally framed decision process might get a more diverse and more comprehensive picture of the organisation than by including only members from one part of the organisation.[67] Another way of influencing the probability of a positive selection is to include in the interaction those members who occupy positions in the organisation from which they can enforce the implementation of the new self-description. Closely connected to this is also the question of the legitimacy of an interaction: if members of the top management team are included in the interaction, the decisions taken within the interactionally framed decision process cannot be easily rejected, as they are generally perceived as more legitimate.[68]

4. Re-Stabilisation

This last section focuses on mechanisms that serve the third evolutionary function: re-stabilisation. Generally, re-stabilisation has to do with the stabilisation of the system as a whole in response to a (positive or negative) selection. Here we shall examine mechanisms that can re-stabilise the organisation after a new self-description has either been accepted or rejected. If a new self-description has been accepted, the re-stabilisation mechanism has to integrate the new self-description into the existing structures. This means, first, that the existing self-description has to be replaced by the new self-description, and second, that all other structures have to be adjusted to it. But the organisation also has to be re-stabilised if the new self-description is rejected: in contrast to a positive selection, here it is not the new self-description that has to be integrated, but the knowledge about the rejection of a possible self-description.[69] Through the (positive or negative) selection the contingency of the (old and the new) self-description becomes apparent. In order for the autopoiesis to continue – that is to say, in order for the autopoiesis to create clear points for further operations to connect to – the contingency of the selected self-description has to be disguised. The self-description has to appear as necessary again. In other words, the organisation has to be able to expect that only *one* of the two self-descriptions will be used.

Probably two of the most important re-stabilisation mechanisms are the cognitive and the normative stabilisation of self-descriptions. Self-descriptions are *normatively* stabilised if one can expect deviations from the self-description to be

---

[66] Luhmann (1997), p. 479.

[67] A simple example: if only production managers were included in the interaction, the financial side of a variation would not be taken into account.

[68] Cf. Walton (1975).

[69] The rejection does not lead to the annulment of the new self-description but only to its potentialisation. The new self-description does not disappear from the organisation but persists as a rejected possibility, and, most importantly, the organisation now 'knows' about it. Cf. Luhmann (1992a), p. 582; Luhmann (2000), p. 60.

compensated in some way.[70] A drastic form of compensation, for example, would be the termination of membership of those members who do not adhere to the 'right' self-description.[71] Another form would be to reject all those decisions which are based on the 'wrong' self-description. The important point of normative stabilisation is not the compensation itself but the *expectation* of compensation. In this sense, normative stabilisation means that one can expect the self-description to remain the 'right' one even in face of potential deviations from it.[72] Normative stabilisation is a mechanism that functions both in the case of positive and of negative selection. In the first case, the normative 'support' for the established self-description is removed and attributed to the new self-description; in the second case the normative support for the established self-description is confirmed.

In contrast to normative stabilisation, *cognitive* stabilisation is not based on the expectation of the persistence of self-descriptions in the face of deviations, but on the expectation of flexibility.[73] In this sense, a self-description is only 'right' as long as it is perceived to represent 'accurately' the organisation to itself. At a first glance this seems to be rather more destabilising than stabilising but, as Luhmann argues, it is not. Theoretically, the 'accuracy' of a self-description could be tested every time it is referred to. Every time a decision is made, which refers to the self-description, the organisation can examine whether the self-description is still able to account for the organisational reality. If the self-description fails the test it will be rejected. The important point now is that if one knows that there were multiple *possibilities* for testing the 'accuracy' of the self-description, and that the self-description would have been rejected if it had failed the tests, the self-description is *assumed* to have been well tested and to be therefore likely to remain valid in the future. One assumes that the self-description would no longer exist if it had not been 'accurate' so far. As Luhmann shows, cognitive stabilisation is based on social trust: one trusts that others have tested and approved of the self-description.[74] Luhmann writes:

> The stabilisation mechanism is based precisely on the permanent readiness to reject and replace knowledge, which in the past has been considered valid. One assumes that the present knowledge is subject to a continuous process of testing and that it would no longer exist, if it were not able to persist in the respective present.[75]

---

[70] Luhmann (1997), p. 551, conceives of normative stabilisation as a central stabilisation mechanism in the societal evolution of ideas.

[71] As Kieserling (1994b), pp. 61ff. writes, by accepting membership of an organisation one is expected to acknowledge the organisational self-description; it is a condition for membership. Thus, the self-description is enforced through being coupled to the decision on membership.

[72] In this respect, Luhmann (1997), 551 writes: 'By putting expectations into a normative form one can claim something to be right even if in single cases it does not apply or is violated' (my translation).

[73] Luhmann (1992a), pp. 588ff. conceives of cognitive stabilisation as a primary re-stabilisation mechanism in the evolution of the system of science.

[74] Cf. Luhmann (1992a), pp. 558f.

[75] Luhmann (1992a), p. 589 (my translation). Here, Luhman refers to the stabilisation mechanism of scientific knowledge. However, the stabilisation of self-descriptions can be seen as an analogous case.

In contrast to normative stabilisation, which becomes effective immediately after the selection, the stabilising effect of cognitive stabilisation develops over time. That is to say, the more time passes after the selection, the stronger the stabilising effect. The reason for this is that the more time passes, in which the self-description persists, the more tests it is *assumed* to have passed successfully.

Like normative stabilisation, cognitive stabilisation can function as a re-stabilisation mechanism both in the case of positive and of negative selection. In the case of a positive selection, cognitive stabilisation will result in the assumption that the new self-description has proved more 'accurate' than the former self-description. In the case of negative selection, it will be assumed that the established self-description has proved more accurate than the new self-description.

A further mechanism of re-stabilisation can be found in the restrictions on reflection, which are achieved through the formal communication channels. This can be seen most clearly in the case of a formal hierarchy. The hierarchy restricts different types of decision communications to different levels within the hierarchy. Operative decisions, for example, are restricted to the lower hierarchical levels, managerial decisions to the managerial levels, and institutional decisions to the highest levels.[76] In this way, all questions concerning the organisation as a whole are (ideally) limited to the top of the hierarchy. In contrast, only locally relevant decisions are to be made at lower levels.

This means that the organisational self-description, which concerns the organisation as a whole, is not open to criticism from lower levels of the hierarchy. If a new self-description has been selected, it is to be accepted without criticism. Similarly, if a variant self-description has been rejected, the former self-description has to be accepted, as it had been accepted before. This formal restriction does not mean that no criticism at all is possible from lower levels of the hierarchy; such criticism, however, is shifted into (informal) interactions:[77] for example, within the context of their regular work, shop-floor workers cannot criticise the organisational self-description, but they can do so at their lunch break. Thus, the contribution to re-stabilisation, after an evolutionary selection has taken place, lies in the fact that the possibilities for criticising the self-description are restricted.

A similar stabilisation mechanism can be found in the habitualisation and concealment of self-descriptions. Habitualisation and concealment restrict the probability of self-descriptions being questioned and criticised. As to the former, if a self-description has been used for some time, members are likely to take it for granted. The contingency of the self-description is no longer visible; the self-description appears as a necessity, to which there are no alternatives. As a consequence, the self-description might be referred to explicitly in the decision communications, but it is not further questioned.[78] In addition to that (and often as

---

[76] For classic works on this topic, see, e.g. Taylor (1947), Simon (1971), Parsons (1960), and Thompson (1967).

[77] There it might initiate a new evolutionary process.

[78] In this respect, Von Krogh and Roos (1995), p. 123, speak of self-descriptions becoming 'socialized organisational knowledge'. As such they can serve, in Toulmin's sense, as paradimatic warrants in organisational arguments.

a consequence of that), self-descriptions might be concealed. That is to say, they are only indirectly communicated about, or, in other words, they are only implied in the communication.[79] As a consequence, the focus of the communication is directed away from the self-description.[80] Similarly von Krogh and Roos observe:

Concealed [self-descriptions] are not exposed to further criticism and questioning [...].'[81]

In contrast to the restriction on reflection through the formal communication channels discussed above, the restabilisation mechanisms of habitualisation and concealment are not effective immediately after the evolutionary selection has taken place. They are mechanisms that already presuppose some stability. In other words, they can only reinforce the stability that has already been achieved.

A further mechanism for re-stabilising an organisation after a positive selection has taken place can be found in the differentiation of the organisation into departments. Organisations, for example, are often differentiated on the basis of functions (e.g. finance department, production department, marketing department) or of segments (e.g. different profit centres).[82] That is to say, different parts of the organisation are to a greater or lesser extent independent of each other. As a consequence, the requirements with regard to structural consistency between different parts are lower than they would be without differentiation. This has particular advantages for the integration of new self-descriptions, as we will show. Once a new self-description has been selected it has to be integrated into the organisation's different parts. Integration here means not only the adaptation of existing structures to the new self-description, but also the adaptation of the self-description to the given organisational structures. It is with regard to this particular point that the differentiation into various departments has a stabilising effect. Due to the organisational differentiation self-descriptions do not have to be used consistently throughout the organisation, so new self-descriptions can adapt differently to the contexts of different departments. In other words, the organisation does not have to find one interpretation of the self-description that fits all contexts. The finance department, for example, can interpret the new self-description differently from the production and marketing departments. For that reason, through differentiation the re-stabilisation of the organisation becomes simpler. Moreover, also in the case of later changes in local structures within different departments the self-description could be adapted *locally*. That is to say,

---

[79] See also Chapter 3, Section 3.c.(2).

[80] Luhmann (2000), p. 244, and Luhmann (1996) discuss a similar phenomenon with regard to values.

[81] Von Krogh and Roos (1995), p. 122.

[82] The differentiation can be understood to be based on different programmes. We are not talking about different subsystems in the form of different autopoietic systems – otherwise we would have to indicate specific modes of operation for them on the basis of which they reproduce themselves.

if the finance department changed structurally it might just change its particular interpretation of the self-description.[83]

A further mechanism for re-stabilisation can be found in organisational culture.[84] According to our explanation above,[85] organisational culture can be understood as the medium of communicative possibilities in which an organisation creates its decision operations. This medium is to some extent the very product of the organisation's own operations. We argued that in the course of its operations every organisation creates its own, particular medium – without being aware of it. In other words, the organisation and its medium adjust to each other: the organisation is restricted by its medium, but the medium is also modified by the organisation. For example, if particular decisions are repeated over and over again, the medium becomes 'rigid' and makes deviations from those decisions difficult. That is to say, the organisational culture limits the possibilities to a greater or lesser extent to the practices already established.[86]

With regard to the organisational self-description, this means that if a self-description is used, the organisational culture will develop around it. For example, organisations often develop a particular language that is adjusted to the self-description and its associated decision practices.[87] If an organisation describes itself as a school, it will communicate in terms of pupils, teachers, or education, and not in terms of customers, sales persons, products, and services. This particular language restricts the organisation to such decision processes that are likely to be consistent with the self-description of 'school'. Thus, organisational culture reinforces the stability that the established self-description has already achieved. This is particularly important in the case of a negative evolutionary selection. As the organisational culture reinforces everything the organisation is used to, it will also reinforce the established self-description, even though the organisation knows about another possible (but rejected) self-description.

What happens if a new self-description has been accepted by the evolutionary selection mechanism? There are two possible effects: the organisational culture may prevent the new self-description from diffusing throughout the organisation, restricting its use to areas where the new self-description does not make much of a difference. At the same time the established self-description will be retained in areas where it does make a difference. For example, in the presence of senior managers one refers to the new, official self-description, while during normal work one refers to the established self-descriptions. Alternatively, the organisational culture might lead to the new self-description being interpreted so as to become

---

[83] Cf. Orton and Weick (1990) with regard to the connection between differentiation and stability in general.
[84] The stabilising function of culture has been noted by many researchers, most notably Parsons (1960) – however, not as part of an evolutionary theory.
[85] See Chapter 2, Section 4.
[86] Cf. Luhmann (2000), p. 245.
[87] Similarly Rüegg-Stürm (1998a); Kieser (1998).

very similar to the former self-description. As a consequence the new self-description will reproduce the status quo.[88]

5. Summary

In this chapter we have sketched an evolutionary model of self-transformation. We started off with an explanation of Luhmann's general concept of evolution. Analogously to the concept of autopoiesis, Luhmann suggests abstracting the concept of evolution from its biological roots and developing it into a concept at the transdisciplinary level of systems theory. At this level, evolution can be conceptualised as the interplay between the three evolutionary functions of variation, selection and retention (or re-stabilisation). These three functions can be explained without reference to any particular type of system.

Variation in the context of self-transformation concerns the production of decisions on new self-descriptions. We argued that the main mechanism for producing these decisions could be found in the exposure of interactionally framed decision processes to the interactional memory. In contrast to the organisational memory, the interactional memory remembers the constitutive uncertainty of earlier decisions. This memory is triggered if inconsistencies with regard to the self-description are experienced. This means that the contingency of the self-description becomes apparent to the organisation and a decision on the self-description is likely to be called for. Thus, the possibility arises that the established self-description is not confirmed, and a new self-description is decided upon instead.

Evolutionary selection in the context of self-transformation concerns the acceptance or rejection of the decision on the new self-description. We argued that the primary mechanism of selection could be found in the differentiation between interactionally framed decision process and organisation. In other words, the selection results from the fact that the structures of the interactionally framed decision process differ from the general organisational ones. We distinguished two forms of selection: latent and manifest selection. Latent selection concerns the question of whether or not a variation is taken notice of outside the interactionally framed decision process. Manifest selection concerns the explicit acceptance or rejection of the proposed new self-description. We argued that with regard to manifest selection, the structure of existing positions was of particular importance. A new self-description would only be accepted if it were seen as compatible with existing positions at least to some extent. As the compatibility for different positions is likely to vary, it is possible that some positions accept and some reject it. We identified and discussed several reinforcement mechanisms, which increase the likelihood for variations to be positively selected.

Re-stabilisation in the context of self-transformation concerns the re-stabilisation of the organisation after either a positive or a negative selection of the

---

[88] Because of these and similar effects, organisational culture is nowadays widely seen as an impediment to innovation. Cf. Luhmann (2000), pp. 245ff., 344.

proposed new self-description has taken place. In the case of a positive selection, the new self-description has to be integrated into the established structures. In the case of a negative selection, the established self-description has to be stabilised against the knowledge that an alternative self-description had been suggested. We identified several re-stabilisation mechanisms with different dispositions. The stabilising effect of cognitive stabilisation and normative stabilisation results from their supporting the expectation that the self-description will remain valid in the future. Habitualisation, concealment of self-description, and formal communication channels stabilise indirectly by restricting the possibilities of communicating about the self-description. Organisational culture and differentiation into departments stabilise by facilitating the adaptation between self-description and other structures.

Conclusion

The Distinctions of the Study

In this conclusion we want to reflect briefly on the nature of our study. As the title indicates, this book is ultimately concerned with *two* issues: organisational identity (and its change) and Luhmann's autopoietic perspective. Consequently, at least two readings of this book are possible: one can read it either as an exploration of the (relatively) new concept of organisational identity, for which Luhmann's autopoietic perspective has been chosen. Or one may read it as an exploration of Luhmann's autopoietic perspective, for which organisational identity (and its change) have been chosen as an exemplary topic that demonstrates the potential of Luhmann's approach. To put it in Spencer Brown's terms, we can say that this study offers two observational distinctions, each of which can be used for observing the other one, and each of which can constitute the primary or secondary distinction, in relation to the other one. In our introduction we highlighted the former reading, and merely hinted at the latter one. It is, however, ultimately up to the reader to choose his or her position with regard to the two distinctions, on the basis of his or her particular interests.[1] At this point, we would like to reflect briefly on the two arrangements of distinctions.

Generally, every observation creates both vision and blindness, as it is based on a distinction with a marked and an unmarked side: it can see what it can see, but it cannot see *what* it cannot see, nor *that* it cannot see what it cannot see.[2] Our study is no exception to this principle. With regard to the two readings we can distinguish two distinctions of vision and blindness. In the reading suggested in the introduction, Luhmann's systems theory served as a primary distinction, according to which organisational identity was observed. This primary distinction allowed us to observe the organisational identity by providing a point of reference, with regard to which problems could be seen and solutions sought.[3] The organisation's autopoiesis served as this point of reference. In this sense, in the third chapter we were able to observe how organisational identity was produced by the organisation's own operations and what function it served for them. We were also able to identify different forms of identity with regard to their functions in the organisational self-reproduction. The significance of this reference was particularly salient in our analysis of self-transformation in the fourth chapter: only because of the reference to the organisational *self*-reproduction were we able to observe the

---

[1] Cf. Spencer Brown (1979), p. 103, who writes that any expression (arrangement of distinctions) is ambiguous unless the position of the observer with regard to it is indicated.

[2] See Chapter 1, Section 3.a.

[3] Cf. Luhmann's (1991a), pp. 9-53, 'equivalence functionalism'.

paradox of self-transformation and, consequently, look for organisational mechanisms that could deal with it. In the last chapter, that reference led us to ask how a change of identity was possible without an author to control the change. We answered this question with an evolutionary model. The particular vision that was created can be summarised as follows: the concept of autopoiesis has allowed us to observe organisational identity and self-transformation *from the perspective of the organisation itself.*[4]

This distinction, however, also created blindness. The other side to a chosen approach are the excluded approaches, which *could* have been chosen: other theoretical approaches (e.g. a socio-psychological approach), or other empirical approaches (e.g. grounded theory). Other approaches would have allowed us to ask other questions, and thus seek other answers. We could have tried to overcome this blindness by choosing different approaches consecutively, observing what each approach would have made us observe.[5] The result would have been either a collection of unrelated, incommensurate observations about organisational identity, or a 'meta-approach' for integrating the observations would have had to be chosen. That, however, would have created its own blindness, because any meta-approach is necessarily selective in the way it interprets and relates the various approaches to each other. In this study we chose a Luhmannian approach, because it promised to lead to very interesting observations. Also, we chose to restrict ourselves to one approach instead of several (integrated or non-integrated), as the latter option would have inevitably meant sacrificing depth for breadth. Logically, these two choices could not but be based on non-scientific criteria; namely personal preferences.[6]

On the basis of the epistemological assumption that all seeing depends on the distinctions chosen,[7] we can say that there are no 'right' or 'wrong' findings, but only findings that are consistent to a greater or lesser extent. That is to say, apart from the 'resistance' of observations with regard to each other,[8] there are no higher principles according to which observations can be evaluated; world knowledge does not exist. The criterion according to which we evaluated our findings was that of internal consistency with other observations that the approach allowed for. In this sense, we are in an analogous situation to the organisation, as described above, which can only select decisions on the basis of other decisions.[9]

According to the second, implicit reading of this book, the concept of identity is used as a primary distinction for observing the potential of Luhmann's

---

[4]   Cf. Luhmann (2000), p. 55.
[5]   For such a procedure, see e.g. Whetten and Godfrey (1998), where organisational identity is studied from a functionalist, interpretivist and postmodern perspective.
[6]   Cf. Kuhn (1962), p. 109 on the impossibility of deciding paradigm debates on a scientific basis.
[7]   The epistemological position expressed here is that of radical constructivism. See Luhmann (1993); Watzlawick (1984).
[8]   Luhmann (2002a).
[9]   This also applies to the present argument about our study, which is only substantiated by our approach. Thus, the argument has a circular structure. This, however, cannot be avoided but merely hidden. On such problems see Luhmann (1992a).

autopoietic perspective, creating its own vision and blindness. On the one side, the focus on identity (and its change) allowed us to demonstrate how Luhmann's approach can conceptualise self-referential and paradoxical phenomena. Apart from that, these exemplary topics provided a criterion for deciding how to present and where to expand the existing theory, especially in the first two chapters. In particular, they led us to explore the concept of organisational interaction and organisational culture. Generally, our choice allowed us to observe a markedly counter-intuitive theory in such a way that it seemed to make sense. On the other side, this choice for observing the theory also created blindness. By choosing another exemplary topic, or by comparing the theory to other theories, one would have been able to observe other aspects of the theory. Again, however, vision with regard to those aspects could only have been achieved by creating blindness elsewhere. From the point of view of the vision we created, the blindness that resulted seemed permissible (but maybe only because we could not see what we could not see – only when we see it will we know what we have missed out!).

We have drawn our distinction. The next distinction has to be drawn by the reader. There are only two possibilities: either confirmation by repetition of the distinction, or cancellation by crossing it.

Bibliography

Abernathy, W., 1978. *The Productivity Dilemma*. Baltimore: John Hopkins University Press.

Adams, T.D., 1990. *Telling Lies in Modern American Autobiography*. Chapel Hill: University of North Carolina Press.

Albert, S., 1998. 'The Definition and Metadefinition of Identity' pp. 1-13 in *Identity in Organizations: Building Theory Through Conversations*, eds. D. Whetten and P.C. Godfrey. Thousand Oaks: Sage.

Albert, S., Ashforth, B.E., and Dutton, J.E., 2000. 'Organizational Identity and Identification: Charting New Waters and Building New Bridges' *Academy of Management Review* 25:13-17.

Albert, S. and Whetten, D.A., 1985. 'Organizational Identity' pp. 263-295 in *Research in Organizational Behavior*, vol. 7, eds. L.L. Cummings and B.M. Straw. Greenwich, CT: JAI Press.

Alvesson, M., 1994. 'Talking in Organizations: Managing Identity and Impression Management in an Advertising Agency' *Organization Studies* 15: 535-563.

Alvesson, M. and Berg, P., 1992. *Corporate Culture and Organizational Symbolism*. Berlin: de Gruyter.

Argyris, C., 1976. 'Leadership, Learning, and Changing the Status Quo' *Organizational Dynamics* 4:29-43.

———, 1992. *On Organizational Learning*. Oxford: Blackwell.

Argyris, C. and Schön, D.A., 1978. *Organizational Learning*. Reading, Mass.: Addison Wesley.

Arndt, M. and Bigelow, B., 2000. 'Presenting Structural Innovation in an Institutional Environment: Hospital's Use of Impression Management' *Administrative Science Quarterly* 45:494-522.

Aschenbach, M., 1996. *Die Reorganisation von Konzernen. Systemtheoretische Beobachtungen des geplanten Wandels*. München: Kirsch.

Ashforth, B.E. and Mael, F., 1989. 'Social Identity Theory and the Organization' *Academy of Management Review* 14:20-39.

———, 1996. 'Organizational Identity and Strategy As a Context for the Individual' pp. 19-64 in *Advances in Strategic Management*, vol. 13, J.A.C. Baum and J.E. Dutton. Greenwich, CT: JAI Press.

Atkinson, M.A., Cuff, E.C., and Lee, J.R., 1978. 'The Recommencement of a Meeting As a Member's Accomplishment' pp. 133-275 in *Studies in the Organization of Conversational Interaction*, ed. J. Schenkein. New York: Academy Press.

Atlan, H., 1979. *Entre le Cristal et la Fumée*. Paris: Seuil.

Axelrod, R., 1976. *The Structure of Decision: The Cognitive Maps of Political Elites*. Princeton: Princeton University Press.

Baecker, D., 1992. 'Die Unterscheidung zwischen Kommunikation und Bewußtsein' pp. 217-268 in *Emergenz: Entstehung von Ordnung, Organisation und Bedeutung*, eds. W. Krohn and G. Küppers. Frankfurt a.M.: Suhrkamp.

————, 1993a. *Die Form des Unternehmens*. Frankfurt a.M.: Suhrkamp.

————, 1993b. 'Im Tunnel' pp. 12-37 in *Kalkül der Form*, ed. D. Baecker. Frankfurt a.M.: Suhrkamp.

————, 1994. *Postheroisches Management: Ein Vademecum*. Berlin: Merve.

————, 1996. 'Kybernetik Zweiter Ordnung' pp. 17-23 in *Wissen und Gewissen: Versuch einer Brücke*, ed. H. Von Foerster. Frankfurt a.M.: Suhrkamp.

————, 1998. 'Einfache Komplexität' pp. 21-50 in *Komplexität Managen: Strategien, Konzepte und Fallbeispiele*, eds. H.W. Ahlemeyer and R. Königswieser. Wiesbaden: Gabler.

————, 1999a. 'Kommunikation im Medium der Information' pp. 174-191 in *Kommunikation, Medien, Macht*, eds. R. Maresch and N. Weber. Frankfurt a.M.: Suhrkamp.

————, 1999b. *Organisation als System*. Frankfurt a.M.: Suhrkamp.

————, 2000. *Die verlernende Organisation*. Unpublished manuscript. Universität Witten/Herdecke.

————, 2001. 'Why Systems?' *Theory, Culture and Society* 18:59-74.

————, forthcoming a. 'Complexity' in *Encyclopedia of Social Theory*, eds. A. Harrington, B.L. Marshall, H.-P. Müller. London: Routledge.

————, forthcoming b. 'Evolutionary Theory' in *Encyclopedia of Social Theory*, eds. A. Harrington, B.L. Marshall, H.-P. Müller. London: Routledge.

Balmer, J.M.T., 1998. 'Corporate Identity and the Advent of Corporate Marketing' *Journal of Marketing Management* 14: 963-996.

Balmer, J.M.T. and Wilson, A., 1998. 'Corporate Identity: There Is More to It Than Meets the Eye' *International Journal of Marketing and Organization* 28:12-31.

Barel, Y., 1989. *La Paradoxe et le Système: Essai sur le Fantastique Social*. Grenoble: Presses Universitaires de Grenoble.

Barney, J., 1986. 'Organizational Culture: Can It Be a Source of Sustained Competitive Advantage' *Academy of Management Review* 11:656-665.

Barney, J.B., Bunderson, S., Foreman, P., Gustafson, L.T., Huff, A.S., Martins, L.L., Reger, R.K., Sarason, Y., and Simpert, J.L., 1998. 'A Strategy Conversation on the Topic of Organizational Identity' pp. 99-170 in *Identity in Organizations: Building Theory Through Conversations*, eds. D. Whetten and P.C. Godfrey. Thousand Oaks: Sage.

Barrett, F.J., Thomas, G., and Hocevar, S.P., 1995. 'The Central Role of Discourse in Large-Scale Change: A Social Construction Perspective' *Journal of Applied Behavioral Science* 31:352-372.

Barry, D. and Elmes, M., 1997. 'Strategy Retold: Toward a Narrative View of Strategic Discourse.' *Academy of Management Review* 22:429-452.

Bart, C.K. and Baetz, M.C., 1998. 'The Relationship Between Mission Statements and Firm Performance: An Exploratory Study' *Journal of Management Studies* 35:823-853.

Bartunek, J.M., 1984. 'Changing Interpretive Schemes and Organizational Restructuring: The Example of a Religious Order' *Administrative Science Quarterly* 29:355-372.

Bateson, G., 1972. *Steps to an Ecology of Mind*. New York: Ballantine.

Beer, S., 1980. 'Preface' pp. 63-72 in *Autopoiesis and Cognition: The Realization of the Living*, eds. H.M. Matuarana and F.G. Varela. Dordrecht: Reidel.

Benoit, W. and Czerwinski, A., 1997. 'A Critical Analysis of USAir's Image Repair Discourse.' *Business Communication Quarterly* 60:38-57.

Birkrigt, K. and Stadler, M., eds., 1993. *Corporate Identity: Grundlagen, Funktionen, Fallbeispiele*. Landsberg a.L.: Verlag Moderne Industrie.

Blau, P.M., 1956. *Bureaucracy in Modern Society*. New York: Random House.

Boden, D., 1994. *The Business of Talk: Organizations in Action*. Cambridge: Polity Press.

Bolina, M., 1999. 'Citizenship and Impression Management: Good Soldiers or Good Actors?' *Academy of Management Review* 24:82-98.

Brinson, S. and Benoit, W., 1996. 'Dow Corning's Image Repair Strategies in the Breast Implant Crisis' *Communication Quarterly* 44:29-41.

Bromley, D.B., 1993. *Reputation, Image, and Impression Management*. Chichester: John Wiley & Sons.

Brown, A., 1997. 'Narcissism, Identity, and Legitimacy' *Academy of Management Review* 22:643-686.

———, 2001. 'Organization Studies and Identity: Towards a Research Agenda' *Human Relations* 54:113-121.

Brown, A. and Jones, M., 2000. 'Honourable Members and Dishonourable Deeds: Sensemaking, Impression Management, and Legitimation in the "Arms to Iraq" Affair' *Human Relations* 53:655-689.

Brown, A. and Starkey, K., 2000. 'Organizational Identity and Learning: A Psychodynamic Perspective.' *Academy of Management Review* 25:102-120.

Brunsson, N. and Olsen, J.P., 1993. *The Reforming Organization*. London: Routledge.

Bryant, J., 1983. 'Hypermaps: A Representation of Perceptions in Conflicts' *Omega* 11:575-586.

Bühler, K., 1934. *Sprachtheorie: Die Dartellungsfunktion der Sprache*. Jena: Fischer.

Buschor, F., 1996. *Baustellen in einer Unternehmung: Das Problem unternehmerischen Wandels jenseits von Restrukturierungen – Resultate einer empirischen Untersuchung*. Bern: Haupt.

Campbell, A. and Yeung, S., 1991. 'Creating a Sense of Mission' *Long Range Planning* 24:10-20.

Campbell, D.T., 1960. 'Blind Variation and Selective Retention in Creative Thought As in Other Knowledge Processes' *Psychological Review* 67:380-400.

———, 1969. 'Variation and Selective Retention in Socio-Cultural Evolution' *General Systems* 14:69-85.

Carter, S. and Deephouse, D., 1998. 'Tough Talk and Soothing Speech: Managing Multiple Reputations' *Working paper*. University of Notre Dame.

Cheney, G., 1983. 'The Rhetoric of Identification and the Study of Organizational Communication' *Quarterly Journal of Speech* 69:143-158.

Cheney, G. and Christensen, L.T., 2001. 'Organizational Identity. Linkages Between Internal and External Communication' pp. 231-269 in *New Handbook of Organizational Communication*, eds. F.M. Jablin and L.L. Putnam. Newbury Park, CA: Sage.

Chia, R., 1994. 'The Concept of Decision: A Deconstructive Analysis' *Journal of Management Studies* 31:781-806.

———, 1999. 'A "Rhizomic" Model of Organizational Change and Transformation: Perspective From a Metaphysics of Change' *British Journal of Management* 10:209-227.

Chreim, S., 2002. 'Reducing Dissonance: Closing the Gap Between Projected and Attributed Identity' pp. 75-90 in *Corporate and Organizational Identities: Integrating Strategy, Marketing, Communication, and Organizational Perspectives*, eds. B. Moigneon and G. Soenen. London: Routledge.

Christensen, L.T., 1995. 'Buffering Organizational Identity in the Marketing Culture' *Organisation Studies* 16:651-672.

Christensen, L.T. and Askegaard, S., 2001. 'Corporate Identity and Corporate Image Revisited: A Semiotic Exercise' *European Journal of Management* 35:292-315.

Christensen, L.T. and Cheney, G., 1994. 'Articulating Identity in an Organizational Age' pp. 222-235 in *Communication Yearbook*, vol. 17, ed. S.A. Deetz. Thousand Oaks: Sage.

Collins, J. and Porras, J.I., 1991. 'Organizational Vision and Visionary Organizations' *California Management Review* 34:30-52.

Cooper, R., 1986. 'Organization/Disorganization' *Social Science Information* 25:299-335.

———, 2006. 'Making Present: Autopoiesis as Human Production' *Organization* 13.

Corley, K.G., 2004. 'Defined by Your Strategy or Culture? Hierarchical Differences in Perceptions of Organizational Identity and Change' *Human Relations* 57:1145-1177.

Corley, K.G. and Gioia, D.A., 2003. 'Semantic Learning as Change Enabler: Relating Organizational Identity and Organizational Learning' pp. 623-638 in *Blackwell Handbook of Organizational Learning and Knowledge Management*, eds. M. Easterby-Smith and M.A. Lyles. Oxford: Blackwell.

———, 2004. 'Identity Ambigity and Change in the Wake of a Corporate Spin-off' *Administrative Science Quarterly* 49:173-208.

Cornelissen, J.P., 2002a. 'On the "Organizational Identity" Metaphor' *British Journal of Management* 13:259-268.

———, 2002b. 'The Merit and Mischief of Metaphor: A Reply to Gioia, Schultz and Corley' *British Journal of Management* 13:277-279.

Coupland, C. and Brown, A., 2004. 'Constructing Organizational Identities on the Web: A Case Study of Royal Dutch/Shell' *Journal of Management Studies* 41:1325-1344.

Czarniawska, B., 1997. *Narrating the Organisation: Dramas of Institutional Identity*. Chicago and London: The University of Chicago Press.

———, forthcoming. 'On Gorgon Sisters: Organizational Action in the Face of Paradox' in *Niklas Luhmann and Organizational Studies*, eds. D. Seidl and K.-H. Becker. Copenhagen: Copenhagen Business School Press.

Czarniawska-Joerges, B., 1992. *Exploring Complex Organizations: A Cultural Perspective*. Thousand Oaks: Sage.

———, 1994. 'Narratives of Individual and Organizational Identities' pp. 193-221 in *Communication Yearbook*, vol. 17, ed. S.A. Deetz. Thousand Oaks: Sage.

———, 1996. 'Autobiographical Acts and Organizational Identities' pp. 157-171 in *Understanding Management*, eds. S. Linstead, R. Grafton-Small, and P. Jeffcut. London: Sage.

David, F.R., 1989. 'How Companies Define Their Mission' *Long Range Planning* 22:90-97.

Davis, S.M. and Lawrence, P.R., 1977. *Matrix*. Reading, Mass.: Addison-Wesley.

Dawkins, R., 1983. 'Universal Darwinism' pp. 403-425 in *Evolution From Molecules to Man*, ed. D.S. Bendall. Cambridge: Cambridge University Press.

Deal, T. and Kennedy, A.A., 1982. *Corporate Culture: The Rites and Rituals of Corporate Life*. Reading, Mass.: Addison-Wesley.

Dennett, D.C., 1995. *Darwin's Dangerous Idea: Evolution and the Meanings of Life*. London: Allen Lane.

Derrida, J., 1968. 'La "Différance".' *Bulletin de la Soçiété Française de Philosophie* 63:73-120.

Down, S. and Taylor, S., 2000. 'Pubs, "Castle Houses", Factories and Offices: The Organisation of Work Space in a Small Firm' *Paper presented at the 16th EGOS Colloquium* (Helsinki, 2-4. July).

Drepper, T., forthcoming. 'Organization and Society' In *Niklas Luhmann and Organization Studies*, eds. D. Seidl and K.-H. Becker. Copenhagen: Copenhagen Business School Press.

Drew, P. and Heritage, J., eds., 1992. *Talk at Work: Interaction in Institutional Settings*. Cambridge, Mass.: Cambridge University Press.

Dukerich, J.M. and Carter, S.M., 1998. 'Mismatched Images: Organizational Responses to Conflicts Between Identity, Shared External Image, and Reputation' *Paper presented at the 14th EGOS Colloquium* (Maastricht, 9-11 July).

Dukerich, J.M., Golden, B.R., and Shortell, S.M., 2002. 'Beauty Is in the Eye of the Beholder: The Impact of Organizational Identification, Identity, and Image on the Cooperative Behaviors of Physicians' *Administrative Science Quarterly* 47:507-533.

Dutton, J.E. and Dukerich, J.M., 1991. 'Keeping an Eye on the Mirror: Image and Identity in Organizational Adaptation' *Academy of Management Journal* 34:517-554.

Dutton, J.E. and Penner, W.J., 1993. 'The Importance of Organizational Identity for Strategic Agenda Building' pp. 89-113 in *Strategic Thinking: Leadership and the Management of Change*, eds. J. Hendry and G. Johnson, with J. Newton. Chichester: John Wiley & Sons.

Dutton, J.E., Dukerich, J.M., and Harquail, C.V., 1994. 'Organizational Images and Member Identification' *Administrative Science Quarterly* 39:239-263.

Elsbach, K.D., 1994. 'Managing Organizational Legitimacy in the California Cattle Industry: The Construction and Effectiveness of Verbal Accounts' *Administrative Science Quarterly* 39:57-88.

————, 2003. 'Organizational Impression Management' *Research in Organizational Behavior* 25:297-332.

Elsbach, K.D. and Glynn, M.A., 1996. 'Believing Your Own "PR": Embedding Identification in Strategic Reputation' *Advances in Strategic Management* 13:65-90.

Elsbach, K.D. and Kramer, R.M., 1996. 'Members' Responses to Organizational Identity Threats: Encountering and Countering the *Business Week* Rankings' *Administrative Science Quarterly* 41:442-472.

Elsbach, K.D., Sutton, R.I., and Principe, K.E., 1998. 'Averted Expected Challenges Through Anticipatory Impression Management: A Study of Hospital Billing' *Organization Science* 9:68-86.

Esposito, E., 1995. 'Illusion Und Virtualität: Kommunikative Veränderungen Der Fiktion' pp. 187-216 in *Soziologie Und Künstliche Intelligenz: Produkte Und Probleme Einer Hochtechnologie*, ed. W. Rammert. Frankfurt a.M.: Campus.

Etzioni, A., 1971. *The Active Society: A Theory of Societal and Political Processes*. London: Collier-Macmillan.

Fiol, C.M., 1991. 'Managing Culture As a Competitive Resource: An Identity-Based View of Sustainable Competitive Advantage' *Journal of Management* 17:191-211.

————, 2002. 'Capitalizing on Paradox: The Role of Language in Transforming Organizational Identities' *Organization Science* 13: 653-666.

Fitzgerald, T., 1988. 'Can Change in Organizational Culture Really Be Managed?' *Organizational Dynamics* 17:5-15.

Fombrun, C., 1996. *Reputation: Realizing Value From Corporate Image*. Boston: Harvard University Press.

Fombrun, C. and Shanley, M., 1990. 'What's in a Name? Reputation Building and Corporate Strategy' *Academy of Management Journal* 33:233-258.

Ford, Jeffrey D. and Backoff, R., 1988. 'Organizational Change In and Out of Dualities and Paradox' pp. 81-121 in *Paradox and Transformation: Toward a Theory of Change in Organization and Management*, eds. R.E. Quinn and K.S. Cameron. Cambridge, Mass.: Ballinger.

Foreman, P. and Whetten, D.A., 2002. 'Members Identification with Multiple-Identity Organizations' *Organization Science* 13:618-35.

Freeman, R.E., 1984. *Strategic Management: A Stakeholder Approach*. Boston: Pitman.

Fuchs, S., 1995. 'The Stratified Order of Gossip' *Soziale Systeme* 1:47-73.

Galbraith, J., 1971. 'Matrix Organisation Design: How to Combine Functional and Project Forms' *Business Horizons* 14:29-40.

Geertz, C., 1973. *The Interpretation of Cultures*. New York: Basic Book.

Gersick, C.J.G., 1991. 'Revolutionary Change Theories: A Multilevel Exploration of the Punctuated Equilibrium Paradigm' *Academy of Management Review* 16:10-36.

Geyer, F., 1992. 'Autopoiesis and Social Systems' *International Journal of General Systems* 21:175-183.

Ghoshall, S and Bartlett, C.A., 1994. 'Linking Organizational Context and Manegerial Action: The Dimensions of Quality of Management' *Academy of Management Review* 15:91-112.

Giddens, A., 1984. *The Constitution of Society: Outline of the Theory of Structuration*. Cambridge: Polity Press.

———, 1991. *Modernity and Self-Identity*. Cambridge: Polity Press.

Ginzel, L.E., Kramer, R.M., and Sutton, R.I., 1992. 'Organizational Impression Management As a Reciprocal Influence Process: The Neglected Role of Organizational Audience' pp. 227-266 in *Research in Organizational Behavior*, vol. 15, eds. L.L. Cummings and B.M. Staw. Greenwich, CT: JAI Press.

Gioia, D.A., 1998. 'From Individual to Organizational Identity' pp. 17-31 in *Identity in Organizations: Building Theory Through Conversations*, eds. D. Whetten and P.C. Godfrey. Thousand Oaks: Sage.

Gioia, D.A. and Poole, P.P., 1984. 'Scripts in Organizational Behavior' *Academy of Management Review* 9:449-459.

Gioia, D.A., Schultz, M., and Corley, K.G., 2000. 'Organizational Identity, Image and Adaptive Instability' *Academy of Management Review* 25:63-81.

———, 2002a. 'On Celebrating the Organizational Identity Metaphor: A Rejoinder to Cornelissen' *British Journal of Management* 13: 269-275.

———, 2002b. 'Metaphorical Shadow Boxing: A Response to Cornelissen's Reply to Our Rejoinder' *British Journal of Management* 13:281.

Gioia, D.A. and Thomas, J.B., 1996. 'Identity, Image and Issue Interpretation: Sensemaking During Strategic Change in Academia' *Administrative Science Quarterly* 41:370-403.

Glassman, R.B., 1973. 'Persistence and Loose Coupling in Living Systems' *Behavioral Science* 18:83-98.

Glynn, M.A., 2000. 'When Cymbals Become Symbols: Conflict Over Organizational Identity Within a Symphony Orchestra' *Organization Science* 11:285-298.

Glynn, M.A. and Abzug, R., 2002. 'Institutional Identity: Symbolic Isomorphism and Organizational Names' *Academy of Management Journal* 45:267-280.

Goffman, E., 1959. *The Presentation of Self in Everyday Life*. Garden City: Doubleday Anchor.

Golden-Biddle, K. and Rao, H., 1997. 'Breaches in the Boardroom: Organizational Identity and Conflict of Commitment in a Non-Profit Organization' *Organization Science* 8:593-611.

Goleman, D., 1985. *Vital Lies, Simple Truths: The Psychology of Self-Deception*. New York: Simon & Schuster.

Greenwood, R. and Hinings, C.R., 1993. 'Understanding Strategic Change: The Contribution of Archetypes' *Academy of Management Journal* 36:1052-1081.

Gregory, K.L., 1983. 'Native-View Paradigms: Multiple Cultures and Culture Conflicts in Organizations' *Administrative Science Quarterly* 28:359-376.

Grinyer, P.H. and J.-C. Spender, 1979. 'Recipes, Crises, and Adaptation in Mature Business' *International Studies of Management and Organization* 9:113-133.

Gustafson, L. and Reger, R.L., 1995. 'Using Organizational Identity to Achieve Stability and Change in High Velocity Environments' *Paper presented at the Academy of Management Meeting* (Vancouver, August).

Habermas, J., 1987. *The Theory of Communicative Action*. Cambridge: Polity.

Hahn, A., 1987. 'Sinn Und Sinnlosigkeit' pp. 155-164 in *Sinn, Kommunikation Und Soziale Differenzierung: Beiträge Zu Luhmanns Theorie Sozialer Systeme*, eds. H. Haferkamp and M. Schmid. Frankfurt a.M.: Suhrkamp.

Hannan, M.T. and Freeman, J., 1984. 'Structural Inertia and Organizational Change' *American Sociological Review* 49:149-164.

———, 1989. *Organizational Ecology*. Cambridge: Harvard University Press.

Hardy, C., Lawrence, T.B., and Grant, D., 2005. 'Discourse and Collaboration: The Role of Conversations and Collective Identity' *Academy of Management Review* 30: 58-77.

Haslam, S.A., Postmes, T., and Ellemers, N., 2003. 'More Than a Metaphor: Organizational Identity Makes Organizational Life Possible' *British Journal of Management* 14:357-369.

Hatch, M.J., 1997. *Organization Theory: Modern, Symbolic and Postmodern Perspectives*. Oxford: Oxford University Press.

Hatch, M.J. and Schultz, M., 2002. 'The Dynamics of Organizational Identity' *Human Relations* 55:989-1018.

Hearit, K., 1996. 'The Use of Counter-Attack in Apologetic Public Relation Crises: The Case of General Motors and Dateline NBC' *Public Relations Review* 22:233-248.

Hedberg, B.L.T. and Jönsson, S.A., 1977. 'Strategy Formulation As a Discontinuous Process' *International Studies of Management and Organization* 7:89-109.

Heider, F., 1926. 'Ding und Medium' *Symposion. Philosophische Zeitschrift für Forschung und Aussprache* 1:109-157.

———, 1959. 'Thing and Medium' *Psychological Issues* 1:1-34.

Heinen, E., 1981. 'Identität: Ein bisher vernachlässigtes Element des Zielsystems der Unternehmung' pp. 125-143 in *Wirtschaftstheorie und Wirtschaftspolitik: Gedenkschrift für Erich Preiser*, eds. W.J. Mückl and A.E. Ott. Passau: Pasavia Universitätsverlag.

Hendry, J. and Seidl, D., 2003. 'The Structure and Significance of Strategic Episodes: Social Systems Theory and the Routine Practices of Strategic Change' *Journal of Management Studies* 40: 175-196.

Herbst, P.G., 1976. *Alternatives to Hierarchies*. Leiden: Martinus Nijhoff.

Hernes, T. and Bakken, T., 2003. 'Implications of Self-Reference: Niklas Luhmann's Autopoiesis and Organization Theory' *Organization Studies* 24:1511-1535.

Hodgson, G., 1993. *Economics and Evolution: Bringing Life Back into Economics*. Cambridge: Polity.

Hogg, M.A. and Terry, D.J., 2000. 'Social Identity and Self-Categorization Processes in Organizational Contexts' *Academy of Management Review* 25:121-140.

Holmes, S., 1987. 'Poesie der Indifferenz' pp. 15-45 in *Theorie als Passion: Niklas Luhmann zum Geburtstag*, eds. D. Baecker, J. Markowitz, R. Stichweh, H. Tyrell, and H. Willke. Frankfurt a.M.: Suhrkamp.

————, 1989. 'The Permanent Structure of Antiliberal Thought' pp. 227-253 in *Liberalism and the Moral Life*, ed. N. Rosenblum. Cambridge, Mass.: Harvard University Press.

————, 1993. *The Anatomy of Antiliberalism*. Cambridge, Mass.: Harvard University Press.

Horvath, L. and Glynn, M.A., 1993. *Owning a Little Piece of Rock: Employee Ownership, Organizational Identification, and Self-Management in Worker Cooperatives*. Unpublished manuscript. Yale University.

Humphreys, M. and Brown, A.D., 2002. 'Narratives of Organizational Identity and Identification: A Case Study of Hegemony and Resistance' *Organization Studies* 23:421-447.

Husserl, E., 1948. *Erfahrung und Urteil: Untersuchungen zur Genealogie der Logik*. Hamburg: Claassen & Goverts.

————, 1950. 'Ideen zu einer reinen Phänomenologie und phänomenologischen Philosophie.' *Husserliana*, vol. 3, The Hague: Nijhoff

Jabri, M., 2004. 'Change as Shifting Identities: A Dialogic Perspective' *Journal of Organizational Change Management* 17:566-576.

Jensen, M.C. and Mecklin, W.H., 1976. 'Theory of the Firm: Managerial Behavior, Agency Costs and Ownership Structure' *Journal of Financial Economics* 3:305-360.

Jefkins, F., 1989. 'Public Relations' pp. 617-627 in *Marketing Handbook*, ed. M.J. Thomas. Aldershot: Gower.

Johnson, G., 1987. *Strategic Change and the Management Process*. Oxford: Basil Blackwell.

Kärreman, D. and Alvesson, M., 2004. 'Cages in Tandem: Management Control, Social Identity, and Identification in a Knowledge-Intensive Firm' *Organization* 11:149-166.

Kibéd, M.V. von, and Matzke, R., 1993. 'Motive und Grundgedanken der "Gesetze der Form"' pp. 58-85 in *Kalkül der Form*, ed. D. Baecker. Frankfurt a.M.: Suhrkamp.

Kieser, A., 1998. 'Über die allmähliche Verfertigung der Organisation beim Reden' *Industrielle Beziehungen* 5:45-75.

Kieserling, A., 1994a. 'Interaktion in Organisationen' pp. 168-182 in *Die Verwaltung des politischen Systems: Neue systemtheoretische Zugriffe auf ein altes Thema*, eds. K. Dammann, D. Grunow, and K.P. Japp. Opladen: Westdeutscher Verlag.

————, 1994b. *Organisationssoziologie und Unternehmensberatung: Sechs Lehrvorträge*. Unpublished Manuscript. Universität Bielefeld.

————, 1999. *Kommunikation unter Anwesenden: Studien über Interaktionssysteme*. Frankfurt a.M.: Suhrkamp.

Kimberly, J.R., 1987. 'The Study of Organization: Toward a Biographical Perspective' pp. 223-237 in *Handbook of Organizational Behavior*, ed. J.W. Lorsch. Englewood Cliffs, NY: Prentice Hall.

Kirsch, W., 1970-1971. *Entscheidungsprozesse*. Wiesbaden: Gabler.

———, 1988. *Die Handhabung von Entscheidungsproblemen: Einführung in die Theorie der Entscheidungsprozesse*. München: Kirsch.

———, 1991. *Unternehmenspolitik und strategische Unternehmensführung*. München: Kirsch.

———, 1992. *Kommunikatives Handeln, Autopoiese, Rationalität: Sondierungen zu einer evolutionären Führungslehre*. München: Kirsch.

———, 1996. *Wegweiser zur Konstruktion einer evolutionären Theorie der strategischen Führung: Kapitel eines Theorieprojektes*. München: Kirsch.

Kirsch, W., Esser, W., and Gabele, E., 1979. *Das Management des geplanten Wandels*. Stuttgart: Poeschel.

Kirsch, W. and Meffert, H., 1970. *Organisationstheorien und Betriebswirtschaftslehre*. Wiesbaden: Gabler.

Kirsch, W. and Zu Knyphausen, D., 1991. 'Unternehmungen als "autopoietische" Systeme?' pp. 75-101 in *Managementforschung I*, eds. W.H. Staehle and J. Sydow. Berlin: de Gruyter.

Klemm, M., Sanderson, S., and Luffman, G., 1991. 'Mission Statements: Selling Corporate Values to Employees' *Long Range Planning* 24:73-78.

Korzybski, A., 1958. *Science and Sanity*. Lakeville, CT: International Non-aristotelian Library Publishing Co.

Kuhn, T.S., 1962. *The Structure of Scientific Revolutions*. Chicago: University of Chicago Press.

Kurland, N.B. and Pelled, L.H., 2000. 'Passing the Word: Toward a Model of Gossip and Power in the Workplace' *Academy of Management Review* 25:428-438.

La Porte, T.R., 1975. *Organized Social Complexity: Challenge to Politics and Policy*. Princeton: Princeton University Press.

Linstead, S. and Grafton-Small, R., 1992. 'On Reading Organizational Culture' *Organization Studies* 13:331-355.

Löfgren, L., 1977. 'Complexity Descriptions of Systems: A Foundational Study' *International Journal of General Systems* 3:197-214.

Luhmann, N., 1975. 'Allgemeine Theorie organisierter Sozialsysteme' pp. 39-50 in *Soziologische Aufklärung 2: Aufsätze zur Theorie der Gesellschaft*, ed. N. Luhmann. Opladen: Westdeutscher Verlag.

———, 1976. *Funktionen und Folgen formaler Organisationen*. Berlin: Duncker & Humblot.

———, 1980. 'Komplexität' pp. 1064-1070 in *Handwörterbuch der Organisation*, ed. E. Grochla. Stuttgart: C.E. Poeschel.

———, 1984. 'Soziologische Aspekte des Entscheidungsverhaltens' *Die Betriebswirtschaft* 44:591-603.

———, 1986. 'The Autopoiesis of Social Systems' pp. 172-192 in *Sociocybernetic Paradoxes: Observation, Control and Evolution of Self-Steering Systems*, eds. F. Geyer and J. Van d. Zeuwen. London: Sage.

————, 1987. 'Tautologie und Paradoxie in den Selbstbeschreibungen der modernen Gesellschaft' *Zeitschrift für Soziologie* 16:161-174.

————, 1988. 'Frauen, Männer und George Spencer Brown' *Zeitschrift für Soziologie* 17:47-71.

————, 1990a. 'Anfang und Ende: Probleme einer Unterscheidung' pp. 11-23 in *Zwischen Anfang und Ende: Fragen an die Pädagogik*, eds. N. Luhmann and K.E. Schorr. Frankfurt a.M.: Suhrkamp.

————, 1990b. 'Meaning As Sociology's Basic Concept' pp. 21-79 in *Essays on Self-Reference*, ed. N. Luhmann. New York: Columbia University Press.

————, 1991a. *Soziologische Aufklärung 1: Aufsätze zur Theorie sozialer Systeme*. Opladen: Westdeutscher Verlag.

————, 1991b. *Soziologische Aufklärung 2: Aufsätze zur Theorie der Gesellschaft*. Opladen: Westdeutscher Verlag.

————, 1991c. 'Wie lassen sich latente Strukturen beobachten?' pp. 61-74 in *Das Auge des Betrachters: Beiträge zum Konstruktivismus*, eds. P. Watzlawick and P. Krieg. München: Piper.

————, 1992a. *Die Wissenschaft der Gesellschaft*. Frankfurt a.M.: Suhrkamp.

————, 1992b. 'Organisation' pp. 165-185 in *Rationalität, Macht und Spiele in Organisationen*, eds. W. Küpper and G. Ortmann. Opladen: Westdeutscher Verlag.

————, 1993a. *Soziologische Aufklärung 3: Soziales System, Gesellschaft, Organisation*. Opladen: Westdeutscher Verlag.

————, 1993b. *Soziologische Aufklärung 5: Konstruktivistische Perspektiven*. Opladen: Westdeutscher Verlag.

————, 1993c. *Gesellschaftsstruktur und Semantik 2: Studien zur Wissenssoziologie der modernen Gesellschaft*. Frankfurt a.M.: Suhrkamp.

————, 1993d. *Gesellschaftsstruktur und Semantik 3: Studien zur Wissenssoziologie der modernen Gesellschaft*. Frankfurt a.M.: Suhrkamp.

————, 1993e. 'Die Paradoxie des Entscheidens' *Verwaltungs-Archiv: Zeitschrift für Verwaltungslehre, Verwaltungsrecht und Verwaltungspolitik* 84:287-310.

————, 1993f. 'Observing Re-Entries' *Graduate Faculty Philosophy Journal* 16:485-498.

————, 1994. *Die Wirtschaft der Gesellschaft*. Frankfurt a.M.: Suhrkamp.

————, 1995a. *Gesellschaftsstruktur und Semantik 4: Studien zur Wissenssoziologie der modernen Gesellschaft*. Frankfurt a.M.: Suhrkamp.

————, 1995b. *Social Systems*. Stanford: Stanford University Press.

————, 1995c. *Soziologische Aufklärung 6: Die Soziologie und der Mensch*. Opladen: Westdeutscher Verlag.

————, 1996. 'Complexity, Structural Contingencies and Value Conflicts' pp. 59-71 in *Detraditionalization*, eds. P. Heelas, S. Lash, and P. Morris. Oxford: Blackwell.

————, 1997. *Die Gesellschaft der Gesellschaft*. Frankfurt a.M.: Suhrkamp.

————, 1998a. *Die Kunst der Gesellschaft*. Frankfurt a.M.: Suhrkamp.

————, 1998b. *Observations of Modernity*. Stanford, CA: Stanford University Press.

————, 1999. 'Sign As Form' pp. 46-63 in *Problems of Form*, ed. D. Baecker. Stanford, CA: Stanford University Press.

————, 2000. *Organisation und Entscheidung*. Opladen: Westdeutscher Verlag.

————, 2002. 'How Can the Mind Participate in Communication?' pp. 169-184 in *Theories of Distinction. Redescribing the Descriptions of Modernity*, ed. N. Luhmann. Stanford: Stanford University Press.

March, J.G., ed. 1989. *Decisions and Organizations*. Oxford: Basil Blackwell.

March, J.G. and Olsen, J.P., 1975. *Choice Situations in Loosely Coupled Worlds*. Unpublished Manuscript. Stanford University.

March, J.G. and Olsen, J.P., eds. 1976. *Ambiguity and Choice in Organizations*. Bergen: Universitetsforlaget.

March, J.G. and Sevón, G., 1989. 'Gossip, Information and Decision-Making' pp. 429-442 in *Decision and Organization*, ed. J.G. March. Oxford: Basil Blackwell.

March, J.G. and Simon, H.A., 1958. *Organizations*. New York: Wiley.

Margulies, W.P., 1977. 'Make Most of Your Corporate Identity – A Well-Managed Programm Involves More Than Just Changing a Name' *Harvard Business Review* 55:66-74.

Martin, J., 1992. *Cultures in Organizations: Three Perspectives*. Oxford: Oxford University Press.

Martin, J. and Frost, P., 1996. 'The Organizational Culture War Games: A Struggle for Intellectual Dominance' pp. 599-621 in *Handbook of Organization Studies*, eds. S.R. Clegg, C. Hardy, and W.R. Nord. London: Sage.

Maruyama, M., 1963. 'The Second Cybernetics: Deviation Amplifying Mutual Causes Processes' *American Scientist* 51:164-179.

Marziliano, N., 1998. 'Managing the Corporate Image and Identity: A Borderline Between Fiction and Reality' *International Studies of Management and Organization* 28:3-11.

Maturana, H., 1978. 'Biology of Language: The Epistemology of Reality' pp. 27-63 in *Psychology and Biology of Language and Thought: Essays in Honour of Eric Lenneberg*, ed. G. Millar and E. Lenneberg. New York: Academic Press.

————, 1980a. 'Autopoiesis: Reproduction, Heredity and Evolution' pp. 45-79 in *Autopoiesis, Dissipative Structures and Spontaneous Orders*, ed. M. Zeleny. Boulder: Westview Press.

————, 1980b. 'Introduction' pp. xi-xxx in *Autopoiesis and Cognition: The Realization of the Living*, eds. H.R. Maturana and F. Varela. Dordrecht: Reidel.

————, 1980c. 'Man and Society' pp. 11-31 in *Autopoietic Systems in the Social Sciences*, ed. F. Bensler, P. Hejl, and W. Köck. Frankfurt a.M.: Campus.

————, 1988. 'Reality: The Search for Objectivity or the Quest for a Compelling Argument' *Irish Journal of Psychology* 9:25-82.

Maturana, H. and Varela, F., 1980. *Autopoiesis and Cognition: The Realization of the Living*. Dordrecht: Reidel.

————, 1992. *The Tree of Knowledge: The Biological Roots of Understanding*. Boston: Shambhala.

Meindl, J.R., 1990. 'On Leadership: An Alternative to Conventional Wisdom' pp. 159-204 in *Research in Organizational Behavior*, vol. 12, eds. B.M. Staw and L.L. Cummings. Greenwich, CT: JAI Press.

Merton, R.K., 1957. *Social Theory and Social Structure*. Glencoe, Ill.: Free Press.

Messick, D.M. and Mackie, D.M., 1989. 'Intergroup Relations' pp. 45-81 in *Annual Review of Psychology*, vol. 40, eds. M.R. Rosenzweig and L.W. Porter. Palo Alto, CA: Annual Reviews.

Meyer, E., 1990. 'Der Unterschied, der eine Umgebung schafft' pp. 110-122 in *Im Netz der Systeme*, ed. ars electronica. Berlin: Merve.

Meyer, J.P., Bartunek, J.M., and Lacey, C.A., 2002. 'Identity Change and Stability in Organizational Groups: A Longitudinal Investigation' *The International Journal of Organizational Analysis* 10:4-29.

Meyer, J.W. and Rowan, B., 1977. 'Institutionalized Organizations: Formal Structure As Myth and Ceremony' *American Journal of Sociology* 83:340-363.

Miller, A. and Dess, G.G., 1996. *Strategic Management*. New York: McGraw Hill.

Mingers, J., 1992. 'The Problems of Social Autopoiesis' *International Journal of General Systems* 21:229-236.

———, 1995a. *Self-Producing Systems: Implications and Applications of Autopoiesis*. New York: Plenum.

———, 1995b. 'A Comparison of Maturana's Autopoietic Social Theory and Giddens' Theory of Structuration' *Warwick Business School Research Papers*.

———, 2002. 'Can Social Systems be Autopoietic? Assessing Luhmann's Social Theory' *Sociological Review* 50:278-299.

———, 2003. 'Observing Organizations: An Evaluation of Luhmann's Theory of Organizations' pp. 103-122 in *Autopoietic Organization Theory. Drawing on Niklas Luhmann's Social Systems Perspective*, eds. T. Hernes and T. Bakken. Copenhagen: Copenhagen Business School Press.

———, 2004. 'Can Social Systems be Autopoietic? Bhaskar's and Giddens' Social Theories' *Journal for the Theory of Social Behaviour* 34:403-426.

Mintzberg, H., 1978. 'Patterns in Strategy Formation' *Management Science* 24:934-948.

———, 1980. *The Nature of Managerial Work*. Englewood Cliffs, NJ: Prentice Hall.

Mintzberg, H. and Waters, J.A., 1990. 'Studying Deciding: An Exchange of Views Between Mintzberg and Waters, Pettigrew, and Butler' *Organization Studies* 11:1-16.

Morgan, G., 1997. *Images of Organization*. Thousand Oaks, CA: Sage.

Nelson, R.R. and Winter, S.G., 1982. *An Evolutionary Theory of Economic Change*. Cambridge, Mass.: Belknap Press.

Nkomo, S.M. and Cox Jr., T., 1996. 'Diverse Identities in Organizations' pp. 338-356 in *Handbook of Organization Studies*, eds. S.R. Clegg, C. Hardy, and W.R. Nord. London: Sage.

Noss, C. and Schreyögg, G., 1997. 'The Nature of Organizational Change: Organizational Development and Beyond' *Paper presented at the 13th EGOS Colloquium* (Budapest, 3-5 July).

Olins, W., 1990. *The Wolff Olins Guide to Corporate Identity*. London: The Design Council.

Ort, N., 1998. 'Sinn als Medium und Form: Ein Beitrag zur Begriffsklärung in Luhmanns Theoriedesign' *Soziale Systeme* 4:207-218.

Ortmann, G. and Sydow, J., 1999. 'Grenzmanagement in Unternehmungsnetzwerken: Theoretische Zugänge' *Die Betriebswirtschaft* 59:205-220.

Orton, J.D. and Weick, K.E., 1990. 'Loosely Coupled Systems: A Reconceptualisation' *Academy of Management Review* 15:203-223.

Osborn, R.N. and Ashforth, B.E., 1990. 'Investigating the Challenges to Senior Leadership in Complex, High-Risk Technologies' *Leadership Quarterly* 1:147-163.

Ouchi, W.G., 1981. *Theory Z: How American Business Can Meet the Japanese Challenge*. Reading, Mass.: Addison-Wesley.

Palmer, R., Welker, R., Campbell, T., and Magner, N., 2001. 'Examining the Impression Management Orientation of Managers' *Journal of Managerial Psychology* 16:35-49.

Parsons, T., 1960. *Structure and Process in Modern Societies*. New York: Free Press.

Peacock, L.J. and Holland, D.C., 1993. 'The Narrated Self: Life Stories in Process' *Ethos* 21:367-383.

Pedler, M., Boydell, T., and Burgeone, J.G., 1991. *The Learning Company: A Strategy for Sustainable Development*. New York: McGraw-Hill.

Peters, J.T. and Waterman, R.H., 1982. *In Search of Excellence: Lessons From America's Best-Run Companies*. New York: Harper and Row.

Peters, T., 1987. *Thriving on Chaos*. New York: Alfred A. Knopf.

Pettigrew, A.M., 1979. 'On Studying Organisational Cultures' *Administrative Science Quarterly* 24:570-581.

———, 1985. *The Awakening Giant: Continuity and Change at ICI*. Oxford: Basil Blackwell.

Phillips, N. and Hardy, C., 1997. 'Managing Multiple Identity: Discourse, Legitimacy and Resources in the UK Refugee System' *Organization* 4: 159-185.

Porac, J.F. and Thomas, H., 1994. 'Cognitive Categorization and Subjective Rivalry Among Retailers in a Small City' *Journal of Applied Psychology* 79:54-66.

Prahalad, C.K. and Hamel, G., 1990. 'The Core Competence of the Corporation' *Harvard Business Review*:79-91.

Prahalad, C.K. and Bettis, R.A., 1986. 'The Dominant Logic: A New Linkage Between Diversity and Performance' *Strategic Management Journal* 7:485-501.

Pratt, M.G. and Foreman, P.O., 2000. 'Classifying Managerial Responses to Multiple Organizational Identities' *Academy of Management Review* 25:18-42.

Quinn, R.E. and Cameron, K.S., eds., 1988. *Paradox and Transformation: Toward a Theory of Change in Organization and Management*. Cambridge, Mass.: Ballinger.

Rajagopalan, N. and Spreitzer, G., 1996. 'Toward a Theory of Strategic Change: A Multi-Lens Perspective and Integrative Framework' *Academy of Management Review* 22:48-79.

Ravasi, D. and Van Recom, J., 2003. 'Key Issues in Organizational Identity and Identification Theory' *Corporate Reputation Review* 6:118-132.

Reinhard, W., 1982. *Die Identität von Organisationen*. Unpublished PhD thesis. Ludwig-Maximilians-Universität. München.

Rindova, V.P. and Fombrun, C.J., 1998. 'The Eye of the Beholder: The Role of Corporate Reputation in Defining Organizational Identity' pp. 62-66 in *Identity in Organizations: Building Theory Through Conversations*, eds. D.A. Whetten and P.C. Godfrey. Thousand Oaks: Sage.

Rindova, V.P. and Schultz, M., 1998. 'Identity Within and Identity Without: Lessons From Corporate and Organisational Identity' pp. 46-52 in *Identity in Organizations: Building Theory Through Conversations*, eds. D.A. Whetten and P.C. Godfrey. Thousand Oaks: Sage.

Robb, F., 1989. 'Cybernetics and Suprahuman Autopoietic Systems' *Systems Practice* 2:47-74.

———, 1991. 'Accounting – a Virtual Autopoietic System?' *System Practice* 4:215-235.

Rodríguez, D.M., 1991. *Diagnóstico Organizacional: Elementos para su Estudio*. Santiago di Chile: Publicidad Universitaria.

Rose, S., 1970. *The Chemistry of Life*. London: Pelican.

Rüegg-Stürm, J., 1998a. 'Neuere Systemtheorie und Unternehmerischer Wandel: Skizze einer systemisch-konstruktivistischen "Theory of the Firm"' *Die Unternehmung* 52:3-17.

———, 1998b. 'Implikationen einer systemisch-konstruktivistischen "Theory of the Firm" für das Management von tiefgreifenden Veränderungsprozessen' *Die Unternehmung* 52:81-89.

Ruesch, J. and Bateson, G., 1951. *Communication: The Social Matrix of Psychiatry*. New York: Norton & Co.

Sandelands, L. and Stablein, R.E., 1987. 'The Concept of Organization Mind' pp. 135-162 in *Research in the Sociology of Organizations*, eds. S. Bacharach and N. DiTomaso. Greenwich, CT: JAI Press.

Schein, E.H., 1984. 'Coming to a New Awareness of Organizational Culture' *Sloan Management Review* 25:3-16.

———, 1985. *Organisational Culture and Leadership*. San Francisco: Jossey-Bass.

Schreyögg, G., 1992. 'Organisationsidentität' pp. 1488-1498 in *Handwörterbuch des Personalwesens*, eds. E. Gaugler and W. Weber. Stuttgart: Poeschel.

Schreyögg, G. and Noss, C., 1994. 'Hat sich das Organisieren überlebt?: Grundfragen der Unternehmenssteuerung in neuem Licht' *Die Unternehmung* 1:17-33.

———, 1995. 'Organisatorischer Wandel: Von der Organisationsentwicklung zur lernenden Organisation' *Die Betriebswirtschaft* 55:169-185.

Schultz, M., Hatch, M.J., and Larsen, M.H., 2000. *The Expressive Organization. Linking Identity, Reputation, and the Corporate Brand.* Oxford: Oxford University Press.

Schulz, M., 1994. *On Studying Organizational Cultures: Diagnosis and Understanding.* Berlin: De Gruyter.

Schulze-Bönig, M. and Unverferth, H.-J., 1986. 'Rationalität in komplexen Sozialsystemen: Zur Entwicklung des Rationalitätsbegriffs in der Systemtheorie Niklas Luhmanns' pp. 14-90 in *System und Selbstproduktion: Zur Erschließung eines neuen Paradigmas in den Sozialwissenschaften*, ed. H.-J. Unverferth. Frankfurt a.M.: Lang.

Schwartzman, H.B., 1986. 'The Meeting As a Neglected Social Form of Organizational Studies' pp. 233-258 in *Research in Organizational Behavior*, vol. 8, eds. B.M. Staw and L.L. Cummings. Greenwich, CT: JAI Press.

———, 1987. 'The Significance of Meetings in an American Health Care Centre' *American Ethnologist* 14:271-294.

———, 1989. *The Meeting – Gatherings in Organizations and Communities.* New York: Plenum Press.

Scott, S.G. and Lane, V.R., 2000. 'A Stakeholder Approach to Organizational Identity' *Academy of Management Review* 25:43-62.

Seidl, D., 2003a. 'Organizational Identity in Luhmann's Theory of Social Systems' pp. 123-150 in *Autopoietic Organization Theory. Drawing on Niklas Luhmann's Social Systems Perspective*, eds. T. Hernes and T. Bakken. Copenhagen: Copenhagen Business School Press.

Seidl, D., 2003b. 'Metaphorical Self-descriptions of Organizations' pp. 165-182 in *Communications in Organisations. Structures and Practices*, eds. A. Müller and A. Kieser. New York: Peter Lang.

Seidl, D., 2004. 'The Role of General Strategy Concepts in the Practice of Strategy'. *Munich Business Research Paper*, No. 2003-10.

Seidl, D., forthcoming a. 'Basic Concepts of Luhmann's Theory of Social Systems' In *Niklas Luhmann and Organization Studies*, eds. D. Seidl and K.-H. Becker. Copenhagen: CBS Press.

Seidl, D., forthcoming b. 'Organization and Interaction' In *Niklas Luhmann and Organization Studies*, eds. D. Seidl and K.-H. Becker. Copenhagen: CBS Press.

Seidl, D. and Becker, K.-H., 2006. 'Organizations as Distinction Generating and Processing Systems: Niklas Luhmann's Contribution to Organization Studies' *Organization* 13.

Selznick, P., 1943. 'An Approach to a Theory of Bureaucracy' *American Sociological Review* 8:47-54.

Shannon, C.E. and Weaver, W., 1949. *The Mathematical Theory of Communication.* Urbana, Ill.: Illinois University Press.

Sills, D.S., 1957. *The Volunteers.* Glencoe, Ill.: Free Press.

Simon, F., 1993a. *Unterschiede, die Unterschiede machen: Klinische Epistemologie. Grundlage einer systemischen Psychiatrie und Psychosomatik.* Frankfurt a.M.: Suhrkamp.

———, 1993b. 'Mathematik und Erkenntnis: *Eine* Möglichkeit die "Laws of Form" zu lesen' pp. 38-57 in *Kalkül der Form*, ed. D. Baecker. Frankfurt a.M.: Suhrkamp.

Simon, H.A., 1957. *Models of Man – Social and Rational: Mathematical Essays on Rational Human Behavior in a Social Setting*. New York: Wiley & Son.

———, 1971. 'Decision Making and Organizational Design' pp. 189-212 in *Organization Theory: Selected Readings*, ed. D.S. Pugh. Harmondsworth: Penguin.

Simon, H.A., Smithburg, D.W., and Thompson, V.A., 1950. *Public Administration*. New York: Wiley & Son.

Skyttner, L., 1996. *General Systems Theory: An Introduction*. Houndsmill: Macmillan.

Slatter, S., 1984. *Corporate Recovery*. London: Penguin.

Smircich, L., 1983. 'Organizations As Shared Meanings' pp. 55-65 in *Organizational Symbolism*, eds. L.R. Pondy, P. Frost, G. Morgan, and T. Dandridge. Greenwich, CT: JAI Press.

Smircich, L., 1983. 'Concept of Culture and Organizational Analysis' *Administrative Science Quarterly* 28:339-358.

Spencer Brown, G., 1979. *The Laws of Form*. New York: E.P. Dutton.

Tacke, V., 1999. 'Wirtschaftsorganisationen als Reflexionsproblem: Zum Verhältnis von Neuem Institutionalismus und Systemtheorie' *Soziale Systeme* 5:55-81.

Tafertshofer, A., 1982. 'Corporate Identity: Magische Formel als Unternehmensideologie' *Die Unternehmung* 1:11-25.

Tajfel, H., 1972. 'La Categorisation Social' pp. 272-302 in *Introduction a la Psychologie Social*, vol. 1, ed. S. Moscovici. Paris: Larousse.

Tajfel, H. and Turner, J.C., 1986. 'The Social Identity Theory of Intergroup Behavior' pp. 7-24 in *Psychology of Intergroup Relations*, eds. S. Worchel and W.G. Austin. Chicago: Nelson-Hall.

Taylor, F.W., 1947. *Scientific Management*. New York: Harper & Brothers.

Tedeschi, J.T., 1981. *Impression Management Theory and Social Psychological Research*. New York: Academic Press.

Tedeschi, J.T. and Melburg, V., 1984. 'Impression Management and Influence in the Organization' pp. 31-58 in *Research in the Sociology of Organizations*, vol. 3, eds. S.B. Bacharach and E.J. Lawler. Greenwich, CT: JAI Press.

Teubner, G., 1987a. 'Episodenverknüpfung: Zur Steigerung von Selbstreferenz im Recht' pp. 423-446 in *Theorie als Passion*, eds. D. Baecker, J. Markowitz, R. Stichweh, H. Tyrell, and H. Willke. Frankfurt a.M.: Suhrkamp.

———, 1987b. 'Hyperzyklus in Recht und Organisation: Zum Verhältnis von Selbstbeobachtung, Selbstkonstitution und Autopoiese' pp. 89-128 in *Sinn, Kommunikation und soziale Differenzierung: Beiträge zu Luhmanns Theorie sozialer Systeme*, eds. H. Haferkamp and M. Schmid. Frankfurt a.M.: Suhrkamp.

Theis, A.M., 1994. *Organisationskommunikation: Theoretische Grundlagen und empirische Forschungen*. Opladen: Westdeutscher Verlag.

Thompson, J.D., 1967. *Organizations in Action: Social Science Bases of Administrative Theory*. New York: McGraw-Hill.

Trux, W., G. Müller, and Kirsch, W., 1984. *Das Management strategischer Programme*. München: Kirsch.

Turner, J.C., 1985. 'Social Categorization and Self-Concept: A Social Cognitive Theory of Group Behaviour' *Adv. in Group Process* 2:77-122.

Turner, J.C., Hogg, M.A., Oakes, P.J., and Reicher, S.D.W.M.S., 1987. *Rediscovering the Social Group: A Self-Categorization Theory*. Oxford: Basil Blackwell.

Turner, J.C. and Oakes, P.J., 1989. 'Self-Categorization Theory and Social Influence' pp. 233-275 in *The Psychology of Group Influence*, ed. P.B. Paulus. Hillsdale: Erlbaum.

Turner, J.C., Oakes, P.J., Haslam, S.A., and McGarty, C., 1994. 'Self and Collective: Cognition and Social Context' *Personality and Social Psychology Bulletin* 20:454-463.

Van Riel, C.B. and Balmer, J.M.T., 1997. 'Corporate Identity: the Concept, Its Measurement, and Management' *European Journal of Marketing* 31:341-355.

Varela, F., 1975. 'A Calculus for Self-Reference' *International Journal of General Systems* 2:5-24.

———, 1979. *Principles of Biological Autonomy*. New York: Elsevier.

———, 1981. 'Describing the Logic of the Living: The Adequacy and Limitations of the Idea of Autopoiesis' pp. 36-48 in *Autopoiesis: A Theory of the Living Organization*, ed. M. Zeleny. New York: Elsevier.

———, 1984. 'Two Principles of Self-Organization' pp. 25-32 in *Selforganization and Management of Social Systems: Insides, Promises, Doubts and Questions*, eds. H. Ulrich and G.J.B. Probst. Bern: Haupt.

Varela, F., Maturana, H., and Uribe, R., 1974. 'Autopoiesis: The Organization of Living Systems, Its Characterization and a Model' *Biosystems* 5:187-196.

Vaughan, D., 1986. 'Structural Secrecy and Organizational Misconduct: NASA and the Space Shuttle Challenger' *Paper presented at the Academy of Management Meeting* (Chicago, August).

Von Bertalanffy, L., 1973. *General Systems Theory: Foundations, Development, Application*. Harmondsworth: Penguin.

Von Foerster, H., 1949. 'Quantum Mechanical Theory of Memory' pp. 112-145 in *Cybernetics: Transactions of the Sixth Conference*, ed. H. Von Foerster. New York: Josiah Macy Jr. Foundation.

———, 1976. 'Objects: Tokens for Eigen-Behaviors' *ASC Cybernetic Forum* 8:91-96.

———, 1981. *Observing Systems*. Seaside, CA: Intersystems.

———, 1991. 'Through the Eyes of the Other' pp. 21-28 in *Research and Reflexivity*, ed. F. Steier. London: Sage.

———, 1992. 'Ethiks and Second-Order Cybernetics' *Cybernetics and Human Knowing* 1:9-19.

———, 1993. 'Für Niklas Luhmann: Wie Rekursiv ist Kommunikation?' *Teoria Sociologica* 2:61-88.

Von Foerster, H. and Pörksen, B., 1998. *Wahrheit ist die Erfindung eines Lügners: Gespräche für Skeptiker*. Heidelberg: Carl Auer.

Von Krogh, G. and Roos, J., 1995. *Organizational Epistemology*. Basingstoke and London: Macmillan.

———, 1996. 'Conversation Management and Knowledge Development' pp. 218-225 in *Managing Knowledge: Perspectives on Cooperation and Competition*, eds. G. Von Krogh and J. Roos. London: Sage.

Walsch, J.P. and Ungson, G.R., 1991. 'Organizational Memory' *Academy of Management Review* 16:57-91.

Walsh, J. and Fahey, L., 1986. 'The Role of Negotiated Belief Structures in Strategy Making' *Journal of Management* 12:325-338.

Walton, Richard, 1975. 'The Difference of New Work Structures: Explaining Why Success Didn't Take' *Organization Dynamics* 4:1-30.

Watzlawick, P., ed., 1984. *The Invented Reality: How Do We Know What We Believe We Know? Contributions to Constructivism*. New York: Norton.

Watzlawick, P., Weakland, J.H., and Fisch, R., 1974. *Change: Principles of Problem Formation and Problem Resolution*. New York: Horten.

Weaver, W., 1948. 'Science and Complexity' *American Scientist* 36:536-544.

Weber, J., 1985. *Unternehmensidentität und unternehmenspolitische Rahmenplanung*. München: Kirsch.

Weick, K.E., 1976. 'Educational Organizations As Loosely Coupled Systems' *Administrative Science Quarterly* 21:1-19.

———, 1977. 'Re-Punctuating the Problem' pp. 193-225 in *New Perspectives on Organizational Effectiveness*, eds. P.S. Goodman and J.M. Pennings. San Francisco: Jossey Bass.

———, 1979. *The Social Psychology of Organizing*. London: Addison and Westley.

———, 1982a. 'Management of Organizational Change Among Loosely Coupled Elements' pp. 375-408 in *Change in Organizations: New Perspectives on Theory, Research, and Practice*, eds. P.S. Goodman and Associates. San Francisco: Jossey-Bass.

———, 1982b. 'Administering Education in Loosely Coupled Schools' *Phi Delta Kappa* 63:673-676.

———, 1986. 'The Concept of Loose Coupling: An Assessment' *AERA Organizational Theory Dialogue*:8-11.

———, 1987. 'Theorizing About Organizational Communication' pp. 97-122 in *Handbook of Organizational Communication: An Interdisciplinary Perspective*, eds. F. Jablin et al. Newbury Park: Sage.

———, 1989. 'Loose Coupling: Beyond the Metaphor' *Current Contents* 20:14.

———, 1990. 'Cartographic Myths in Organizations' pp. 1-10 in *Mapping Strategic Thought*, ed. A.S. Huff. Chichester: John Wiley and Sons.

———, 1995. *Sensemaking in Organizations*. London: Sage.

Weick, K.E. and Roberts, K.H., 1993. 'Collective Mind in Organizations: Heedful Interrelating on Flight Decks' *Administrative Science Quarterly* 38:357-381.

Westley, F.R., 1990. 'The Eye of the Needle: Cultural and Personal Transformation in a Traditional Organization' *Human Relations* 43:273-293.

Westley, F. and Mintzberg, H., 1989. 'Visionary Leadership and Strategic Management' *Strategic Management Journal* 10:17-32.

Westley, F.R. and Vredenburg, H., 1996. *The Perils of Precision: Managing Local Tensions to Achieve Global Goals* 32:143-159.

Whetten, D.S. and Godfrey, P.C., eds., 1998. *Identity in Organizations: Building Theory Through Conversations*. Thousand Oaks: Sage.

Whetten, D.A. and Mackey, A., 2002. 'A Social Actor Conception of Organizational Identity and Its Implications for the Study of Organizational Reputation' *Business and Society* 41:393-414.

Whitehead, A., 1979. *Process and Reality: An Essay in Cosmology*. New York: Free Press.

Whitehead, A. and Russell, B., 1913. *Principia Mathematica*. Cambridge: Cambridge University Press.

Williamson, O.E., 1975. *Markets and Hierarchies: Analysis and Antitrust Implications. A Study in the Economics of Internal Organization*. New York: Free Press.

Wilson, I., 1992. 'Realizing the Power of Strategic Vision' *Long Range Planning* 25:18-28.

Wimmer, R., 1992. 'Die Steuerung komplexer Organisationen: Ein Reformulierungsversuch der Führungsproblematik' pp. 131-56 in *Politische Prozesse in Unternehmen*, ed. K. Sandner. Berlin: Springer.

————, 1995. 'Die permanente Revolution: Aktuelle Trends in der Gestaltung von Organisationen' pp. 21-41 in *Veränderung in Organisationen*, eds. R. Grossmann, E. Kraintz, and M. Oswald. Wiesbaden: Gabler.

————, 1999. 'Wider den Veränderungsoptimismus: Zu den Möglichkeiten und Grenzen einer radikalen Transformation von Organisationen' *Soziale Systeme* 5:159-180.

Zeleny, M. and Hufford, C., 1992. 'The Application of Autopoiesis in Social Analysis: Are Autopoietic Systems Also Social Systems?' *International Journal of General Systems* 21:145-160.

Zu Knyphausen, D., 1988. *Unternehmen als evolutionsfähige Systeme: Überlegungen zu einem evolutionären Konzept für die Organisationstheorie*. München: Kirsch.

————, 1991. 'Selbstorganisation und Führung: Systemtheoretische Beiträge zu einer evolutionären Führungskonzeption' *Die Unternehmung* 45:47-64.

————, 1992. 'Paradoxien und Visionen: Visionen einer paradoxen Theorie der Entstehung des Neuen' pp. 140-159 in *DELFIN – Konstruktivismus: Geschichte und Andwendung*, eds. G. Rusch and S.J. Schmidt. Frankfurt a.M.: Suhrkamp.

Zu Knyphausen-Aufsess, D., 1995. *Theorie der strategischen Unternehmensführung: State of the Art und neue Perspektiven*. Wiesbaden: Gabler.

Index

For Product Safety Concerns and Information please contact our EU
representative GPSR@taylorandfrancis.com
Taylor & Francis Verlag GmbH, Kaufingerstraße 24, 80331 München, Germany

www.ingramcontent.com/pod-product-compliance
Ingram Content Group UK Ltd.
Pitfield, Milton Keynes, MK11 3LW, UK
UKHW021611240425
457818UK00018B/506